Jesus the Messiah in the Hebrew Bible

Jesus the Messiah in the Hebrew Bible

EUGEN J. PENTIUC

Paulist Press
New York/Mahwah, N.J.

Cover design by Elenie M. Poulos
Book design by The HK Scriptorium

Library of Congress Cataloging-in-Publication Data

Pentiuc, Eugen J., 1955-
Jesus the Messiah in the Hebrew Bible / Eugen J. Pentiuc.
p. cm.
Includes bibliographical references.
ISBN 0-8091-4346-1 (alk. paper)
1. Jesus Christ—Messiahship. 2. Bible O.T. — Theology. I. Title.
BT230.P46 2006
232'.12—dc22

2005023259

Published by Paulist Press
997 Macarthur Boulevard
Mahwah, New Jersey 07430

www.paulistpress.com

Printed and bound in the
United States of America

The world was created for the sake of the Messiah.

—*Babylonian Talmud, Sanhedrin* 98b

For Flora

אֵשֶׁת־חַיִל מִי יִמְצָא

What a rare find is a virtuous woman! (Prov 31:10)

Contents

Abbreviations xii

Preface xiii

Part A
The Fallen Messiah 1

I. Three Steps in Fashioning Humanity 5
1. The First Step: Humanity as a Reflection, or Image, of the Triune God 5
(1) Unity in Diversity (Gen 1:26–27) 6
(2) God's Living Breath (Gen 2:7) 10

2. The Second Step: Reshaping the Face of Humanity 14
(1) A Help like Humanity's Opposite (Gen 2:18) 14
(2) Playing God (Gen 2:19–20) 16
(3) A Help from Inside Humanity (Gen 2:21–22) 18
(4) Man's Identity (Gen 2:23) 20

3. The Third Step: Humanity's Unity Regained 21
Made One for Another (Gen 2:24) 21
Notes 23

II. Swinging between Life and Power 25
1. God's Enticement 25
(1) A Garden, a Steppe, and Chaos (Gen 2:8) 25
(2) "The tree of life in the midst of the garden, and the tree of knowledge of good and evil…" (Gen 2:9) 26

2. Mixed Feelings 26
(1) Happiness and Insecurity in the Garden (Gen 2:15–17) 26
(2) The Serpent's Guile (Gen 3:1) 28

3. The Fall of Humanity 30
(1) A Preamble to Sin: Eve's Three Mistakes (Gen 3:2–3) 30
a. Entering into Dialogue with the Serpent (Gen 3:1–2) 30
b. Creating Her Own Universe (Gen 3:3a) 31
c. Defending God (Gen 3:3b) 31
(2) Original Sin (Gen 2–3) 31
Notes 32

III. Humanity's Fate Revealed (Gen 3:15) 34
1. Harassment between Serpent and Humanity 34
2. The Seed of the Woman: Another Chance 36
Notes 38

Part B
The Rising Messiah 41

I. The Preexistence of Messiah 43
1. Within the Godhead 43
(1) Poured Out as a Libation (Prov 8:23; Ps 2:6 [LXX and pre-MT]) 43
(2) Acquired by God (Prov 8:22 [MT]) 45
(3) Brought Forth in Labors (Prov 8:24) 46
(4) A Source of Delight for God (Prov 8:30b//Matt 3:17) 47
(5) God's Partners in Dialogue (Gen 1:26–27; Isa 9:5; Zech 13:7; Ps 110:1; Prov 8:30a) 48
a. Messiah: A "Wonder-Counselor" or an "Angel of a Great Council" 49
b. The Man: God's Fellow 50
c. Melchizedek: Co-regent with God 51
d. Wisdom: God's Confidant 52
(6) "Son of Man" or "Son of Weakness" (Dan 7:13–14 //John 3:13; 5:27; 6:27, 53, 62; Matt 24:30; 26:64; 25:31; Acts 7:56; Rev 1:13; 14:14) 52

2. God's Propensities toward Incarnation 56
(1) The "Angel of Yahweh" (Gen 32:25, 27; Hos 12:4–5 [Eng. 3–4]; Exod 3:2–4; Josh 5:13–15; Judg 2:1–5; 13:17–20) 57
Other Occurrences of the "Angel of Yahweh" 63
(2) *Yahweh,* a Name for All Seasons (Exod 3:13–15) 65
(3) Two Yahwehs? (Gen 18:33; 19:1, 24; cf. Exod 34:5–6; Ps 22:2 [Eng. 22:1]) 68
(4) Walking To and Fro (Gen 5:21–24; 6:9; 24:40) 71
(5) The Tabernacling Glory (Exod 33:18–23; Num 12:8a; Isa 6:1–3//John 1:14) 74
(6) Vibrant Silence: From Thunder to a Soft Whisper (1 Kgs 19:11–12; cf. Exod 19:16, 18–19) 77
(7) The Occurrence of God's Word (Hos 1:1; *et passim* in prophetic books) 79
(8) Melchizedek (Gen 14:17–24; Ps 110:4 //Heb 7:1–3) 80
Notes 84

II. The Birth of Messiah 90
1. The Mother of Messiah 90
(1) The Woman (Gen 3:15) 91
(2) The Royal Consort (Ps 45:8–10) 93
(3) The Veiled One (Isa 7:14//Matt 1:18, 22–23; Luke 1:26–27, 30–31) 95

2. Virginal Conception and Birth (Isa 7:14 [LXX]; Ezek 44:1–3; Jer 31:22; Exod 3:2; Isa 49:1, 5 //Luke 1:34–35) 99

3. Time of Birth (Gen 49:10; Num 24:17; Dan 9:24–27; Mal 3:1; Hag 2:6–9; Ps 118:25–27) 106

4. Place of Birth and Other Places in Christ's Itinerary (Mic 5:1 [Eng. 5:2]; Isa 8:23–9:1; 11:1; Hos 11:1) 117
Bethlehem 117
Nazareth 119
Galilee 120
Egypt 122

5. The Forerunner of Messiah's Birth (Isa 40:3; Mal 3:1) 123

6. The Lineage of Messiah (Son of Man: Dan 7:13–14; of Shem: Gen 9:25–27; of Abraham: Gen 12:1–3; of Isaac: Gen 26:4–5; of Judah: Gen 49:10; of Jesse: Isa 11:1; of David: 2 Sam 7:16) 124

Son of Man 125

Son of Shem 125

Son of Abraham 127

Son of Isaac 130

Son of Judah 131

Son of Jesse 131

Son of David 132

Notes 134

III. The Suffering, Death, and Resurrection of Messiah 139

1. The Betrayal 141

(1) Betrayer's Profile (Ps 41:10 [Eng. 41:9]; 55:13–15 [Eng. 55:12–14]) 141

a. Colleague 142

b. Trusted One 143

c. Meal Sharer 144

d. Despiser 144

e. Co-equal 145

f. Compatriot 146

g. Confidant 146

h. Participant in a Secret Gathering 147

(2) Sold for Thirty Pieces of Silver (Zech 11:12–13 //Matt 26:15–16; 27:3–10) 148

2. The Passion 151

(1) Forsaken by His Disciples (Zech 13:7 //Mark 14:27) 151

(2) Accused by Fanatic Witnesses (Ps 35:11–12; 109:2; 38:13–15 [Eng. 38:12–14]; 39:2; Isa 53:7 //Matt 26:59–60; 27:12, 14; 1 Pet 2:23) 153

(3) Smitten with a Rod upon His Cheek (Mic 4:14 [Eng. 5:1]; Isa 50:6a//Matt 26:67–68; 27:30) 155

(4) Spat Upon (Isa 50:6b//Matt 26:67a; 27:30a) 157

(5) Pierced in Hands and Feet (Ps 22:17 [Eng. 22:16] //John 20:25) 158
(6) Crucified with Thieves (Isa 53:9, 12 //Mark 15:27, 28; Luke 22:37; 23:39–43) 159
(7) He Prayed for His Persecutors (Ps 109:4–5; Isa 53:12//Luke 23:34; cf. Acts 7:59) 160
(8) He Became the Object of Ridicule (Ps 109:25; 22:7, 8, 13 [Eng. 22:6, 7, 12]; Isa 52:14; 53:2–3 //Matt 27:39; Luke 23:35) 161
(9) His Garments Were Gambled for (Ps 22:19 [Eng. 22:18]//John 19:23, 24) 163
(10) Abandoned by God (Ps 22:2 [Eng. 22:1]; Isa 49:14; 54:7–8//Matt 27:46; Mark 15:34–35) 163
(11) He Agonized with Thirst (Ps 22:16 [Eng. 22:15]; 69:3, 21//John 19:28; Matt 27:34, 48) 166
(12) He Entrusted His Spirit to God (Ps 22:21 [Eng. 22:20]; 31:6//Matt 27:43; Luke 23:46; Acts 7:59) 167
(13) His Friends Stood Afar Off (Ps 38:12; 88:8; Isa 63:3//Luke 23:49) 170
(14) They Did Not Break His Bones (Ps 22:18 [Eng. 22:17]; 34:20–21 [Eng. 34:19–20]; Exod 12:46; Num 9:12//John 19:36) 171
(15) He Was Pierced between His Hands (Zech 12:10; 13:1, 6//John 20:25–27; cf. 19:34; Rev 1:7) 173
(16) Darkness over the Whole Earth (Amos 8:9; Ps 22:3 [Eng. 22:1]//Matt 27:45) 174

3. The Death 175
(1) He Died a Voluntary, Substitutionary Death (Isa 53:5, 6, 11, 12; 50:6; Dan 9:26 //John 10:11, 18; Matt 20:28; 1 Cor 15:3; Gal 2:20; Heb 1:3; 1 Pet 2:24; Rev 1:5) 175
(2) He Was Buried with the Rich (Isa 53:9 //Matt 27:57–61) 178

4. The Resurrection 179
The Third-Day Resurrection and the "Sign of Jonah" (Hos 6:1–3; Jonah 1:17 //Matt 12:39–40; 1 Pet 3:18–20) 179
Notes 184

BIBLIOGRAPHY 186

Abbreviations

CAD	Gelb, I. J., et al., eds. *The Assyrian Dictionary of the Oriental Institute of the University of Chicago.* Chicago, Ill.: University of Chicago Press, 1956–.
EA	El-Amarna tablet(s). Moran, W. L., ed. *The Amarna Letters.* Baltimore/London: Johns Hopkins University Press, 1992.
HALOT	Koehler, L., and W. Baumgartner, eds. *The Hebrew and Aramaic Lexicon of the Old Testament.* 5 volumes. 3rd edition. Leiden: Brill, 1994–2000.
LXX	Septuagint (the Greek translation of the Old Testament)
MT	Masoretic Text (the vocalized Hebrew text)
PG	Migne, J. P., ed. *Patrologiae cursus completus.* Series Graeca. 221 vols. Paris, 1844–66.
PL	Migne, J. P., ed. *Patrologiae cursus completus.* Series Latina. 217 vols. Paris, 1844–64.
TODT	Botterweck, G. J., H. Ringgren, and H.-J. Fabry, eds. *Theological Dictionary of the Old Testament.* 14 vols. Grand Rapids: Eerdmans, 1974–.
V	Vulgate (the Latin version of the Old Testament)

Preface

THIS BOOK REPRESENTS A KEY INTEREST OF MINE, and I am pleased to have been given the opportunity to write it. Although the approach of this work falls under the traditional rubric, it does not have anything to do with fundamentalist treatments of the messianic topic. I have tried to shift away from conventional paradigms to develop a new way of understanding the presence of Christ in the Old Testament. I call this approach *ontological*, and I emphasize that it is distinct from *royal messianism* and other scholarly conventions of analysis. The ontological approach is based on the view that Jesus the Messiah was preexistent, and that he appeared in manifold forms throughout the Hebrew Bible prior to his human incarnation in the New Testament. My approach is based on the idea that Christ is the "last Adam" referred to by Paul in 1 Corinthians 15:45, while the first Adam, that is, the primeval humanity, was a kind of messianic agent appointed by God as his representative on earth. This bipartite division accords with the structure of the book: the first agent is the *fallen Messiah*, the second agent is the *rising Messiah*. Ontological, therefore, refers to this duality: Adam's status as the first Messiah, and the preexistent, last Messiah, who incarnated as Jesus Christ. The path through salvation history which leads fallen humanity back into communion with God is guided by the manifestations of the preexistent Messiah, and especially by the life and ministry of Christ. I call these manifestations, Messiah's propensities toward incarnation and his willingness to share in our human weaknesses.

Ontological also refers to the relationship between the *fallen* and the *rising Messiah*, for without the lapse of primeval humanity, the advent of the rising Messiah would have been unnecessary. This relationship is a central locus of my text. My vision of the role and the appearances of Messiah throughout the Old Testament, and in the New Testament as well, is distinct. I hope that my presentation will convince the reader that the ontological view of Messiah is a more comprehensive way of understanding his existence and his enactment of God's will on our behalf.

In this book, I have relied primarily on the Hebrew texts of Scripture. These texts and my interpretations are then brought into dialogue with ancient Jewish theological writings, the Septuagint version of the Bible, the Vulgate version, and early Christian patristic sources. I will address these materials in more depth below. Let me say here that I have surveyed the breadth of messianic literature because I firmly believe in the general virtue of finding a common point of discussion between Jews and Christians with respect to the topic of messianism. Part of my intent in writing this book has been an effort to find just such commonality between our two great faiths.

Not a few consider the Septuagint a quasi-inspired version of Scripture, and my own Eastern Orthodox Church holds this version in the highest esteem. My primary reliance on the Hebrew Bible should not, therefore, be read as an indication of my lack of respect for that venerable Greek text. On the contrary, my regard for the Septuagint has been demonstrated in my years of teaching the Old Testament and in my published academic writings. However, my desire has always been an ardent one: to understand the portrayals of Messiah as found in the Hebrew Bible. The early Christian fathers, in their christological interpretations, reconstructed the portrait of Christ from the Septuagint version of the Old Testament, as viewed through the lens of the gospels. I have long wanted to parallel these interpretive precursors, but in the light of the Hebrew Bible.

During my academic pilgrimage, I have spent time learning at the École Biblique in Jerusalem, Bucharest University, and Harvard University. I have studied theology, Old Testament, and philology so that I could marry Semitic and Greek philology and tie these to the Hebrew Bible in order to return to the biblical texts, read them in their earliest languages, compare the extant versions, and reconstruct the original content as closely as possible. It was in this milieu that the idea of this book was born. This has been a tremendously exciting endeavor that has resulted, in part, in this book. My goal here is to bring this vision to you, to convey my joy to you, to offer my labor of love to you, so that you may also understand the depth and breadth of the Messiah's presence in salvation history.

I would like to emphasize that I intend this book to be primarily a pastoral work, based on theology and biblical exegesis. I do not intend for it to be a scholarly text of biblical exegesis, although I believe the dichotomy between pastoral applications and intellectual endeavors to be a false one. I respectfully disagree with those who assert that there can be no marriage between scholarship and faith. On the contrary, I am certain that scholars have an important role to play in lending greater depth to our faith. Faith is not merely blind belief; rather, it is belief supported by knowledge. The presentation of pastoral guidance supported by rigorous scholarly research and dedication is an additional focus of my work in this book.

I should include here a few particular points. In order that the reader may orient to the materials I have used in the text, let me address some of the specifics. I will refer throughout to the Hebrew Bible and the Masoretic Text. These should not be conflated: the Hebrew Bible is not simply the Masoretic Text. Rather, the Hebrew Bible predates the Masoretic Text, and has been meticulously reconstructed by a multitude of scholars using various surviving versions. The Masoretic Text, on the other hand, is a later version of the Hebrew Bible that was vocalized between AD 500 and 700; that is, it has had the symbols for vowel sounds added to the consonantal text. In fact, all versions of the Hebrew text operate as text witnesses, a technical label for various forms (versions) of the original text (the autograph) of the Bible, which was lost in the process of copying and transmitting the text. Today, evaluating all sources, and building on the Qumran discoveries, we are in a much better position to reconstruct the pre-Masoretic Hebrew text, owing to the larger palette of text witnesses, including the Qumran copies. We are also better positioned to understand the place of the Septuagint in the history of the sacred text. All of these considerations enable us to get closer to the autograph, which is proof of the value of the Septuagint and Qumran traditions in reconstructing the Hebrew Bible. This process is technically known as textual criticism, and some of my own reconstructions and translations have benefited from such text-critical endeavors. In any case, in staying with the Masoretic Text, or reconstructing the pre-Masoretic text, I have tried to remain within the letter and spirit of the Hebrew language of the autograph.

No matter how good a translation is, its value pales in comparison with the original language in which the autograph was fixed in writing. One of my primary goals in this work is to regain the freshness of the original language. Pertaining to my topic, the main objective is to grasp the nuances missing from Messiah's previously rendered portraits, which have been fashioned in many instances based on the language and metaphor of the Septuagint. The present work, it is hoped, will make its case in showing the importance of detail and fidelity in contouring Messiah's profile. The reader will therefore understand why I have devoted such care to the words and the syntax of the authors of the sacred text. There is no better way than through the careful reading of the Hebrew text to reveal the metaphorical nuances of the Bible and to savor them. To this end, I have applied my philological training. I have attempted to keep the most technical analysis out of the text, confining it to notes in order to facilitate the reading of my narrative. The reader should remember that my goal is not merely exegetical; I also hope to convey a more accurate rendering of the sacred text into English, because such accuracy is the best way to provide a clear and reliable text. This in turn facilitates not only the production of the best material for further exegetical work; it also grounds the nonspecialist in a more realistic understanding of the imagery, intent, and breadth of the sacred text. This subsequently has the power to contribute to the vitality and strength of our common faith in God and the realities conveyed to us through the Bible.

Another characteristic of this work lies in my use of ancient Jewish interpretations, among which are included the Targumim, the Midrashim, the Talmud, Mishnah, and the Septuagint itself. The Septuagint is the first Greek translation of the Hebrew Bible, produced by Jewish scholars in Alexandria, Egypt, beginning with the translation of the Pentateuch around 250 BC. In addition to being the oldest Greek translation of the Old Testament, the Septuagint is also one of the earliest Jewish interpretations of the Hebrew Bible. When we approach the Hebrew Bible, I consider the most appropriate interpretations to be those produced in Jewish (that is, Hebrew-speaking) circles. All of the interpretive sources I use, then, are specifically brought to bear in order to strengthen our understanding of the historical and linguistic contexts of the biblical text.

To those who consider my endeavors merely an attempt to Christianize the Hebrew Bible, I would respond that we have benefited from having the New Testament and viewing the Hebrew Bible through its literary-theological prism. This is doubly so, when we consider the efforts of some of our early Christian interpreters, such as Justin Martyr. There is a certain commonality between Jews and Christians in seeing messianic prophecies in almost all the same biblical texts. There is a notable extent of Christian reading into the Hebrew Bible, but this is the result of the canonical shape of the Christian Bible, as well as the propensity of the Hebrew Bible to conform to christological interpretation. This is largely due to the high degree of similarity between the prophetic and typological dimensions of these texts and the New Testament recordings of Jesus' exploits and utterances.

There are, in general, three factors that the early Christian writers sought in the Old Testament to demonstrate the truth of messianic readings culminating in Christ's life, ministry, and salvific death. The first is that certain texts (*proof texts*) are apprehended as specific prophecies of Jesus' role as Messiah. The second is the *typological approach*, in which Old Testament figures, events, and institutions were seen to foreshadow Jesus. The third is the interpretation of Old Testament *theophanies* as appearances of the pre-incarnate Son of God. All these approaches were perhaps best articulated by second-century writers, but their presence can also be detected in the New Testament canon, and their application of these criteria were strongly influenced by an understanding of the Hebrew interpreters who had gone before them. I have attempted in this book to return to such criteria for interpretation and for fullness of comprehension.

Finally, let me say a few words about my view of the interrelationship between the Old Testament and the New. In any discussion pertaining to Christ's view of the Old Law, the text of Matthew 5:17 is commonly quoted, "Do not think that I have come to abolish the law or the prophets; I have come not to abolish but to fulfill" (NRSV). The "fulfillment" to which Jesus refers should not be viewed as an end point, as is customary. Rather, it is a long, intricate, and gradual process beginning with the incarnation of the Logos and continuing throughout Christ's life and the various phases of the church's history. The *vertical paradigm* long in vogue, in which the Hebrew Scripture exists at the bottom and the New Testament triumphs at the top of history, overlooks the Jewishness of the Old Testament and ignores the reality of a living, vibrant Jewish community of faith. If we conceive of the messianic "fulfillment" as a *process* inaugurated by Christ, and not simply as an end point, then the vertical scheme must be replaced by a *horizontal paradigm*. I envision this horizontal model to consist of two concentric circles: one circle that circumscribes the entire history of salvation as recorded and hinted at by the Hebrew Bible; and another circle, situated in the center of the first, that represents the activities of Messiah in all his scriptural incarnations. This latter circle I label *divine mercy* as intimated by the New Testament.

I would designate the coming of Christ as a circle of divine mercy because, as Paul puts it in Hebrews 1:2, Messiah was expected "at the end of those days." John the Baptist's question directed to Jesus, "Are you the one who is to come, or are we to wait for another?" (Matt 11:3 NRSV), mirrors a similar belief in an eschatological Messiah. That Christ came before the end of time one may see from the account of the two demoniacs: "Suddenly they shouted, 'What have you to do with us, Son of God? Have you come here to torment us before the time?'" (Matt 8:29 NRSV). Thus, Christ represents the appearance of Messiah prior to the eschatological expectation. In this eschatological expectation, time and history will be consummated in the eschaton, and God's judgment and mercy will be revealed then. However, Jesus the Messiah "tabernacled (*eskēnōsen*) among us" (John 1:14) prior to the advent of the eschaton, and this demonstrated the reality of God's mercy prior to the fulfillment of time. Similarly, divine mercy is shown to us in the manifold appearances of Messiah throughout recorded history, and this is the *crux* of my horizontal paradigm.

The circle of divine mercy exists at the center of the other circle, and through the course of history it will expand to the point at which the two overlap. This will be the culmination of the history of salvation, the eschaton. Jesus' observation is specific on this point, "The kingdom of God is in the midst of you" (Luke 17:21). The *kingdom*, represented in my horizontal model by the interior circle of divine mercy, is at the center and gains more space by expanding among nations and throughout its temporal development. When the second advent is upon us, then, divine mercy and salvation history will be a single unified and complete circle of God's love for his creation. This love has been shown to us visibly throughout salvation history, prior to the eschaton, and this is the meaning I hope to convey by my horizontal model. God and Messiah are and have been with us, beside us, throughout our history, showing us his mercy at all times, and joining us in the flow and ebb of our experiences as humanity.

The history of salvation is recorded narratively, poetically, and prophetically by the texts of Scripture. It is a circle larger than divine mercy that lies at the center, or heart, of the history of salvation. Salvation history is not merely a chronological progression, but is a wholeness that exists both *in* time and *beyond* time, dimensions that are joined by the work and the manifestations of God in our midst. The culmination of time and history will be the eschaton, ushered in by Messiah at his glorious coming. In the interim, however, we remain within salvation history, linked by the mercy of God to what has gone before and what is to come. I offer this book as witness to that mercy and to our place in God's history of salvation.

FEAST OF THE HOLY APOSTLES PETER AND PAUL
JUNE 29, 2004

* * *

The author is indebted to Andrew Scott Catey (PhD candidate), whose assistance on matters of English style is obvious on nearly every page.

Part A
The Fallen Messiah

WE HOLD IT TO BE TRUE THAT, in order to understand Old Testament messianism, or the hope in the coming of Messiah, we must first look to humanity. The Messiah was God's anointed. A careful and critical evaluation of the Hebrew text reveals that this anointed one was God's chosen, who was to represent him on earth. In the first instance, this was humanity itself. Such a notion is revealed in the creation narrative of Genesis, through the use of the Hebrew term *ʾādām*. This term connotes "humanity" as a totality, not a particular person or individual gender. The original *ʾādām* was, then, a single human collective, an undifferentiated aggregate of the male and female individuals created by God. It was this collective that received the commission to care for the rest of God's creation.

It is very important to underscore here the fact that the narrative uses the term *humanity* in the broadest sense, rather than *man* or *male, woman* or *female*. We will see how, according to the Book of Genesis, God first created humanity as this collectivity of individuals, and how at a certain point, the separation, or division, of humanity into the specificities of man and woman came about. Based on this formulation, then, there are three critical elements in our understanding of messianism: God, the Creator; the anointed One, God's representative; and God's crowning creation, humanity. This section of our work will focus on the idea of humanity as God's original representative.

In our view, the first Messiah, the first anointed one, was the primeval human collective. Humankind, made in God's image, was created to represent his kingship on earth, as we can see in Genesis 1:28, "And God blessed them, and God said to them, 'Be fruitful and multiply, and fill the earth and subdue it'" (NRSV). Since the term *māšîaḥ* (Messiah) means "anointed one," that is, the chosen or appointed one, one may conclude that humanity as it was originally created was commissioned by God to represent him in his new creation. It is the same idea the first book of Holy Scripture conveys when it states that "humanity," not the individual genders, was created in the image of God (Gen 1:26–27). Thus, Adam, the primeval human collective, can be considered the first Messiah. As we know from the events of Genesis 3, and as the title of this section suggests, humanity ultimately becomes the *fallen Messiah*. This fallenness precipitates the requirement of the *rising Messiah*, who atones for humanity's errors and restores it in the godly relationship. This may sound odd, but the distinction is crucial to understand the relationship between the fallen Messiah and the rising Messiah. This relationship and the figure of the rising Messiah are fundamental elements of the Hebrew Bible viewed through the Christian prism. The rising Messiah is that mysterious figure prophesied in the Hebrew Bible (Old Testament), and interpreted by the early church as Jesus of the gospels. This theme will be explored more fully later in this work. For now we turn to our consideration of humanity as the fallen Messiah.

After God refashioned humanity by splitting, or reshaping it into the dynamic man–woman relationship (Gen 2:18–23), and subsequent to the two first humans' act of disobedience, the need for a rising Messiah was gradually felt. This need was for an ideal reflection and representative of God, one able to restore the unregenerate *ʾādām* to its initial beauty as God's image on earth, and one able to restore the correct relationship between God and his creation. There is, then, a wealth of messianic texts in the Hebrew Bible, and these texts are to be read as allegories, or signposts, that direct us toward a fuller interpretation of God's appointed and God's will as expressed through the law, prophets, and wisdom and consummated in the person of Jesus Christ. Any attempt to discuss biblical messianism must therefore start by looking closely at primeval humanity. More precisely, we should look at the way in which God fashioned humanity and designated it as his chosen representative.

God designed and initially created primeval humanity according to his own ontological pattern: unity in diversity. This ontology is the foundation for the triune Godhead Christians have come to know. God then apportioned humanity into its familiar complementary roles: the dynamic male-female pair. God's intent was for primeval humanity to regain its being, and most fully reflect his own ontological reality, through marriage. However, the fall into sin fragmented the fragile unity created by God. The creative context is characterized by the following sequence: *unity*, represented by the primeval humanity; *dialogical disunity*, represented by the prosopic relationship of male and female; *conjugal unity*, portrayed by the cleaving together of husband and wife (Gen 2:24); and *fragmentation*, which arises from disobedience and the expulsion from paradise. Throughout this book, we are going to examine the juxtaposition of the contours of the fallen Messiah and the profile of the rising Messiah as these are revealed in the Hebrew Bible. This scriptural and prophetic vision will be supplemented with the historical and theological interpretations found in the New Testament and early church. This early interpretation realized the reality of Jesus Christ as the anointed one sent to restore humanity's fragmented unity and its disconnected relationship with our creative God. The realized reality has been passed to us through the church tradition. References to the Jewish interpretive tradition made throughout this work are meant to show that between the Jewish synagogue and early church there was an obvious *commonality*, to a certain degree, in selecting which biblical texts were messianic.

It is worth noting that the apostle John reports Jesus' first miracle and associates it with the marriage at Cana in Galilee (John 2). The miracle of transforming water into wine might be read as a prophetic allusion to Jesus' mandate of *restoring* the primeval humanity. John implicitly connects the revelation of Christ as the Messiah with the venerable institution of marriage. This is meant to signify Christ's role as the mediator of the restoration of humanity's relationship with God (through conjugal unity). It also is meant to illustrate how humanity's primeval unity can be regained and preserved. Christ's miracle at Cana thus has a vertical dimension (between God and humanity) and a horizontal one (between members of humanity). Christ is the fulcrum, the agent through which all of this healing/restoration occurs.

If we read further into the event and the biblical text, we can see that there is a qualitative difference between water and wine, just as there is such a difference between primeval humanity and its fallen self. Restored humanity is more than a simple copy of the first humanity. It is an improved, sweeter, and more godly being. The primeval unity in diversity, willed, designed, and realized by God on the sixth day of creation, is restored by Christ so that it may be eternally preserved in him. As Paul rightly summarizes in Colossians 3:11, in Christ there is no division or fragmentation, but simply equality and harmony of the parts. Paul also witnesses that the primitive Adam was a physical manifestation, and the life-giving Adam was a spiritual one (1 Cor 15:46). Through his own baptism and other saving acts, Christ, the rising Messiah and life-giving spiritual being is also *eschatos Adam,* "the last Adam" (1 Cor 15:45), and as such incorporates all humanity in his mystical body. In this way our primeval humanity is refashioned and restored. This idea has a Jewish analog in the Midrash's interpretation of Messiah as the one who incorporates all humans, "The royal Messiah will not come until all the souls which [God] contemplated creating have been created" (*Genesis Rabbah* 24:4). That is, only for the sake of the souls he has made will God send forth his royal Messiah.

I

Three Steps in Fashioning Humanity

THE FIRST TWO CHAPTERS OF THE BOOK OF GENESIS present the making of humanity as an act that occurs in three phases. The text is silent with respect to the time elapsed between these steps, or if, in fact, there was any time between them. With any fragment or link of creation there was only one act or word of God. For instance, the Creator says on the first day, "'Let there be light'; and there was light" (Gen 1:3). Or on the second day, the same Creator utters the powerful word, "'Let there be a firmament....' And God made the firmament..." (Gen 1:6, 7). Just one word or one step initiates creation and serves as a link between these acts. Contrary to this pattern, in the case of humanity, God uses a different way, a creative endeavor consisting in three steps. This pattern shows the enormous care God took in planning and making humanity, and how deliberative he was in designing and bringing to life his plan and humanity's role in his creation.

1. The First Step: Humanity as a Reflection, or Image, of the Triune God

What makes humanity quite different from the rest of the living world is the fact that we were created in the *image of God*. Throughout time, the biblical concept of the "image of God" has received various interpretations, some of them having nothing to do with the sacred text, some of them completely ignoring it in order to fit into one or another philosophical, systematic, or dogmatic scheme. The most popular interpretation remains the one that equates the image of God with the human soul or reason. Yet one of the unfortunate practical consequences of such an interpretation is the Manichaean dichotomy that results from this type of thinking, and which tends to develop a state of conflict between the soul and the body. At best this is alien to both the letter and the spirit of biblical anthropology, which emphasize the indissoluble unity between soul and body. In addition, as we will see from Genesis 2:7, humanity, fashioned from dust (not ground!), becomes a living breath only through God's breathing into its nostrils. We may add that, by equating the image of God only with the soul, the proponents of this Platonic interpretation fail to take into account the texts of Genesis 1:20–24, 30, which plainly remark that animals, birds, and reptiles also have souls in them. The soul is not to be considered the distinguishing feature of human being. The soul is, rather, the principle of life that sets all living creatures *in motion* (distinguished from plants, which lack mobility and thus a soul). What distinguishes humans from animals with respect to the soul is the way in which the soul is given to these creatures. We will discuss this further below.

If the image of God cannot and should not be restricted to the soul, then what else may this concept refer to? An interpretation based on a contextual, careful reading of Genesis texts regarding the creation of humanity suggests that the image of God should be understood as a cross, with both vertical and horizontal dimensions. The image of God is, on the one hand, unity in diversity, or the diversity of persons and the unity of human nature (the horizontal dimension). On the other hand, this image is also a constant dialogue between God and humans (the vertical dimension). In its horizontal dimension, the image of God connects us to one another as a large family whose unity is dynamically supported by the diversity of the human persons. In its vertical dimension, the image of God confirms our position in a living, unpredictable, yet always wonderful, relationship with our Creator.

(1) Unity in Diversity (Gen 1:26–27)

> *Gen 1:26–27: And God said, "Let us make humanity in our image, according to our likeness. It shall rule the fish of the sea, the birds of the sky, the cattle, the whole earth and all creeping things that creep on earth." And God created humanity in his image, in the image of God he created it, male and female he created them.*

This short fragment speaks of God's deliberation and his creation of humanity in his own image. The plural "Let *us* make humanity..." was variously understood by the ancient interpreters. From the outset, the explanation of the plural as a royal "we" should be avoided because this kind of plural rarely occurs in biblical Hebrew. Given this, the wealth of interpretations shaped throughout the centuries may be generally reduced to two schools of thought.

On the one hand, according to Jewish interpreters, God was addressing some beings, such as the personified Wisdom or the angels, and inviting them to take part in the act of the creation of humanity. Thus Wisdom of

Solomon 9:1–2 states, "O God of my ancestors and Lord of mercy, who have made all things by your word, and by your wisdom (*sophia*) have fashioned (*kataskeuasas*) humanity (*anthrōpon*) to rule the creatures that you have made...." For Philo, the inclusion of the angels in humanity's creation would explain humanity's sins. These sins are due to the angels' influence; the sins are thus distinct from humanity's right deeds, which should be attributed to God. Philo eloquently sums up this notion, "For it seemed to be unfitting to God, the ruler of all, that the road to wickedness within the reasonable soul should be of his making, and therefore he delegated the forming of this part to his inferiors" (*Confusion of Tongues* 179).[1] Similarly, "Rabbi Ḥanina said, 'When God set out to create the first human being, he consulted with the ministering angels. He said to them, 'Let us make man'" (*Genesis Rabbah*, 8:3–4).

On the other hand, and distinct from their Jewish counterparts, Christian interpreters suggested that God the Creator was addressing the second person of the Trinity, the Son of God, in whose image humanity was created. Thus, Ephraem the Syrian explains, "The Father commanded with his voice; it was the Son who carried out the work" (*Commentary on Genesis* 1:28). The singular "our image," instead of our images, is a strong argument defending the thesis that God spoke those words to a person equal in rank rather than to his servants. The verb used in deliberation is *ʿāśâ*, a generic verb for the idea of "making, doing," but when God started fashioning humanity, the biblical author employs *bārāʾ*, meaning "to create." This is the same verb that is found in Genesis 1:1 with respect to the creation of heavens and earth. It is worth noting here that in the Hebrew Bible, *bārāʾ* is used exclusively with God as subject, thus expressing God's creative power. The presence of this verb for the second time in the first chapter of Genesis is meant to show how unique and dignifying was the divine act undertaken by God in his creation of humanity.

As for our proposed rendering of *ʾādām* with "humanity" instead of "man," as several modern translations choose to do, some clarification may be warranted at this juncture. Our translation is not determined by the desire to be politically correct regarding gender issues raised by the first three chapters of the Book of Genesis. It is rather dictated by the peculiar character of the creation account in Genesis, which insists on humanity rather than individuals. We have chosen humanity, and not mankind, because the latter contains the male gender element, which narrows the undifferentiated collective reality of *ʾādām*. In addition, humanity, which derives from the Latin *homo* (from *humus,* "ground") would be a good match for the folk etymology suggested by Genesis 2:7 (cf. 3:19), which emphasizes the origin of *ʾādām,* "humanity," from *ʾădāmâ,* "ground." We believe that fidelity to the original intent is paramount, and so we use the term humanity.

There is extant extrabiblical evidence, such as the most important ancient Near Eastern myths, that proclaims in unison that gods, from the very beginning, created humans in one-act creation. The Hebrew Bible, specifically Genesis 1–2, diverges from this normative assumption and proposes a three-phase scenario of fashioning humanity: first, the genderless collectivity; second, the male–female polarity; and then the conjugal unity. This reality is recursively witnessed within the Bible itself: Genesis 1:27 is supported by Genesis 5:2, which refers to the two humans, male and female, as the collective "humanity" (*ʾādām*), "Male and female he created them. He blessed them and gave them the name humanity (*ʾādām*) when they were created" (Gen 5:2).

This is further interpretively supported by the Midrashim: "Rabbi Jeremiah bar Leazar said, 'When the Holy One, blessed be he, created the first humanity (*ʾdm*), he created it as androgynous, for it is said, 'Male and female created he them and called their name humanity' [Gen 5:2]. Rabbi Samuel bar Nahman said, 'When the Lord created the first humanity he created it double-faced, then he split it and made of it two backs, one back on this side and one back on the other side'" (*Genesis Rabbah* 8:1).

The Hebrew word *ʾādām* literally denotes a collective, designating "mankind," "humanity," or "people." It should be remembered that it is only sporadically that *ʾādām* has been employed with the meaning of "individual man" (e.g., Lev 22:5; cf. 13:2; Num 19:14; Prov 27:19), and even in these instances the noun can also be read to indicate a collective entity. The Septuagint correctly chose to translate the Hebrew with the word *anthrōpos,* "human being," which does not indicate gender, and not *anēr,* which denotes "man" or "male."

Regarding the meaning of the expression *ṣelem ʾĕlōhîm,* "image of God," we also draw the reader's attention to the Hebrew term *ṣelem,* meaning "image." This term most frequently was used to designate a statue, with respect to a god or a king, or an inscribed column.[2] In ancient times, kings used to commission the creation and erection of statues with their own effigies in remote territories in order to demonstrate to their subjects that they were also the masters of those faraway regions. Concerning the creation of humanity "in the image of God" (Gen 1:27), the idea we underscore here is that the destiny of this humanity was to be God's viceroy or representative on earth. In order to fulfill its mission, humanity needed first to be anointed with a special blessing, which began with the inspiration of God's breathing into humanity (Gen 2:7), and culminated in the mandate in Genesis 1:28.

It should be noted also that there are in the Hebrew text of Genesis 1:26 two apposite terms, *ṣelem,* "image," and *demût,* "shape, likeness." This duality gives us the familiar formula "in our image, according to our likeness." The use of both of these designates overlapping or coextensive entities. The Septuagint confirms this for us by inserting the conjunction *kai,* "and," which renders the phrase as a pair of distinct concepts that complement each other, "according to our image *and* according to [our] likeness." In addition, the Hebrew text of Genesis 1:27 states that God created humanity "in his image," and Genesis 5:1 conveys to us that God created humanity "in the likeness of God" (*bidmût ʾĕlōhîm*). These contingent uses underlie the rationale for the Septuagint's efforts to harmonize the two texts: the Septuagint translation of Genesis 5:1 reads "in the image of God" (*kat' eikona theou*), rather than the more correct literal translation, which should read "in the likeness of God." Therefore, from a correct reading of the Hebrew texts of Genesis 1:26–27 and 5:1, we may conclude that the notions of "image" and "likeness," as used in the Primeval History (Gen 1–11), are interchangeable. Based on the Septuagint reading, which differentiates between the two notions, patristic interpreters were inclined to explain these lexical peculiarities by resorting to an ingenious type of analysis: "image" was given to humanity in the act of creation, while "likeness" had to be reached by humanity's cooperation with God or, rather, humanity's actions in conjunction with the divine will or grace.[3] This understanding of likeness and image as interchangeable is reified when coupled with the fact that Genesis 1:27 disregards the use of "likeness" and explains the creation of humanity only as being "in the image of God."

The text of Genesis 1:26–27 deals with the notion of image in the horizontal dimension discussed above; that is, as the unity in diversity of humanity. In short, these verses inform us about the content of our diversity, and how the content and expression of this diversity are managed by our original, primordial unity. The diversity mentioned in v. 27 may be understood as a gender distinction, or the creation of distinct persons from the fundamental human collectivity. This is the only distinction willed and designed by God with respect to humans. In terms of the critical academic interpretation of Scripture, the *documentary hypothesis*[4] designates the text of Genesis 1:26–27 as originating with the Priestly source, owing to its majestic, transcendent, or abstract style. However, such a source-critical conclusion is contradicted by the presence of two graphic terms in v. 27 that define the distinct polarity between male and female. We might mention that Hebrew has several pairs of words that are used with respect to the man–woman distinction. These terms underscore the gender differences[5] or the social differences.[6] In our text, the author highlights the gender distinction. The division of the biblical texts into sources created and advocated by the proponents of the literary (source) criticism does not work in the context of this particular pericope, in which graphic terms defining the male/female distinction coexist with God's majestic description so appropriate to the Priestly source. In any event, the unity precedes and puts its imprint on the human being prior to any distinctiveness that arises from gender differentiation.

(2) God's Living Breath (Gen 2:7)

> *Gen 2:7: And Yahweh God fashioned the humanity* of *the dust of the ground, and breathed into its nostrils the breathing of life, so the humanity became a living breath.*

Since the term *nĕšāmâ* indicates a "movement of air,"[7] the whole phrase, *nišmat ḥayyîm*, which occurs here in conjunction with the root *n-p-ḥ,* "to breathe," should be rendered as the "breathing of life."[8] This conceptual notion of the method of bestowing life has significant and consistent analogs in other creation narratives in the ancient Near East. In Hebrew terms, in Genesis 2:7, the phrase *nepeš ḥayyâ* may be translated as "living breath," which corresponds to God's act of "breathing" (*nĕšāmâ*). The rendition "living being," found in some modern translations, makes the content too abstract for source-critical approaches, as the text in Genesis 2:7 relies on metaphorical language for its defining feature. This is an additional rationale for choosing breath rather than being in rendering *nepeš*. Note the difference between the two phrases *nišmat ḥayyîm,* "breathing of life," and *nepeš ḥayyâ,* "living breath"; the first phrase indicates an action, breathing, performed by God, the source of "life" (*ḥayyîm*), while the second phrase describes the result of God's action, namely, the bringing to life of humanity, introduced metaphorically as a living breath. As can be seen, the biblical account has nothing to do with any sense of a philosophical dichotomy between soul and body, or spirit and matter, with respect to the human person. Humanity does not receive a soul, but rather humanity becomes a living breath.[9] The adjective *ḥayyâ,* "living," employed in the phrase *nepeš ḥayyâ* underscores the reality that humanity has been a living breath since the first moment of its creation, and this humanity enjoys its dignified nomenclature as long as it struggles to preserve its dynamic relationship with the source of life. It is also interesting to note that humanity in Genesis 2:7 is presented not merely as the end product of God's action, as an object, or as the artifact of the action of creation. Humanity is, rather, a continuing part of the creative action of God, a living breath among so many other living breaths, all together constituting God's breathing, the personal openness of the Creator toward the created world. Thus, the depiction of humanity is as fluid and as dynamic as it must be to convey the underlying theological premise of God's interest and immanence in this world. This mandates that we accept that humanity's fashioning or becoming does not stop with the sixth day. Having entered into the world through God's breathing of life, humanity is continually refashioned and persistently accommodated to God, its prototype. Thus, humanity is a part of God in this world, his representative, and is therefore called to take an active part in God's creative and providential activities. This is demonstrated to us early in the Genesis narrative, when we are told of humanity's duties in the Garden of Eden, one of the first of which was "to work and to guard the garden" (Gen 2:15).

In order to understand better humanity's place and role within God's creation, we might take a brief look at another realm, that of the other living creatures. According to Genesis 1:20–24, 30, these living creatures, namely, beasts, birds, reptiles, fish, all *have*, or *possess*, a "living breath" (*nepeš ḥayyâ*). This is in distinction to the method of human creation: humanity *became* a living breath; it does not simply have such a breath. Nowhere in the Book of Genesis are we told that living creatures, except humanity, became a living breath; rather, all other living creatures simply *possess* or *contain* such a principle of life. Genesis 1:30 equates "every thing that creeps upon earth" with "every thing that *has* living breath (*nepeš ḥayyâ*) in it." Thus, all living creatures, except humanity, represent end products of God's creative action, not co-sharers with him in his creative activity. Only with humanity does such a role obtain.

We may say, then, that humanity can be defined in one sense by answering the question, Who is humanity? The answer that follows from our discussion is: Humanity is the living breath within God's creative breathing. Thus, being close to God in what he is best defines humanity's being, its existence. Yahweh, the God of Israel, identifies himself as "I am" (*ʾehyeh*) (Exod 3:14), and in a way humans are also defined through such an ontological term, "They *are* (rather than *have*) living breaths" of the "One Who Is" (*Yahweh*) (Exod 3:15).

Another important detail of Genesis 2:7 (Yahwist source) is the fashioning of humanity out of the "dust" (*ʿāpār*) of the "ground" (*hāʾădāmâ*). Humanity is not fashioned out of the solid ground or clay, as in other ancient myths, but rather out of a volatile, unstable substance, the dust of the ground. The theological significance attached to this metaphor holds that humanity, unlike the rest of the living realm, is less firmly attached to the physical reality. The nature of humanity is flimsy, fragile, yet powerful through the reality of its spiritual origin and relation to God.

The Yahwist account, with its anthropomorphic language, has the merit to underscore one facet of God's profile that is missing from the Priestly source, namely, God's direct, intimate involvement in humanity's creation and his personal interest in the continued existence of humanity. Throughout the six days of creation, God exercises his kingly power either through word or act, but nowhere else in the scriptural texts did he demonstrate the willingness to enter into such close relations with his handiwork as in the case of humanity. Genesis 2:7 depicts God as an ancient king, a shepherd king, who left his throne for the sake of his subjects. He shaped humanity out of dust because he wanted to be intimately involved in its creation as he had never been before. At the same time, however, he wanted his new creature to involve itself physically and spiritually in God's own creative life. In short, God wanted to bring humanity closer to him, in order to share with it the creative and sustaining life he enjoys. Thus, with creation, humanity became a constituent of God's breathing, and from that starting point forward, at birth, each human person is brought into God's breathing circle. Immortality is the natural consequence of such an involvement of the humanity in God's creative breathing.

The Genesis accounts do not tell us whether humanity was created mortal or immortal, but the conclusion that may be drawn from Genesis 2:7 is that humanity cannot avoid immortality because of God's willingness to attract it into his creative life. This harmonious relationship was weakened by the first humans' fall into the sin of disobedience. This fallen Messiah, then, must be restored to the fullness of the relationship of life with God. Through his life of perfect submission to the Father, his passion and resurrection, Christ will be able to effect the restoration of the edenic harmony between humans and their Creator. But this restoration should not be understood as a simple return to a temporal or spatial locus in paradise. Restoration through Christ translates into perfection. At both the Last Supper and on the Sunday of resurrection, Christ referred to the peace other than that which this world may offer (John 14:27; 20:21). This peace echoes Christ's perfection; literally, the Hebrew word *šālôm,* commonly translated "peace," comes from a root *š-l-m,* meaning "to be complete, to restore, to finish." In other words, the continual, persistent fashioning of humanity in the image of God was brought to perfection by Christ's life, his death, and his willingness to do the Father's will to bring humanity back into the fullness of its relationship with the Creator. (Jesus' peace refers primarily to the restoration of fallen humanity and its reconciliation with the Creator.)

Breathing life into humanity's nostrils means, on the one hand, that the new creature is not only touched but rather is formed, infused, filled with God's breathing of life. On the other hand, the imagery underscores the personal relationship between the Creator and its creature. God treats humanity with respect, as a partner in dialogue, in a face-to-face relationship, as one person to another. There is a hierarchy of relationships in the early Genesis narrative; namely, God creates the human collective in order to share in a personal, prosopic, dialogic relationship with it. Similarly, Eve was created to stand in the same kind of relationship with her counterpart. Her primary role was to engage in dialogue with her partner. Only after the establishment of this communicative relationship was procreation to follow. This particularity further differentiates humans from the other living creatures: the thirst for communion and reciprocal respect, the face-to-face dialogue that sustains us as social-spiritual beings. Humanity's destiny, therefore, depends exclusively on God's attitude toward it. The biblical account of Genesis 2:7 eloquently depicts the dynamic, fluid, and almost volatile aspect of humanity's fabric: the body is taken from dust, while the entire human person may be understood as the ambiguous, never controllable, always sustaining, living breath of God. The main point, the one that counts for us in this section of our text, is that humanity has been, from its very first moment, sustained by God's creative breathing, as a part of the Creator's own respiration.

Summing up then, the image of God in which the humanity was created may be represented by a cross, an image with both vertical and horizontal dimensions. Horizontally, the image of God translates into humanity's unity in diversity: the unity of our nature and the diversity of genders and persons. Vertically, the image of God refers to humanity's involvement in God's creative, inspirational being. According to Genesis 1:26–27 and 2:7, as long as someone preserves the unity in diversity of the human race while continuing to be(come) a living breath or co-sharer in God's creative breathing, that person is advancing toward the likeness with God in whose image we have been created. The choice of the cross as the instrument of salvation likely serves to remind us of our responsibilities as those created by God, in his own image, with an obligation to pursue and develop our face-to-face, dialogic relationship with him and our neighbors. In a similar vein of thought, Hosea 6:6 (cited in part by Jesus in Matt 9:13 and 12:7) shows what God really does want from us, "knowledge of God" and "kindness" among humans. These mean a personal, intimate, loving relationship with God (the vertical dimension), and kindness, consideration, and long-suffering love toward other living breaths of God (the horizontal dimension). The same bi-dimensionality of the image of God understood as a mandate may be discerned in Jesus' statement on the two great commandments (Matt 22:34–40; Mark 12:28–34; Luke 10:25–28), "You must love your God" (Deut 6:4–5) and "You must love your neighbor" (Lev 19:18), commandments on which "hang the whole Law, and the Prophets too" (Matt 22:40).

In addition, the Midrashim also underscore very well the two dimensions of this image in its interpretation of the unity of genders and their cooperation with God's glory (*Shekinah*): "In our image, after our likeness (Gen 1:26): neither man without woman nor woman without man, nor both of them without the *Shekinah*" (*Genesis Rabbah* 22:2).

The paradigm for humanity, therefore, is the *acquisition of perfection in time*. This is the goal and obligation of all members of the human collective. All other living creatures were made in one instance, but humanity was created in three steps. This illustrates the perfection given, or bestowed, in time, and it announces the phases of the development of the human person as he or she grows and strives to attain the fullness of the relationship with God. For animals, perfection was given in the moment of creation, and the serpent tries to inculcate in humans the notion that perfection is something that should be acquired at once. The unregenerate fallen pair accedes to this idea and loses its edenic privileges, a condition that has subsequently passed to all humanity and which must be overcome through Christ.

2. The Second Step: Reshaping the Face of Humanity

If we may borrow this metaphor, God, the great artist, painted humanity with the strokes of his creative brush. This was the first step in the genesis of humanity. The second step came when the artist looked anew at his adorned canvas. The freshness, and goodness, of his initial brushstrokes evoked contentment in him, but at the same time kindled the sense of a work unfinished. God perceived that something was missing. His canvas seemed a mere palette, crowded with shapes and drops of color but not quite yet a painting, for it lacked order, harmony, and structure. Details of content and nuances of shape were still to be added to his effort. This was the moment in which God realized that no matter how reliably his mysterious way of being, his unity of nature, and his diversity of persons, were reflected in humanity, his creation would not have been able to survive in the world as it existed. In the world, companionship, comfort, assistance, and multiplication are required. The second step in God's creation of humanity, therefore, was the fashioning of an opposite, one to act as comforter, helper, and conjugal companion. This other, this mirror in which the human person became able to know itself, was drawn from within God's creation itself, shaped from the substance of itself. This fashioning of the other is followed immediately by man's discovery of his own identity.

(1) A Help like Humanity's Opposite (Gen 2:18)

> ***Gen 2:18:*** *And Yahweh God said, "It is not good for humanity to be isolated. I will make for it a help like its opposite."*

In the creation narrative, in which God wills an orderly world into existence, he molds from chaos the elements of his creation, and, except for the second day, he reiterates that each constituent of his creation was "good" (*ṭôb*). The implication of this is, namely, that the creative result of each day fits according to his plan. At the end of the account, we learn that everything God had created was "very good" (*ṭôb mĕʾōd*), hallowed, and perfect in his eyes (Gen 1:31). Following this assessment of his efforts, God rested. In Genesis 2:18, however, for the first time the Creator realizes that something is "not good" (*lōʾ ṭôb*). The adjective *good,* as it is used here, in both positive and negative contexts, has an ontological connotation; that is, what is good is in harmony with God's original intent and the design he brought forth based upon that intent. This is an important linguistic device, and the use of "good" and "not good" is significant. Had the term "bad, evil" (*raʿ*) been used, it would have meant that God's creation, or part of it, was bad and that his work of fashioning humanity was bad as well. As it has come to us, however, Genesis asserts, "It is not good for humanity to be isolated." This is not something ontologically bad or evil; rather, it is the opportunity for the completion of humanity to be fulfilled.

The word *lĕbad,* which derives from the Hebrew term *bad,* meaning "part" or "portion," is commonly rendered "alone" or "solitude" (e.g., "It is not good for man to be alone"). In the present context *lĕbad* should be translated as "isolated" or "separated." God is not a selfish Creator. He understands that the human collectivity he created, even though it reflects the divine unity shared equally by the three persons of the Godhead, cannot survive within a living world dominated by a reproductive imperative. An isolated humanity might refer to either an isolation from the rest of the living creatures in terms of mechanisms of procreation, or to a solitude, the lack of social intercourse, which is one of humanity's greatest burdens. Humanity was fashioned by God as a dialogical and social being, positioned face to face with the Creator. Woman was created to complement the immediate role of the Creator in communication and relationship with man. Woman's role in salvation history is therefore as great as man's, in her role as an equal companion.

The text of Genesis 2:18 uses the term *ʿēzer,* meaning "help, assistance," rather than "helper" as some of the modern translations would choose. Scripture is again ambiguous, because the term *ʿēzer* is somehow abstract. The accent falls not on the concrete typology of help or of the purpose of help; rather, the emphasis is on God's own promise that, "I will make a help(er)" or "I will help" humanity. Help thus corresponds to God's designed standards and his will in bringing forth and sustaining his creation.

The word *negdô* may be rendered "its opposite."[10] The *Targum Pseudo-Jonathan* has *qblyh,* "in front of it," while the Septuagint opts for "according to him" (*katʾ auton*). The development of culturally specific gender assumptions is becoming evident with the transmission of the Greek text.

The Septuagint reflects the attitude of Hellenized Alexandria towards women, seen as servants whose purpose was to meet men's needs.

It is important to note that Genesis 2:18 portrays God not as a weak or uncertain being but as an active, thoughtful, and insightful Creator. He is compelled by his love of his creation to admit that something did not go well or according to his initial intention, and he therefore takes the measures necessary to correct or, better, to improve the situation. God is not a selfish artist, interested in admiration or esteem. He is, rather, our caring, loving father, for whom the well-being of his children represents the most important purpose. In addition, this text shows that the perfection of humanity occurs in the course of time; it is a *process* rather than a single event, as it was in the case of the other living creatures. Humanity merits the ontological recognition of "good" only after Eve was shaped and the communicative relationship between human persons was initiated.

(2) Playing God (Gen 2:19–20)

> *Gen 2:19–20: And Yahweh God formed out of the ground all the wild beasts and all the birds of the sky and brought them to the humanity to see what it would call them; and whatever the humanity called [each creature with] living breath that would be its name. And the humanity gave names to all the cattle, all the birds of the sky and all the wild beasts. As for humanity, it found no help like its opposite.*

Regarding the creatures created by God, the phrase *nepeš ḥayyâ*, "living breath," in Genesis 2:19 can be understood as a linguistic shortening of something akin to "[each creature] which has a living breath in it." It should therefore be rendered "living creature" (Gen 1:30; cf. 1:20, 24). Our point here is to highlight the difference regarding humanity and the other animals emphasized within the Bible itself. Genesis 2:7 underscores this fundamental difference. While the other animals *possess* (or *have*) a "living breath" and are therefore called (that is, defined as) "living creatures," humanity *becomes* a "living breath" only as a result of God's enlivening of it through his act of "breathing" into its nostrils. Humanity *is* a "living breath (creature)" as long as it stands face to face, in a personal, dialogical, relationship with its Creator. After the creation of Eve, the circle of personal communion of humans expands from a sacred relationship between humanity and its Creator, to an interpersonal, social-spiritual relationship among human persons and between them and their Creator. These widening circles of relationality define the process of perfection for humanity and will culminate with the rising Messiah's advent and his willingness to sacrifice in order to bring salvation history to its zenith. It is through love of others and the love of God that human persons achieve *theōsis* ("deification"); this is most eloquently expressed in both vertical and horizontal dimensions through Christ's life, ministry, and death.

Genesis 2:19–20 reiterates for us God's intention to fashion humanity as his reflection on earth, and the passage demonstrates the bringing to fruition of his will. This passage should be read as a complement to Genesis 1:26 for the most comprehensive understanding of the fullness of God's intent and the timing involved in achieving his goals. The Yahwist source (Gen 2:19) condenses into a single verse the details offered by the Priestly source (Gen 1) pertaining to the creation of animals. The Yahwist source instead dwells on what its writer considers to be most important in these verses: humanity's ability to give names, that is, to use the creative power of the language. That is, the Yahwist source clarifies humanity's sacred capacity to act as a co-creator with God (cf. Gen 2:7), and to exercise its stewardship over all living beings, over all those creatures that possess the "living breath." By giving names to these creatures, humanity engages in its role and duty as God's representative on earth. This parallels God's own naming of the light ("day") and the darkness ("night") and is one of the paramount responsibilities bestowed by God upon his created children (Gen 1:5). It is a critical element of the relationship shared by God and humanity, the relationship that humanity ultimately abrogates, and the restoration of which is enabled by the rising Messiah.

The end of Genesis 2:20 could be translated from the Hebrew text in either of two ways, "But for humanity (*ʾādām*) was not found a help like its opposite," or, "As for humanity, it found no help like its opposite." The first rendering is amplified in the Septuagint's understanding that help was not found in the realm of the animals.[11] The second option relies on linguistic markers[12] to convey the notion, in context, that humanity went far beyond the mandate entrusted to it by God, namely, to give names to all creatures. In this formulation, humanity has seized the opportunity to attempt, unsuccessfully, to find for itself a help. In the process of this effort, humanity has committed two mistakes, both of which are founded on the hasty and narrow understanding of God's promise as it was articulated in Genesis 2:18, "I will make a *help* like its opposite." Although God was not specific on the nature and profile of the "help" (*ʿēzer*), humanity immediately equated the ambiguous, abstract "help" with the more concrete "helper," assuming that its "helper" (!) should be found among any of the living creatures. Thus humanity foolishly believed in its own ability to anticipate God's mind, will, and actions, and was disappointed when such anticipation was unrealized. This is a common biblical theme, which we will return to later. In addition, humanity also believed, incorrectly, that it could understand the mystery of God; that is, humanity heard in God's words that the source of its "help(er)" would be outside of itself, because of God's description of the help "like its opposite" (*kĕ-negdô*) (Gen 2:18). Hence, humanity multiplied its mistake of trying to predict and thereby reducing the magnificence of God's activity on its behalf.

Humanity comes across in this brief episode as an entity that is eager, anxious to fulfill God's promise in its own time and manner. Such haste and misdirection have plagued humanity from the outset and have resulted in its expulsion from Eden. A similar situation obtains later with Abraham. The patriarch is told in Genesis 12:2 that he will become the father of a great nation, but the reality with which he is confronted is quite contrary to this, for Sarah was barren and could not bear his children (Gen 11:30; 16:1). Like humanity in Eden in Genesis 2:19–20, Abraham attempted to fulfill God's promise through his own actions. Urged by Sarah, Abraham takes to himself the maidservant Hagar, who gives birth to Ishmael. But Yahweh intervenes and promises Abraham that it is Yahweh himself, the one who promised a great nation out of Abraham, who will ensure the fulfillment of that promise through Isaac's birth, "But my covenant I will establish with Isaac, whom Sarah shall bear to you at this season next year" (Gen 17:21 NRSV). These biblical narratives reveal to us a reliable God, one who always delivers as he promises. The impatient human being, always inclined to play God by seeking to bring God's promises to their fulfillment in his own way, fails in such endeavors. Even in such failure and the implicit mistrust that humans' efforts reveal, God maintains his fidelity to his promise and to his children, regardless of their cursing, muttering, and intransigence.

(3) A Help from inside Humanity (Gen 2:21–22)

> ***Gen 2:21–22:*** *So Yahweh God caused a deep sleep to fall upon the humanity; and, while it slept, he took one of its ribs and closed up its place with flesh. And Yahweh God fashioned the rib that he had taken from the humanity into a woman; and he brought her to the humanity.*

Up to Genesis 2:18, the Septuagint follows the Hebrew text (MT) very closely and views the first human entity as a neutral, genderless, collective entity. This explains the Septuagint's rendition of the Hebrew *ʾādām* as *anthrōpos*, "human being." Beginning in v. 19, where this entity exercises its power over the rest of the living creatures, the Septuagint switches from *anthrōpos* to *Adam* written with capital *A*, pointing to a male individual, Adam. Thus, in the Septuagint's reading of v. 21, God takes the rib, out of which he will fashion the woman from *Adam*, the "man," and not from "humanity" (*ʾādām*), as in the reading of the same verse in the Hebrew text. This lexical choice in the Septuagint was most likely triggered by the folk etymology of Genesis 2:23b, which plays on the similar sounding Hebrew words for "woman" (*ʾiššâ*) and "man" (*ʾîš*).[13] However, there is no etymological relation between these words.

The *Targum Onkelos* adds, "God fashioned the rib...into a woman *for marriage*," in order to show that in fashioning Eve, God meant to provide man with a wife, to preserve the unity of the first entity through marriage. A similar interpretation is found in one of the Midrashim, "Rabbi Aibu said, 'He [God] adorned her like a bride and brought her to him [Adam], for there are places where coiffure is called building'" (*Genesis Rabbah* 18:1). The Midrash relies on the meanings of the Hebrew verb *bānâ,* "to build," which in some foreign dialects of Aramaic connotes "to plait" (of hair). This interpretation is made more significant by an additional text from the same work, "'And the rib, which the Lord God had taken from the man, made he (*wayiben*) a woman, and brought her unto the man (Gen 2:22)'—this teaches that the Holy One, blessed be he, plaited Eve's hair and brought her to Adam, acting as groomsman to them, because in the sea-towns they call 'plaits' *binyata*" (*Genesis Rabbah* 7:6).

The above ancient Jewish interpretations are based on the biblical text itself, which says that the Creator "brought her [Eve] to the humanity" (Gen 2:22). This demonstrates that the Creator is, above all, interested in preserving the horizontal dimension of the image of God in humans, namely, unity in diversity. "God caused a deep sleep to fall upon the humanity" (Gen 2:21). Humanity, who previously played God trying to find a "helper" for itself (Gen 2:19–20), is now brought to a complete state of passivity so that in the future it might not credit Eve's creation to itself. The word *tardēmâ,* "deep sleep,"[14] reflects quite precisely humanity's state, which appears similar to lethargy or numbness. Humanity itself has no share or role in Eve's creation. Both male and female are creatures fashioned by God, and humanity's earlier temporal advent does not translate into an indication of the gender superiority of its default element, man.

The text of Genesis 2:22 represents the climax of the second step in refashioning humanity: the creation of the helper from *inside* rather than *outside* of the human collective. By creating a helper from within humanity, God evidences that he wants to preserve the unifying principle of the two, that both may share in their common nature, the nature of humanity. This biblical datum has critical significance for understanding some of the tenets of our Christian faith. For instance, when we speak of original sin, the first sin that *ʾādām,* "humanity," committed was embodied by both male and female. This is possible because of the unity of humanity's common nature. Therefore, salvation of both is also possible: because of the unity of essence between the two elements of humanity. The fundamental considerations of biblical anthropology, origin, sin, and salvation, are comprehensible only if we know that all humans share one essence and that our common fates are linked because of this essence.

As can be seen, humanity's example places much emphasis on the unity of nature. When God created his other living creatures, he fashioned them according to their kinds, or species (cf. Gen 1:21). Thus, in the case of the living creatures, the biblical emphasis is on the diversity of species. From their first moments, the living creatures were created in their diversity. Humanity, conversely, first appears as a unity with gender diversity implied. It is only after God realized that humanity must not be isolated that the diversity of two genders and persons became a reality. We might add that, in humanity's case this diversity cannot be reduced solely to genders. Humanity, as we have shown, was created by God as a *person*, in a face-to-face dialogue consisting of the "breathing of life" (Gen 2:7). When this humanity is reshaped as male and female, the gender distinction enriches this personal, horizontal dimension. The other living creatures do not have such a distinction, as they were brought into existence by a simple creative act without God's personal involvement (compare Gen 1:20–21 with, e.g., Gen 2:7). The living creatures have, therefore, a unity of species, but not the unity of a personalized nature God intended for humanity.

In the biblical texts, the word for "rib," *ṣēlāᶜ*, is used frequently with the meaning "side" (e.g., of a mountain [2 Sam 16:13] or of a building [1 Kgs 6:5, 8]). In this semantic context, Eve's creation presents itself in a more ambiguous light. She is not simply the discrete element of a "rib" drawn from humanity, but one side of it (cf. *Genesis Rabbah* 80:5). In effect, Eve is a mirror in which humanity finds itself reflected. Furthermore, if Eve is one side of the original totality, then the perfect image, or portrait, of humanity is obtainable only through the consideration of both male and female components.

(4) Man's Identity (Gen 2:23)

> ***Gen 2:23:*** *Then humanity said, "Finally, this one is bone of my bones and flesh of my flesh. This one shall be called woman, for from man was she taken."*

Note that the noun *hap-paᶜam,* "at once," rendered here "finally," was translated by the Septuagint as *nyn,* "now." Perhaps humanity was thinking of several ways of getting a helper, and when God created Eve, humanity recognized that this new creation was "at last, finally," after all of its pretensions, the only one able to share in its nature and to be a genuine companion and mate. Jewish interpretation falls mainly along the same lines, as evidenced in the *Targum Onkelos*, which renders the text as *hdʾ zmnʾ*, "this time," which is in the same vein of thought as the Midrashim.

Woman is brought by God to humanity so that it might exercise its role as co-creator, by giving her a name. Again, out of his love for humanity, God honors it with this privilege, even though humanity was totally passive at Eve's creation! But what is humanity's response? As was the case when it searched for a helper among the living creatures, this time also humanity goes beyond God's mandate. Man realized his own identity only after woman's creation, but instead of identifying himself with the default part of humanity, man marked a distinction between himself and original humanity. He stated, contrary to all that had been said previously in Genesis 2, that "woman was taken from man" rather than from humanity. This statement, found in the second half of v. 23, may be attributed to man's arrogance, or may simply be a later addition, a folk saying based on a popular etymology.[15] If we accept v. 23b as a folk saying, then we may assume that the Septuagint, based on this verse, redacted Genesis 2:19 by replacing the word *anthrōpos*, a good match for the Hebrew *ʾādām*, with the word *Adam*, written with capital *A*, and referring to "Adam" as a male person. Another important detail is the distinction that arises from man's semantic usage. When he spoke of himself and the woman God created from a rib, he used the pair of words *ʾîš* /*ʾiššâ*, "man/woman" which highlights the social differences between the two.

According to Genesis 1:26–27, gender characteristics (*zākār/nĕqēbâ*, "male/female") is a distinction willed and designed by God as constitutive elements of primeval humanity. Therefore, the distinction is one of complementarity, not of social hierarchy, exclusiveness, or subordination. Man, in emphasizing the difference as a social one, abrogates his fidelity to God's original purpose once again.

3. The Third Step: Humanity's Unity Regained

Made One for Another (Gen 2:24)

> ***Gen 2:24:*** *Hence a man leaves his father and mother and clings to his wife, so that they become one flesh.*

The verb *dābaq*, meaning "to cling, stick to," designates a complete intertwining of male and female, a divinely ordained union that is difficult to destroy. A similar usage of the same verb is found in Job 38:38, where clods of earth stick tightly together by rain.

As previously, when humanity overstepped God's mandate, a lesson in humility followed. The first lesson was the deep sleep; the second was man's obligation to leave his family and everything familiar to join the woman and her family.[16] This is a reversal of ancient custom and makes for an interesting turn of phrase. Man stated, incorrectly, that woman had been the one taken from him. God, to attenuate man's arrogance, reorders tradition and places the priority of familial origins with the woman. These familial, or social, origins and man's instruction to leave his family therefore serve as a reminder that God's will, not humans', is preeminent.

In addition, the phrase *ʿal–kēn,* "hence, that is why," is somewhat awkward here, since there is no logical connection between Adam's statement in v. 23 and the command for man to leave his parents in order to cleave to his wife in v. 24. However, marriage (conjugal union) was instituted in the Garden of Eden as a mechanism by which humanity's original unity was to be kept intact. The Book of Genesis hints at the natural character of this institution, since the words reproduced in v. 24 are a continuation of man's statement in v. 23. In any event, marriage appears in the context of the Yahwistic narrative of man's creation and is certainly intended by the Creator to keep the male/female polarity unified. Unfortunately, this mechanism did not long prove successful. Humans' transgression of God's commandment not to eat from the tree of knowledge of good and evil precipitated a rapid and deep fragmentation of the created world, beginning with the union between male and female. Adam's accusation of Eve in front of the Creator (Gen 3:12) mirrors this fragmentation. Moreover, God's sanctioning of Eve's misdeed (Gen 3:16) implies a gloomy future for the conjugal union. This will be marked by a situation of tension: to woman's longing for her man (*tĕšûqâ,* "longing, burning desire"),[17] man will respond with a rude attitude, trying "to rule" (*māšal*) over her. This same pair of words (*tĕšûqâ–māšal*) is used to define the relationship between man and the personified Sin in Cain's story (Gen 4:7). Longing and sin are tensely associated in both narratives. Strangely, woman's longing for man is compared to Sin's longing for the human being, while man's domination over his wife is seen in terms of man's ruling over Sin. In these circumstances, as the narratives imply, an impaired conjugal union puts in jeopardy the unity in diversity of humanity, and all are menaced by a deepening crisis. The image of God in humanity is at risk, and the original Messiah, humanity, is fallen. Sin divides man from woman and humanity from God. The rupture in these horizontal and vertical personal relationships is the core of the nature of sin and is that which we are called to overcome through love, patience, and care for others. In this world, however, in our state of sinfulness, this is a task few are able to achieve completely. Therefore, God devises a new means of restoring relationships and reestablishing the unity of his creation: the rising Messiah. As we mentioned above, Jesus the Messiah, the perfect one, "the last Adam" (1 Cor 15:45) came to restore humanity to its natural state of unity in diversity (Col 3:11).

Marriage is depicted here as a complete entwining of male and female resulting in *bāśār*, one "flesh." Based on Gen 2:7, in which humanity is introduced as the "living breath" (*nepeš ḥayyâ*) of God, one may expect that the unity of male and female will be, finally, in a "living breath." Contrary to this, they become one "flesh." This concrete imagery is intended to underscore the material union between the two, which was originally meant to reaffirm and preserve the initial unity of primeval humanity with its two gender elements implied. Thus, the single "flesh" achieved by marital union reminds us that the purpose of such conjugality is to restore our common, unified humanity in its primeval beauty: a perfect unity in diversity.

Notes

1. Quoted in James L. Kugel, *The Bible as It Was* (Cambridge, MA: Belknap Press of Harvard University Press, 1997), 62.

2. For a discussion of the various meanings of the term *ṣelem*, "image," see Claus Westermann, *Genesis 1–11: A Commentary*, trans. John J. Scullion (Minneapolis: Augsburg, 1984), 147–55.

3. Diadochus of Photice explains, "All men are made in God's image; but to be in his likeness is granted only to those who through great love have brought their own freedom into subjection to God" (*On Spiritual Perfection* 4); quoted in Andrew Louth, ed., *Genesis 1–11*, Ancient Christian Commentary on Scripture, Old Testament 1 (Downers Grove, IL: InterVarsity, 2001), 30.

4. The proponents of the documentary hypothesis discern four main sources or documents behind the present text of the Pentateuch. These sources are: J (Yahwist source), ca. 950–850 BC, in Judah, which is distinct for its anthropomorphic language; E (Elohist source), composed in Israel around 750 BC, known for its emphasis on God's transcendence; D (Deuteronomist source), making up the book of Deuteronomy, was composed toward the end of the seventh century BC, in Jerusalem, and is known for preaching of the law; P (Priestly source), written during the Babylonian exile (ca. 550 BC), shows a special interest in worship.

5. For instance, the pair *zākār*, "male" (basic meaning, "phallus," perhaps from a root *z-k-r* II, "to be strong") and *nĕqēbâ*, "female" (*perforata*, as sexual being, from a root *n-q-b*, "to make a hole, to perforate").

6. For instance, *ʾîš*, "male" (perhaps from **ʾ-š-š*, Arab. *ʾaṯṯa*, "to grow profusely") and *ʾiššâ*, "female" (unknown etymology, but see below for some attempts).

7. Cf. *nišmat rûaḥ* (2 Sam 22:16//Ps 18:16). The word *nepeš* may designate "throat, neck, breath, being" (from the root *n-p-š*, "to inhale, breathe").

8. Cf. Genesis 7:22: *nišmat rûaḥ ḥayyîm*, literally, "breathing of the living spirit"

(of animals). A similar phrase is found in the Amarna Letters (fourteenth century BC), e.g., *šar balāṭi,* the "breath of my life" (*EA* 141:6); or "the breath of the mouth of the king" (*EA* 137:7); in both examples, it is said of the sovereign king of Egypt.

9. Note that *Targum Pseudo-Jonathan*'s interpretation maintains that the "soul," namely, the ability to speak, is located in humanity, "and it [God's breathing] became in humanity a speaking spirit (*rwḥ mmll*ʾ)."

10. From the verbal root *n-g-d,* "to be in front, to be opposite"; hence the noun *nāgîd,* "leader," literally means "the one who stands in front" of a gathering.

11. The passive *ouch heuretē,* "it was not found," used in the Septuagint, does not say who was trying to find a help for Adam, probably God.

12. That is, if one takes the consonant *lamed* (*l-*) prefixed to *ʾādām* as a topicalization particle, that is, turning the first part of the sentence into a topic, "As for/with respect to *ʾādām*"; yet the prefixed *lamed* may also function as a dative marker, "to, for," hence the Septuagint reading, "For / to (*tō*) Adam was not found...." We may mention that within the context of Genesis 2, the former alternative (*lamed* as a topicalization particle) seems more likely.

13. "This one shall be called woman (*ʾiššâ*), for from man (*ʾîš*) was she taken." Although the etymology of these terms is still debated, *ʾiššâ,* "woman," might derive from a root *ʾ-n-š* I, meaning "to be weak," while *ʾîš,* "man, male," should be traced back to a root **ʾ-w-š,* meaning "to give"(?) or "to be strong"(?); or *ʾ-š-š,* as in Arabic *ʾaṯṯa,* "to grow profusely," or *ʾ-n-š* II, "to be intimate" (see *HALOT,* 449).

14. The noun *tardēmâ* derives from the root *r-d-m,* which connotes the idea of "numbness." Note Genesis 15:12, where the same word appears with reference to Abraham during a theophany about Israel's future servitude in a foreign land (i.e., Egypt).

15. The popular etymology would derive the word *ʾiššâ,* "female," from the word *ʾîš,* "man, male," but as we saw above, these words are similar to one another only in sound; otherwise they relate to different verbal roots.

16. In customary terms this was an innovation: in the ancient Near East, women were to leave their parents' household and join the man's; in the biblical reversal, the man is commanded to leave everything for the woman.

17. Isaiah 29:8: pulsating throat; from the root *šāqaq,* "to strive, long for," a by-form of *š-w-q* II.

II

Swinging between Life and Power

1. God's Enticement

(1) A Garden, a Steppe, and Chaos (Gen 2:8)

> ***Gen 2:8:*** *Yahweh God planted a garden in Eden, in the east, and placed there the humanity that he had fashioned.*[1]

As this passage indicates, the geography of the Yahwist who wrote Genesis 2 is quite simple. It consists, essentially, of three concentric circles, each of which is associated with a specific group of living creatures. The first circle is the garden, or oasis, associated with humanity. The garden[2] was planted by God to shelter the newly created humanity, whose food was restricted to vegetables and tree fruit.[3] The text of Genesis 2:8 locates the garden in *ʿēden,* "Eden." The proper noun *Eden*[4] may be related to the Hebrew word *ʿēden,* meaning "bliss, delight, jewelry," with the carried meaning of "a garden of delight, or bliss." But "Eden" may also be connected to the Sumerian-Akkadian word *edinu,* designating "steppe, open land" (*CAD* E:27). This steppe is the second circle, and its etymology fits well in the Yahwist's context: God planted the garden, the oasis, in the steppe. In this context, the name of the garden was drawn from the region in which it was situated. "Eden," as a steppe, constitutes in the Yahwist's geographical knowledge, the habitat of animals. The Garden of Eden, then, is the garden that was created, or planted, by God in the steppe of Eden. In this sense, the meaning of "oasis" takes on greater significance. A critical reading of the texts and parallel interpretations brings us to the knowledge that, after the transgression of eating from the tree of knowledge, humans were evicted from the garden into Eden, or from the oasis into the steppe, to live in toil and to subsist on the food of animals. Jewish interpreters comment on this period of human existence and the changes that affected this world as a result of human error, "Abba Cohen Bardela said, 'The mountains became [barren] rocks, the dead began to feel [the worms], men's faces became ape-like, and they became vulnerable to demons'" (*Genesis Rabbah* 23:6). The third circle, the wilderness, is the land of Nod,[5] located to the east of Eden (Gen 4:16). The wilderness, throughout Israel's history, is reminiscent of the primeval chaos (Gen 1:2), and is thus the dwelling place of Azazel (Lev 16) and evil, unclean spirits. There is no place for man, no place for animals in this wilderness.

(2) "The tree of life in the midst of the garden, and the tree of knowledge of good and evil..." (Gen 2:9)

> ***Gen 2:9:*** *And from the ground Yahweh God made to grow every tree that was pleasing to the sight and good for food. The tree of life was in the midst of the garden, and the tree of knowledge of good and evil....*

It is critical that we correct a common misreading of the second part of Genesis 2:9, since several modern translations[6] render the text as if the two trees were both located in the middle of the garden. According to the syntax of Hebrew text,[7] the tree of life is in the midst of the garden, while the specific location of the tree of the knowledge of good and evil remains unknown. This ambiguous way of referring to the two trees is meant to bring the reader to a very important theological point. Prior to the serpent's guile aimed at the destruction of man, God sought to *entice* the humans by leading them to life. This is why he placed the tree of life in the middle of the garden. This tree, which sustained life, necessarily had to become the focus of attention for humans. The tree of the knowledge of good and evil, which bestowed power and control,[8] was dangerous, and its fruit carried the seeds of death. This one was placed by God in a unknown location in the garden, but not in its middle. In his omniscience, God knew that humans would fall into sin, and thus, as a loving, caring father, God placed the tree of life in the middle of the garden, so humans would be attracted to it and, having taken from it, would live forever. He placed the tree of the knowledge of good and evil elsewhere, away from the focal point of the garden, so that temptation and danger were far removed.

2. Mixed Feelings

(1) Happiness and Insecurity in the Garden (Gen 2:15–17)

> ***Gen 2:15–17:*** *Yahweh God took the humanity and gave it rest in the garden of Eden, to work it and guard it. Then Yahweh God commanded the humanity, saying, "Of every tree of the garden you are free to eat;*

but as for the tree of knowledge of good and evil, you must not eat of it; for as soon as you eat of it, you shall surely begin to die."

God is depicted in this text as a father who cares for his children and puts them to rest in a garden of bliss. For this great gift, God asks his child to do two things, to work[9] and guard[10] the garden. Working the garden is not the same thing as tilling the ground, which will come later as the punishment inflicted on man for his role in the primary sin (Gen 3:23). Working the garden, as it appears in this passage, equates with something pleasant, that is, easy, fulfilling work. God also asks humanity to guard the garden. It is here that anxiety[11] and the lack of security are introduced, and we learn that the garden of Eden was not simply a locus of happiness but was, rather, influenced by dense affect, with a jumble of emotions hovering within. Happiness mingled in the garden with feelings of insecurity and unease. The need for the garden to be guarded or protected gives rise to a pertinent question: *From what?* Or, *From whom?* What dangers lurked in the darkness beyond the bounds of the garden, roaming about, seeking to sneak inside?

This sense of anxiety is heightened by the command not to eat from the tree of knowledge of good and evil. This clear order[12] and the reason God gives for abstinence cause an obvious dilemma. On the one hand, the tree of knowledge of good and evil can provide humanity with the power to fight against insecurity, and a logical extension of this is the potential to impart a remedy for danger and anxiety. On the other hand, any eating from this tree will cause humanity to begin to die. This dilemma effects an intensification of the feelings of insecurity. Dangers are everywhere. Death is waiting, even in the edenic garden. An enemy is perhaps waiting outside ready to get in the garden when a good opportunity will occur. We may ask, along with the primeval humanity, an important question: *Which is worse? Death or a permanent sense of insecurity?* This question was, no doubt, in the mind of the original humans when approached by the serpent (Gen 3:1). It may be obvious, but worth stating, that the humans did not take into account the only sure way to rid themselves of their anxiety and insecurity, namely, by placing their complete trust in God. Instead of seeking the assistance of their Creator, the humans wrongly interpreted God's words in their narrow, naive framework dominated by fear and, ultimately, temptation.

This is an excellent point at which to address God's warning. Correctly translated, God said, "You shall surely *begin* to die," which is conventionally rendered, "You shall surely die." The latter rendering creates a problem. As we know, following the fall into sin and expulsion from the garden, Adam did not soon die but lived many years, until the age of 930 (cf. Gen

5:5). Did God lie? Of course not, but interpreters have tried to find an answer to this puzzle. Their answers encompass all conceivable alternatives, from allegorical to spiritual interpretations. The allegorists quote Psalm 90:4, "For a thousand years in your [God's] sight are like yesterday when it is past" (NRSV) and argue that Adam would have died at the sunset of the first day. Proponents of spiritual interpretations hold that God referred here to spiritual death, namely, the separation between humans and their Creator caused by sin. We believe that the text, and more precisely the grammar, offers a more satisfying answer. The Hebrew phrase *môt tāmût,* "you shall surely *begin to die,*" consists of an infinitive absolute, *môt,* "to die," for emphasis, rendered here by the adverb, "surely," and an imperfective, *tāmût,* "you shall die." Both verbal forms derive from the same root *m-w-t,* expressing the idea of "dying." The imperfective aspect designates an incomplete action, one in the process of occurring, with an unidentified starting point. It is unclear whether this starting point is in the past, the present, or the future. We suggest that a correct rendering of the imperfective *tāmût* must indicate a continuous future, such as "you will be dying," or the phrase as we have translated above, "you shall begin to die." This translation makes more sense in the context of the narrative and, more importantly, depicts death in its basic characteristic, as a *process* rather than a precise point in time. The interpretation with respect to spiritual death finds a good home with this new translation, since separation from God is one important step in the long process called death or, more precisely, *dying.*

(2) The Serpent's Guile (Gen 3:1)

> ***Gen 3:1:*** *And the serpent was the shrewdest of all the wild beasts that Yahweh God had made. He said to the woman, "Did God really say, 'You shall not eat of any tree of the garden'?"*

This passage introduces a quite interesting being, a talking serpent defined as "the shrewdest of all the wild beasts that Yahweh God had made." The Hebrew adjective *ʿārûm,* "shrewd, cunning" may have a negative connotation if one takes into account its connection with the Arabic word *ʿaruma,* "to be malicious." The Septuagint renders this adjective with a neutral word, *phronimos,* "prudent, wise," but Paul, speaking of the primeval serpent, resorts to a stronger term to characterize his profile, "The serpent deceived Eve by its cunning (*panourgia*)" (2 Cor 11:3 NRSV). The *Targum Pseudo-Jonathan* demonstrates that the serpent's wisdom was geared toward evil; the serpent was, in the *Targum*'s view, "wiser unto evil (*ḥkym lbyš*) than all the beasts." It was initially believed that the serpent had an upright stature, that it behaved like a human, standing and talking to others. According to Genesis 3:14, the serpent lost its erect posture after it was cursed by God. The evidence for the belief that this shrewd beast was transformed first into a dragon and then into Satan is articulated through a technique called *inner-biblical exegesis.* The Bible is replete with such recursive sequences of internal logic. For instance, Proto-Isaiah (Isa 27:1) juxtaposes the "coiling serpent" (or the "fleeing serpent," Job 25:13) with the "Leviathan" (cf. Amos 9:3).

The association of this serpent, or beast, with water is based on popular belief that the watery deep was a potential enemy in the beginning of creation (Gen 1:2). In the Hebrew text, Wisdom 2:23–24 identifies the serpent of Genesis 3 with "Satan," which the Septuagint rendered *diabolos.* The Greek term *diabolos* means "the one who separates," and English translations render this term "devil." There is an interesting contrast between *diabolos* and the God of the Bible: God is the one who creates and then preserves humanity as unity in diversity. Although God's creation implies separation or division of its elements (e.g., God divides the light from darkness [Gen 1:4]), this act of separation/division serves a benefic goal, to produce and sustain the dynamic unity of such a complex creation. As regards the "devil" (*diabolos*), he is responsible for fomenting the act that separates humans from each other, from God, and from paradise. Separation in this case aims at destroying the unity of God's creation. Through the serpent's guile the fragile male/female unity was fragmented, and the primeval humans were evicted from Eden (Gen 3:12). Passages in Revelation bring this inner exegesis to its fullness, "The great dragon was thrown down, that ancient serpent, who is called the Devil and Satan, the deceiver of the whole world—he was thrown down to the earth, and his angels were thrown down with him" (Rev 12:9 NRSV); and, "He seized the dragon, that ancient serpent, who is the Devil and Satan, and bound him for a thousand years" (Rev 20:2 NRSV). These texts represent the peak of the theological development from a shrewd serpent to Satan, the devil, and the great dragon.

The identification of the serpent as the shrewdest of all the wild beasts makes its objective much easier to achieve. The serpent's goal was to relativize God's warning regarding the death that humans would experience once they had eaten from the tree of the knowledge of good and evil. What other creature was more fit to speak of knowledge and its consequences for human destiny, if not a shrewd one? The tempter, in fact, went further in posing itself as the one who knew everything, even God's intentions. He portrays God as a jealous individual whose intent was to keep his creatures far from knowledge and, by consequence, without power. He planted the seed of doubt in Eve's heart, and it took root, prompting her to disobey God's commandment. The serpent began his conversation with Eve on a general note of doubt, "Did God really say…?" and ended up casting specific doubts on God's purpose vis-à-vis his dialogical creatures. Without the serpent's duplicity, the humans might never have taken action, but rather would likely have remained at their original level of naïveté in their thinking.

3. The Fall of Humanity

(1) A Preamble to Sin: Eve's Three Mistakes (Gen 3:2–3)

> *Gen 3:2–3: The woman* **said to the serpent,** "*We may eat of the fruit of the trees of the garden. But of the fruit of* **the tree in the midst of the garden** *God said, 'You shall not eat of it or* **touch** *it, lest you die.'*"

The sin of disobedience committed by the humans was preceded by three mistakes committed by Eve. These mistakes constituted a preamble to sin and an open door to the serpent's machinations. Each mistake was centered on the idea of doubt. For a better evaluation of these mistakes, one may turn to the New Testament scene of Jesus being tempted by the devil, as found in the Synoptics (Matt 4:1–11; Mark 1:12–13; Luke 4:1–13). For each of Eve's three mistakes, there is an analog in the New Testament; for each of Eve's inadequate replies, there is a correct way of responding to the accuser, namely, the way of Christ. In the text quoted above, Eve's mistakes are hinted at by the boldface words.

a. Entering into Dialogue with the Serpent (Gen 3:1–2)

Eve's first mistake was that she allowed herself to enter in dialogue with the serpent, even though she knew that her interlocutor was the shrewdest among all the wild beasts. Thus, when the serpent raised doubt, she replied at once (v. 2), demonstrating her weakness and her obsession with the tree of knowledge of good and evil. Her words betray weakness, which the serpent notices immediately, and he prepares a new, more devious assault. In contrast, in Jesus' case there is no evidence that he entered into dialogue with the devil. Jesus does not address the tempter; he only quotes from Scripture using a passive, or neutral, formula of speech, "It is written…" (e.g., Matt 4:4). Eve's engagement with the serpent is contrasted with Jesus' almost complete ability to ignore the tempter. In Eve's willingness to respond, the serpent found the opportunity to engage her in dialogue; in Jesus' case the tempter was blocked from conversation by the living word of God.

b. Creating Her Own Universe (Gen 3:3a)

Scripture is silent with respect to the precise location of the tree of the knowledge of good and evil. The inspired word points out only that the tree of life was in the midst of the garden (Gen 2:9). That the tree of the knowledge of good and evil was not located in the midst of the garden, as Eve alone suggested (Gen 3:3), may be seen from Genesis 2:9 and from the way God defines this tree after humanity's fall, "The tree from which I had commanded you not to eat" (Gen 3:11), with no additional information regarding its location. Yet Eve was very concerned with the issue of insecurity in the garden, and of overcoming this insecurity, and in her mind God had located the forbidden tree in middle of the garden. In the universe Eve had constructed therefore, the focus is on the tree of the knowledge of good and evil, rather than on the tree of life. Building this universe of her own, and then throwing herself into it, makes Eve vulnerable to the serpent's subsequent attacks. The serpent finds itself at home in Eve's universe and attempts to maneuver in order to poison the relationship between God and humanity.

c. Defending God (Gen 3:3b)

Eve's third mistake was her presumptuous effort to defend God. Such an effort evinces arrogance and a lack of awareness. Eve perhaps thought that she was taking a preventive measure, but it was futile and clumsy. She portrayed God as a harsh judge inclined to punish every transgression, with no meaningful understanding of man's weaknesses. Her evidence in this accusation is that God forbade the humans from eating the fruit of the tree of knowledge of good and evil. But she misunderstood the command, and in her ignorance misspoke on God's behalf. The divine interdiction did not include the act of touching, as Eve stated it did (see quote above). In his omniscience God knew that the temptation to touch would be too great. Even Christ, the perfect One, could not avoid temptation, and even he was touched by it. But Jesus refused to fuel Satan's trickery, because he knew that God does not need to be defended. Jesus knew this well and used God's living word as the most efficient resistance to Satan's assault. Eve, on the contrary, tried to defend God with her own words, leaving the door open to the tempter.

(2) Original Sin (Gen 2–3)

We may draw a few conclusions on the observations regarding the sin committed by Adam and Eve. This brief presentation of the *original sin* will be done in parallel with the sin committed by Lucifer and metaphorically depicted in Isaiah 14:12–15.

(a) The sin of Lucifer followed great deliberation and was seemingly for no reason at all. The sin of first humans came with no obvious deliberation, but for a serious reason, to get rid of the insecurity that dominated their life in the garden. Lucifer's sin was committed out of too much goodness, or too many gifts, lavished upon him. The primeval humans transgressed God's commandment trying to end their anxiety.

(b) In Lucifer's case, the sin may be described as an open rebellion against the Most High, aimed at usurping God's throne. Adam and Eve did not go so far; what they wanted was to gain a state of security. They did not target God at all. With God or without him, they wanted to have control over their own destiny.

(c) Lucifer did not have any tempter to mislead him from without, to compel him to rebel against God. Adam and Eve sinned through fear and insecurity, instigated and amplified, by the work of the envious serpent who exercised the role of outside tempter.

(d) Based on the above observations, one may say that humans' sin is forgivable, because it was naïve and motivated by a concern for self-preservation and security. Lucifer's sin, on the other hand, cannot be forgiven because it is an open rebellion against God, a serious and malicious attempt to usurp and replace God. In view of the nature of the humans' sin, God designed a plan of salvation for his creatures. At the core of this plan lies the restoration of humanity to its primeval beauty as image of God. In order to put his plan of salvation into practice, God determined to send his Messiah bodily into this world, so that he may restore the relationship of creation with its Creator. This coming unfolds prophetically in the messianic texts of the Old Testament.

Notes

1. This general statement using the common verbal root *ś-y-m,* "to place," will be revisited in a slightly different way in Genesis 2:15. In the latter case, in technical linguistic terms, the root *n-w-ḥ* was vocalized by the Masoretes as a Hiphil B, *yannîaḥ*, meaning "to place, leave." Nevertheless, if one makes a minor orthographic change, from *pataḥ* (short *a*) to *qāmeṣ* (long *ā*), beneath the preformative *yod* (*y*), one reaches a different form, *yānîaḥ*, Hiphil A, meaning "to give rest, to cause to rest." This new reading would impose an interesting metaphor, namely, God acting as a father who places Adam, his child, in a garden to rest.

2. Hebrew *gan,* "[fenced] garden," from a root *g-n-n,* meaning "to fence, protect"; Septuagint: *paradeisos*, transliteration of a Persian word, meaning "orchard."

3. Genesis 1:29: "every plant yielding seed...and every tree with seed in its fruit..."; but note Genesis 3:18, "You shall eat the plants of the field," which demonstrates the change in humans' diet in a post-fall milieu (i.e., a diet similar to animals' [Gen 1:30]: "grass" (*ʿēśeb*) of the field for beastlike humans).

4. Read *Edem* in the Septuagint.

5. From root *n-w-d,* "to be aimless, homeless."

6. For example, *New International Bible, New International Version.*

7. The Septuagint is only a calque, and therefore the Hebrew is authoritative.

8. The Hebrew idiom *ydʿ ṭôb wārāʿ*, "to know good and evil," may be rendered "to be powerful" or "to have control of everything," where *ṭôb wārāʿ,* "good and evil," was taken as expressing "everything."

9. For "to work," the text uses a generic verb *ʾābad.*

10. For "to guard," the text uses the verb *šāmar.*

11. Walter Brueggemann offers a superb analysis of anxiety triggered by prohibition that gradually took over the first humans (*Genesis,* Interpretation [Louisville: John Knox, 1982], 52–54).

12. The verbal root found here, *ṣ-w-h* (Piel conjugation), "to give orders," is frequently used in military scenarios.

III

Humanity's Fate Revealed (Gen 3:15)

Gen 3:15: I will set harassment between you and the woman, and between your seed and her seed; he shall strike at your head, and you shall strike at his heel.

THE TEXT OF GENESIS 3:15 has been always read as messianic, both by Jews (see below the references from the Targumim) and Christians. For this reason it is frequently referred to as the *Proto-Gospel* or the *First Good News*. It hints at Messiah's birth, the struggle between humanity and sin, and the ultimate triumph of the Messiah over human weaknesses. This text is not only messianic, however. First of all, it is a great text about human fate; that is, it reveals humanity's fate in this world. And as can be seen, this fate has remained profoundly unchanged through time.

1. Harassment between Serpent and Humanity

The text of Genesis 3:15 reiterates God's punitive words addressed to the serpent after the humans' fall into sin. The words of this passage outline the relationship between humans and the one who led them astray. This relationship may be characterized as harassment initiated by God himself in response to the first dialogue between Eve and the serpent. We must underscore that this harassment is only that; it is not a battle or a war. Neither is it merely a mental or an abstract enmity. Rather, it is a perpetual harrying, both mental and physical, which is always concrete in its target and means. It is important to note that the Hebrew word *ʾê(y)bâ* that was rendered as "harassment" is related to the name *ʾiyyôb*, "Job," the righteous sufferer who was repeatedly harassed by Satan.[1]

There are four attributes that define the harassment found in Genesis 3:15: *conspicuous, continuous, reciprocal*, and *ambiguous in outcome.*

(a) Conspicuous[2]

This is the primary characteristic. It seems universal, based on the human experience, that such harassment is not simply a subjective evaluation of life's events, but is rather an objective, conspicuous reality with which we must all cope daily. It is at times a cruel reality, presenting extraordinary difficulties to each of us, contradicting our most cherished beliefs and ideals and challenging our faith in divine justice and hope for order in this world. Yet the realism of a text such as Genesis 3:15 helps us to grasp the theological significance of our common fate and to comprehend the value of the wisdom imparted to us as a result of these daily miseries. Ignoring the truth of Genesis 3:15 causes us to remain vulnerable to Satan's continuous assaults while struggling to solve the conflict between God's justice and the tribulations occurring to God's people. This struggle or tension of theodicy is a core element of human existence, and one of the great mysteries of our presence in God's cosmos.

(b) Continuous[3]

The antagonism between Satan and his human quarry does not stop with the victory of the messianic agent, namely, Christ at his resurrection. Rather, it continues beyond this climactic or, more precisely, central moment in salvation history until the end of time. This is the destiny of humanity in its historical unfolding. Although Christ's resurrection did not fundamentally change the relationship between tempter and humans, it did betoken a new hope and a renewed faith in the ultimate victory of God over evil. In this victory, humanity will achieve *theōsis* ("deification"), and the relationship between ourselves and our God will be fully restored. The personal, charismatic oneness that was our original gift in Eden will be reestablished, and we will return to the communion for which we were originally created. Beyond this, the great event of Christ's resurrection also changed the balance of forces between the two actors: humanity now has a powerful and loving advocate, the messianic agent, on its side, one who is intimately familiar with both the tempter's shrewdness and humanity's weaknesses.

(c) Reciprocal[4]

This relationship is not merely a dyad of attacker and victim. It is, rather, bilateral. There is neither pure harasser, nor pure harassed. Roles change; the quarry may become the prey, and vice versa, and both inflict wounds on the other. On the one hand, as in the garden of Eden, the tempter is seized with jealousy for humans because they bear the image of God. This is why he is fated to strike at the heel of the humans: in order that he might deter them from the realization of their likeness with God and their advance toward *theōsis*. On the other hand, humans strike back whenever they do God's will. In response, the tempter strikes again, and so the process of harassment goes on as a reciprocal enterprise.

(d) Ambiguous in outcome

Since the roles of the two adversaries are in constant flux, it is impossible to know who is, or will be, victorious. The biblical text is quite silent regarding the identity of the victor in this world. The harassment appears to us as an endless endeavor with no clear outcome. In addition, there is no difference in its intensity or in its consequences with respect to the wounds inflicted by either combatant on the other. The text does not say explicitly that the messianic agent will be the final victor. The text does allow for one logical observation, however: Since God has set a beginning to this harassment, he will also be able to end it. We may assume, then, that God, the *initiator*, will be the final victor, and so the glorification of the Messiah, and the hope he brings to us, are critical weapons in our battle against the demonic forces. As victor, God will share this role with the humanity he created in his image, who will be restored to primeval beauty by the messianic agent.

2. The Seed of the Woman: Another Chance

There are two extremes in the history of interpretation of Genesis 3:15. On the one hand, the ancient Christian interpreters call this text the *prōton euangelion*, "Proto–Gospel," by regarding it exclusively as a messianic text pertaining to the victory of the woman's son, and the defeat of the serpent.[5] Modern scholars, however, refute such a christological interpretation on the assumption that in this text the Hebrew word *zeraᶜ*, meaning "seed, offspring," cannot refer to a single person, and that the meaning of the passage is therefore a curse (*TDOT* 4:150). It is true that *zeraᶜ* usually designates "offspring" in collective terms, but it is important to note that in Genesis 4:25 the same word *zeraᶜ* indicates Seth, Adam's son, whom Eve perceived to be the replacement for Abel.[6] It is not unlikely that reference to a single individual is intended by the term in Genesis 3:15. The assertion that Genesis 3:15 represents a curse is suspect, not least because God has already cursed the serpent in Genesis 3:14. In addition, in verse 15, God switched from cursing the serpent to warning him and the woman regarding their newly destined relationship.

The rebuttal of both Christian arguments is best expressed by ancient Jewish interpretation. The *Targum Pseudo-Jonathan* reads, "And I will set enmity between you and the woman, and between the seed of your son, and the seed of her sons; and it shall be when the sons of the woman keep the commandments of the law, they will be prepared to smite you upon your head; but when they forsake the commandments of the law, you will be ready to wound them in their heel. Nevertheless, for them there shall be a medicine, but for you there will be no medicine; and they shall make a remedy for the heel in the days of the King Messiah."

This passage counters both the purely messianic content of ancient Christian interpretation and the curse of the modern version. First, by using the plural "her [the woman's] sons,"[7] the Targum refutes the christological interpretation, which is based primarily on the Septuagint reading of the text. The Septuagint renders the Hebrew *zeraᶜ* as *sperma,* "seed, offspring," and maintains that it must be read in conjunction with *autos,* "he," and therefore the text might hint at Christ. Second, the Targum argues that the prophecy will be fulfilled at the end of time, "in the days of the King-Messiah," and there is no mention or indication of a curse having been repeated. Interestingly enough, both Jewish and Christian interpretive traditions read into the text more than is found in the words themselves. This is because both groups of interpreters assumed the ultimate victory of the Messiah, even though the text is ambiguous regarding the outcome of the mutual harassment between humanity and the serpent's offspring. The Targum underlines that there will be a remedy only for humans and this will occur in the days of King-Messiah. If the text is messianic or if it alludes to God's (or his agent's) victory, then this idea can be gleaned only from the fact that God is the one who initiates the harassment, as we pointed out above. No one involved in this fight, not the serpent nor its progeny, not the woman nor her offspring, and not even the messianic agent himself is in charge of the beginning and the end of the harassment. Only God governs the final outcome of the hostility and the final victory of his agent. The full and principal role of God in the messianic saga is not unfolded until the texts of the New Testament, especially God's role in the resurrection of Christ. This role is emphasized by the authors of the New Testament when they alternate between the phrases "Jesus rose again" (1 Thess 4:14; cf. John 2:22; Acts 17:3) to "God raised him [i.e., Jesus] from the dead" (Acts 13:34; cf. Rom 4:25; 6:4).

What, then, is the identity of the woman's seed? The Hebrew text uses the pronoun *hûʾ,* "he, it," which may refer to both "seed" (i.e., "it") or Messiah (i.e., "he"). As early as the time of the Targumim, this pronoun was understood as pointing to a male messianic agent, "the King-Messiah." According to the Septuagint, the messianic agent will be a male individual (*autos,* "he"), and so we see the origin of the christological interpretations that dominated the thought of the early church fathers. Additionally, the Vulgate, or Latin version of the Bible, reads *ipsa,* "herself, the very one (feminine)," which may be a reference to a female messianic agent. This has given rise to the great emphasis on the role of the Virgin Mary in Roman Catholic doctrine and spirituality.

Another messianic feature may be detected in the parallel between the serpent vis-à-vis the woman and the serpent's seed vis-à-vis the woman's seed. The encounter between humanity and the serpent does not end in the garden but continues throughout history. Out of his love for humanity, God is ready to grant humanity another opportunity to restore itself to the right relationship with its Creator. The primeval humanity failed to follow God's commandment and was led astray by the serpent's guile; Adam and Eve failed to recognize their Creator's superiority and desired to become like God as swiftly as possible (Gen 3:5). With the potential for behavioral reform, the offspring of the fallen humanity is given another chance to obey God. Unfortunately, they displayed the same brokenness of nature and the same obstinacy of spirit. The messianic agent was therefore required for humanity's redemption. In the New Testament, Jesus was victorious over his threefold temptation. He received his baptism from John, and willingly took upon himself the sinful nature of humanity. He permanently identified himself with us and incorporated us into himself. He thus became the last version of humanity or, more literally, *eschatos Adam,* "the last Adam" (1 Cor 15:45). In his human manifestation, he experienced and triumphed over the very forces that had previously led humanity into the wilderness. He encountered Satan and conquered temptation, and rather than struggling to be like God, Jesus humbled himself unto death and acted in accord with the divine will at all times. His perfection cleansed us and returned to us the possibility that we might reestablish communion with the Most High, our original creative purpose. Jesus' victory over the tempter is an anticipation of the final victory of God over the evil forces of this world.

Notes

1. We should add that both words derive from the same root *ʾ-y-b,* "to be hostile, to harass."

2. The *conspicuous* attribute is underscored by the use of the root *š-y-t,* "to set, put" ("I will set...") that may designate the act of erecting a wall, fence, or monument, something visible to everyone. Thus, God initiates this harassment as an evident, tangible enactment that characterizes the relationship between the tempter and humans.

3. The use of the imperfective aspect for the root *š-w-p,* "to bruise, to strike," which defines both the activities of the tempter and of the humans, points to the continuous character of the tension inherent in the relationship between the two actors. The best translation of the Hebrew is, "He will strike" or "He will be striking."

4. *Reciprocity* is underscored by both the repetition of *bê(y)n,* "between," and the use of the same root *š-w-p,* "to bruise, to strike," when one refers to the wounds inflicted by either combatant.

5. Ancient Jewish interpreters also saw in Genesis 3:15 a messianic prophecy referring to an eschatological King-Messiah, but these interpreters felt compelled to engage in polemics with their Christian counterparts' claim that the woman's offspring alluded to Christ, and that this figure was the Messiah. Several Targums

added specific explanatory words, *in the days of the King-Messiah*, in order to project the messianic ideal into the eschaton (the end of time); e.g., *Pseudo-Jonathan*, *Neophyti*.

6. The word *zeraʿ* is translated in most cases, when associated with humans, as "offspring." However, in at least two instances, Genesis 3:15 and 4:25, *zeraʿ* appears in conjunction with Eve and should probably be rendered "seed." In Genesis 4:25, *zeraʿ* refers to an *individual* (not collective "offspring") who supplanted Abel. In both cases, "seed" is uncommonly associated with a woman, Eve. Also in both cases, the role of mother is exclusively underscored. There is no word about the physical father's role. Moreover, in Genesis 4:25 (similarly to Gen 4:1), Eve states that God gave her a "seed"—God is presented as instrumental in the birth of Seth, although this is not as clear as in Genesis 4:1, where the same Eve declares that she "acquired" (root *q-n-ʾ*, not *y-l-d*, "to give birth") a "man," *ʾîš* (not a "son" or "child"), "with the help" (*ʾet*) of Yahweh. If this association between *zeraʿ* and Eve does not allude to virginal birth, as some traditionalists would suggest, then at least this association underscores the primordial role of Eve in the history of salvation as the source of the coming of Messiah (note that Abel and then Seth are types of Christ). We should add that the Midrashim suggest a certain relationship between Genesis 3:15 and 4:25, both of which were considered by the ancient Jewish interpreters to be messianic texts, "And she [Eve] called his name Seth, 'For God has appointed me another seed (*zrʿ*),' etc. Rabbi Tanhuma said in the name of Samuel Kozith, '[She hinted at] that seed which would arise from another source, viz., the King Messiah'" (*Genesis Rabbah* 23:5).

7. In Aramaic, *bnhʾ*.

Part B
The Rising Messiah

WE SWITCH NOW FROM THE *FALLEN MESSIAH* to the *rising Messiah*. Our objective is to address the prophecies of the preexistence of the Messiah. It may be worth repeating here that *Messiah* comes from Hebrew word *māšîaḥ*, meaning "anointed" or "appointed," and that the primeval humanity was the first Messiah. Humanity was appointed by God to represent him on earth, but failed to do so, and having failed to bring God's mandate to fruition, lost the dignity of being God's Messiah. The first Messiah stepped away from the relationship with its Creator, and this created the need for the advent of the rising Messiah. In the present work we call this second anointed agent of God the rising Messiah for two reasons: first, to distinguish him from the fallen Messiah; and, second, because this agent of God moves only gradually to the forefront of the scriptural narrative. He therefore rises perceptually through time in the texts, and his persona and role culminate in the resurrection and ascension of Christ. His coming was announced in texts we call *messianic* and this preparation unfolded throughout the centuries of Israel's history. Thus, the final Messiah (or the "last Adam" of 1 Cor 15:45) was continually rising from eternity and transcendence into the realm of historical time and immanence, up to that day when the "Logos took flesh and tabernacled among us" (John 1:10).

I

The Preexistence of Messiah

He [Messiah] is pure from sin.
(*Psalms of Solomon* 17:36;
second century BC)

UNLIKE THE FALLEN ADAM, the rising Messiah has a prehistory, not only a history or a biography. Human persons have a history, including birth, the span of life, and death, but Messiah also has a prehistory, a great deal of which is subtly manifest in the texts of the Old Testament. One of these moments of manifestation is John the Baptist's address to the crowds coming to him to receive the baptism. John makes this observation, "After me comes a man who ranks ahead of me because he was before me" (John 1:30 NRSV). He referred, of course, to Jesus Christ, and his statement underscores the idea that Christ, in reality, was the preexistent one. Similarly, the evangelist remarked, "Jesus said to them, 'Very truly, I tell you, before Abraham was, I am'" (John 8:58 NRSV). This text paraphrases Revelation, "'I am the Alpha and the Omega,' says the Lord God, who is and who was and who is to come, the Almighty" (Rev 1:8 NRSV), and both passages emphasize the preexistent and eternal reality of the Messiah.

This chapter on the preexistence of the Messiah contains two sections. In the first part, we will discuss specific texts that attest to the preexistence of Messiah within the Godhead. The second part will address texts that pertain to the Messiah's pre-incarnate manifestations in salvation history.

1. WITHIN THE GODHEAD

(1) Poured Out as a Libation (Prov 8:23; Ps 2:6 [LXX and pre-MT])

Prov 8:23: *From everlasting, I was poured out as a libation, from the beginning, before the earth [was made].*

Ps 2:6: As for me, I was poured out (anointed) king by him on Sion, his holy mountain.

The central verb in both of the above quotations is *nāsak*, meaning "to pour out [liquid] as a libation, to anoint, to appoint, to set."[1] In Proverbs 8:23, the personified Wisdom, which corresponds to the Logos found in John 1, declares majestically that she "was poured out as a libation." The immediate question that arises is, *By whom?* A careful reading indicates that it was by the Creator, whose intense love for his Wisdom is portrayed as a font bursting forth, unable to be contained. It is not simply Wisdom that pours out, however; it is also abundant fatherly love, goodness, and power. God begets his Wisdom (Prov 8:22) as is summed up so precisely in the Nicene Creed referring to Christ, the incarnate Logos: he is "begotten and not made." The Creator begets his Wisdom "from everlasting,"[2] or "from the beginning,"[3] but since the latter phrase may seem quite ambiguous, the author adds, "before the earth [was made]."[4] In addition to giving us a temporal framework in which to understand the original expression of God's Wisdom, this phrasing also serves to eliminate any assumption that Wisdom was "poured out" at the same time as the earth or other elements of the creation were brought into reality. Unlike the earth, Wisdom was not created but was begotten before time, poured out by the eternal fountain of love, that is, the Father.

The text of Proverbs 8:23 offers us insight into a quite important theological idea. Since everlasting, Wisdom (or Logos) has had a propensity toward sacrifice. Thus, Wisdom is depicted in Proverbs 8:23 as a libation, a flowing offering from eternity. Moreover, the Creator begets Wisdom as a pouring out of himself, as a self-offering: the cause of Wisdom is presented here as the Father's self-offering. This depicts the continuity of the persons of the Trinity; just as the Father offers himself to beget Wisdom, so Wisdom, as the Son, offers himself to restore the balance and harmony of a creation tilting toward perdition. The text also emphasizes the purity of the divine sacrifice, as witnessed in Christ's words to Mary Magdalene at the tomb very early on Sunday morning, "Do not hold on to me, because I have not yet ascended to the Father" (John 20:17 NRSV). Jesus refers to himself in this vignette as a sacrifice that must not be sullied by any human hands prior to its presentation to the Father. This is a very important consideration in the liturgical context.

In Psalm 2:6 the verb *nāsak* is used with reference to God's king on Sion, another messianic title. The king on Sion is the royal Messiah, who declares, as Wisdom, that he was "appointed as leader (with a libation)." He was "anointed," in other words, with the liquid chrism. The particular grammatical form used in this passage[5] might be taken as a hint of sacrifice, of the shedding of Messiah's blood on Sion; if this holds correct, then this prophetic message has its historical fulfillment in Christ's crucifixion. Wisdom, begotten before time, is also the Logos of the New Testament, and his eternal birth from the Father (Prov 8:22-23) and his birth in time and dwelling among humans (Ps 2:7) speak of the Messiah's sacrificial propensities and commitments on humanity's behalf.

The particular meaning of the verb *nāsak*, "to pour out" or "to bring a libation (liquid offering)," specifically designates a liquid offering. We note that an important corollary appears in the New Testament, when Jesus presents himself as a source of living water and affirms his readiness to share this living water with his disciples. This living water will, according to Jesus' own testimony, become a well in the disciples and will spring into eternity. Thus, there is a circle of living water flowing from everlasting with the Creator's begetting of Wisdom and returning to eternity with Messiah's disciples, who have been incorporated into the cycle of eternal life, that is, a cycle of loving self-offerings: "But those who drink of the water that I will give them will never be thirsty. The water that I will give will become in them a spring of water gushing up to eternal life" (John 4:14 NRSV); or, "He who believes in me, as the Scripture said, out of his heart will flow rivers of living water" (John 7:38; cf. Rev 22:17). That the metaphor of living water may be extended into eternity can be deduced from the Book of Revelation, "Then the angel showed me the river of the water of life, bright as crystal, flowing from the throne of God and of the Lamb" (Rev 22:1 NRSV). The use of verb *nāsak* and its variants are therefore crucial to our theological understandings of time, the divine unity, and the role of Messiah as an agent operating in this world on behalf of humanity.[6]

(2) Acquired by God (Prov 8:22 [MT])

> ***Prov 8:22:*** *Yahweh acquired (begot) me as (at) the beginning of his journey, before his works of old.*

The idea of self-offering or self-sacrifice is also found in Proverbs 8:22, in the imagery of the Creator begetting Wisdom.

The basic meaning of the Hebrew verb *qānâ* is "to acquire."[7] Note, though, that in the earlier uses in Semitic languages (for instance, Ugaritic and Old Hebrew), the same root is used to indicate "birthing, begetting," which accords well with the basic idea of the later Hebrew root, "to acquire," inferring, namely, the acquisition of something or someone that existed before but did not belong to the acquirer. A similar semantic development occurred with respect to things that may be acquired through creation or purchase. This gave rise to secondary meanings inherent in the Proto-Semitic root **q-n-y* (Hebrew: *qānâ*), specifically, "to create" and "to buy." Since Proverbs 8:22 depicts Wisdom as a person, we may consider that the meaning "to acquire, to beget" is more suitable than "to create." The Septuagint's[8] choice of *ktizō*, "to create," is explainable from the perspective of the third-century BC Jewish translators, for whom monotheism was the most important dogmatic tenet of their faith. The Hebrew text, then, is more ambiguous than the Septuagint and leaves greater room for interpretation. Therefore, for practical reasons, and holding tightly to monotheism, the Septuagint intended to make a clear distinction between God the Creator and Wisdom, the principle of creation, "made" rather than "acquired/begotten" by God.[9] It is worth remembering that the same root is used by Eve at the birth of Cain, "I have acquired (*qānîtî*) a man" (Gen 4:1). This formulation underscores the idea that Eve is not the creator of her offspring; that at each birth, it is God who continues to act as the Creator.[10]

With respect to the time of bringing forth Wisdom, Proverbs 8:22 states that this occurred before the acts of God, his works of old, "as (at) the beginning" of God's activity[11] from inside to outside. In this case, Wisdom was the beginning, the principle, or the means by which God created the entire world. This reading has triggered a long line of interpretations emphasizing Wisdom's role in the act of creation. This is an especially cogent construal when coupled with other biblical texts, such as Psalm 104:24, "Oh Lord, how great are your works, with Wisdom you have made them all." Additionally, in his prologue, the evangelist John combines an understanding of both interpretive possibilities of the term *rēʾšît*, "beginning," as it is found in Proverbs 8:22, namely, "as (at) the beginning," stating emphatically, "In the beginning (*en archē*) was the Word, and the Word was with God, and the Word was God. He was in the beginning with God. All things came into being through him (*di' autou*), and without him not one thing came into being" (John 1:1–3 NRSV).

(3) Brought Forth in Labors (Prov 8:24)

> ***Prov 8:24:*** *There was still no deep, when I was brought forth (through labor pains), no springs rich (heavy) in water.*

The meaning of the verbal root *ḥ-w-l* used in Proverbs 8:24 is "to writhe, to tremble, to be in labor."[12] This verse depicts the acquisition of Wisdom by the Creator through the birth mechanism, but not in the sense of a conventional birth.[13] Wisdom is brought forth through labor pains; that is, the birth occurs as an act of volition by the Creator, which implies that the birth of Wisdom (Logos) is an act of self-offering, an offering of love, on God's part.

Regarding the time, verse 24 tells that the bringing forth of Wisdom happened "before the deep."[14] The "deep" in ancient cosmogonies is the watery abyss on which rest both the earth's disc and the canopy of heaven (Hebrew *tĕhōm,* "deep": Gen 1:2; Job 38:30; Ps 104:6). Reference to this abyss in Proverbs 8:24 signifies that Wisdom was begotten before the abyss existed. Wisdom, in other words, was preexistent and instrumental in God's domination over chaos and his creation of the cosmos. Specifically, from Genesis 1:2 we learn that the "deep" (*tĕhôm*) was there when God began to create the visible world; but both the Hebrew text and the Septuagint are reluctant to use the verb "to be" when they mention the presence of the deep. The watery deep and the darkness sealing off this deep[15] are neutral realities, which were allowed by God to exist (or rather, to attend) as instruments to test the freedom of angels and humans.[16] From that point on, the deep became the dwelling place of the evil spirits and their followers.

(4) A Source of Delight for God (Prov 8:30b//Matt 3:17)

Prov 8:30b: *I was daily his delight, playing in his presence at all times.*

The text of Proverbs 8:30b provides us with a partial answer to an ageless inquiry: *What was Messiah's role vis-à-vis God before incarnation?* One answer, based on this text, may be that he was a perpetual source of delight for God. In Proverbs 8:30b, it is Wisdom, the Son of God, the Logos before the incarnation, who speaks, "I was daily his delight, playing in his presence at all times."[17] Wisdom, in this passage, constitutes a continuous source of delight for God, the same way a child makes its father rejoice. In addition, the notion of delight is intensified by the phrase "at all times," which connotes the idea of perpetuity.

The metaphor of "a pleasing child" is reinforced by the term defining the activity of Wisdom: She is playing in God's presence. The verb *śāḥaq,* "to laugh,"[18] conveys the image of a child playing in front of his father, while the latter is watching him with an obvious sense of joy. Peace, joy, and harmony are the constitutive elements of the relationship between the Creator and his Wisdom. A similar relationship is depicted in the New Testament's scene of Jesus' baptism, when the voice of the Father is heard naming Jesus "my beloved son."

> ***Matt 3:17:*** *This is my beloved son in whom I take delight (*eudokēsa*).*

These are God's words addressed to Christ on the day of his baptism by John at Jordan River. Christ receives the baptism offered to sinners desiring renewal, and in so doing he identifies his intimate relationship with humanity, the relationship that affords him such compelling insight into the human condition, and into the temptations and sins that characterize our lives. Nevertheless, Jesus Christ is, was, and will remain the perfect One, both God and man, and he is an endless source of delight for God the Father. He is, using Jeremiah's phrase, the "pleasing son" of God (Jer 31:20). In his revelation of Christ as his beloved son, God reveals himself as the Trinity for the first time. Speaking from heaven, the Father affirms both his essence of unity in diversity and his rejoicing in the existence in time of his Son, "This is my beloved Son, in whom I take delight." One of the meanings of the verb *eudokeō* ("to consider someone good and therefore worthy of choice") is "to take delight." In this parallel text, the Father confirms what we have read in Proverbs 8:30b, that Wisdom, or the Son of God before incarnation, was his eternal joy. He wants to say, "Look, the one who identifies himself with the sinners, and who receives the baptism of repentance is my beloved Son in whom I find delight. His *kenōsis* (emptying of himself) did not change my attitude toward him. He is still for me what has been from all eternity: a source of joy and delight, and worthy of my choice."

(5) God's Partners in Dialogue (Gen 1:26–27; Isa 9:5; Zech 13:7; Ps 110:1; Prov 8:30a)

> ***Gen 1:26–27:*** *And God said, "Let us make humanity in our image, according to our likeness. It shall rule the fish of the sea, the birds of the sky, the cattle, the whole earth and all creeping things that creep on earth." And God created humanity in his image, in the image of God he created it, male and female he created them.*

It may be worth restating the interpretive basis of this passage for our exploration of Messiah's preexistence. With respect to the plural "let us make" (*naʿăśeh*) there are at least three main avenues of interpretation: (1) the Jewish tradition, in which the plural refers to God and his angels;[19] (2) the ancient Christian tradition, in which the plural comprises God the Father and the other two persons of the Holy Trinity; and (3) the modern scholarly camp, in which the plural reflects remnants of archaic polytheistic beliefs incorporated into the biblical corpus. In this last formulation, God and other divine beings, perhaps lesser gods, are gathered together in a council. An alternate, or fourth, interpretation holds that the plural is a royal formula. This so-called *plural majestatis* (a royal "we") is uncommon in the Bible, however, and is therefore doubtful as a viable interpretive standard.[20]

What, then, does Genesis 1:26–27 say about the identity of God's dialogical partners? Who are these partners? What role did they have in the act of humanity's creation? The text is nearly silent in this matter, but the way God addresses the other persons makes us believe that they are virtually equal to him. God calls upon his partners to take an active role in the most important chapter of his creative work, and this in itself implies parity. In addition, equality of persons is demonstrated by the use of the singular "image" in conjunction with the creative work of the plurality. This illustrates that all members of the Godhead act together and share the same image, or essence. Had God addressed the angels or other beings, then we would expect God to speak in terms of plural, that is, images.

The following Old Testament texts are connected to Genesis 1:26–27 and should be brought to bear in order to answer the above questions regarding the identity of God's partners in the act of humanity's creation.

a. Messiah: A "Wonder-Counselor" or an "Angel of a Great Council"

Isa 9:5: *For a child has been born to us, a son has been given us; dominion has been on his shoulders; and he has been named, "Wonder-Counselor, Mighty-God, Everlasting-Father, Prince-of-Peace."*

The text of Isaiah 9:5 was interpreted as a messianic text as early as the time of the *Targum Jonathan*.[21] In the Aramaic translation of the Hebrew, the name "prince of peace" was replaced by the following phrase, which is deeply imbued with messianic flavor, *mšyḥʾ dšlmʾ ysgy ʿlnʾ bywmwhy*, "Messiah whose peace will grow upon us in his days." In addition to christological interpretations of this passage, the Jewish messianic applications of Isaiah 9:5 may also be found in the Midrashim, for example, *Deuteronomy Rabbah* 1, and *Numbers Rabbah* 1. The unison of Jewish and Christian voices on the understanding of this prophetic text lends substantial credence to the authenticity of its truth.

Furthermore, if we read the Genesis texts through the prism of Isaiah 9:5, then we can perceive, correctly in our opinion, that the partners in dialogue in Genesis 1:26–27 are likely to be either a "wonder-counselor" or an "angel of a great council." These two alternatives are consistently offered by the two main versions of the Old Testament, namely, the Masoretic Text and the Septuagint. According to the Masoretes, the partner is a "wonder-counselor" (*peleʾ yôʿēṣ*), while the Septuagint maintains that he is an "angel of great council" (*megalēs boulēs angelos*). The Hebrew text is quite ambiguous regarding the identity of God's partner; calling him "wonder-counselor" evokes the image of a counselor who supplies advice to his king. The deeper linguistic implication of this term indicates that this advice may in fact be surprising to the king, or unexpected.[22] The Septuagint, in distinction, tries to construct more concrete imagery and narrows the interpretive possibilities to a special kind of angel. This angel is one very close to God, a member of God's high council, where the most important issues are considered. The Septuagint is here one of the oldest interpretations of the Hebrew texts of both Genesis 1:26–27 and Isaiah 9:5. It may be useful here to include a reconstruction of the methodology employed by the composers of the Septuagint. First, the Hebrew text of Isaiah 9:5 was interpreted as a prophetic reflection on Genesis 1:26–27, where God's addressee in the Genesis passage was equated with the "wonder-counselor" of Isaiah's text. As we noted above, at the time of *Targum Jonathan,* Isaiah 9:5 was seen as a messianic text, and therefore the Septuagint proceeds to its second interpretive step, namely, equating the "wonder-counselor" with Messiah. In order to do this convincingly, the Septuagint renders the Hebrew phrase for "wonder-counselor" as *megalēs boulēs angelos,* "angel of great council." We might wonder why the writers of the Septuagint employed this particular lexical choice? The likely answer lies in biblical, or more precisely, Hebrew norms of presentation. It should be well known that most of the appearances of Messiah in the Hebrew Bible occurred in the guise of the so-called "angel of Yahweh" (*malʾak Yahweh*). Thus, the "angel of great council" is, in the Septuagint's lexical choice, identical with the "angel of Yahweh." This is a special angel of God, the messianic agent.

The Septuagint view, however, was interpretively expanded in the decades after its transmission, to include all angels. This was probably due to the onset of polemics, especially with the development of the christological interpretation of this passage by the early church. The Jewish understanding is found in one ancient interpretation, such as, "When God set out to create the first human, he consulted with the ministering angels. He said to them, 'Let us make man'" (*Genesis Rabbah* 8:3–4). The Christian convention maintains, of course, that God spoke to his consubstantial persons and that angels are a specific and distinct category of creation.

b. The Man: God's Fellow

> ***Zech 13:7:*** *Sword, awake against my shepherd, against my fellow man (*geber ʾămîtî*)—declares Yahweh Sabaoth! Strike the shepherd and the sheep will be scattered! Then I shall turn my hand against the young.*

Zechariah presents the messianic agent here as a man[23] close to God, namely, God's "companion" or "fellow man."[24] Thus, God's partner of dialogue is a human being with special divine features, similar to the "Son of Man" of Daniel 7:13–14. This is someone very close to God, depicted in the Hebrew text as God's fellow man. Note that the *Targum Jonathan* replaces the Hebrew phrase *geber ʾămîtî,* "my fellow man," which seems too anthropomorphic, with the Aramaic phrase *ḥbryh dkwtyh ddmy lyh,* "the friend equal to him, who is very similar to him," namely, a royal character.[25]

c. Melchizedek: Co-regent with God

Ps 110:1: *Yahweh whispered to my Lord, "Sit at my right hand until I make your enemies your footstool."*

The Hebrew root *n-ʾ-m* is related to Arabic *naʾama*, meaning "to growl, to sigh, to whisper,"[26] which clarifies for us the Psalmist's use of the image that "Yahweh whispered." There is a strong biblical convention that uses the prophetic phrase *nĕʾum Yahweh*, "the word [or, whisper] of Yahweh," which is attested 372 times in the Hebrew Bible. This formula is traditionally interpreted as a likely allusion to the prophetic inspiration as an inner, whisper-like process. God speaks directly to one's soul, a communication that necessarily translates into the metaphor of a whisper.

There are three characters presented in this Psalm: David, the psalmist, who narrates; Yahweh, who whispers; and the messianic agent represented in the Psalm by the mysterious king-priest Melchizedek (Ps 110:4). Yahweh "whispers" into Melchizedek's ear, distinguishing him as a secret (wonder) counselor (cf. Isa 9:5 MT) and as a prophet of God's works. In addition, this special counselor is invited by Yahweh to share with him in his power and dominion. God promises his co-regent that he will one day put all enemies beneath him, as a footstool. Until that day, Messiah will rejoice in God's glorious partnership of dialogue.

That this co-regent of God is more than an angel is seen in the Letter to the Hebrews, "But to which of the angels has he ever said, 'Sit at my right hand until I make your enemies a footstool for your feet?'" (Heb 1:13 NRSV). The evangelist Matthew also suggests equality between God in heaven and his Messiah, called "the Lord," "He said to them, 'How is it then that David by the Spirit calls him Lord, saying, "The Lord said to my Lord, 'Sit at my right hand, until I put your enemies under your feet'"?'" (Matt 22:43–44; cf. Acts 2:34–36 NRSV). These recursive New Testament reflections on the texts and images of the Hebrew Bible are evidence for us that those most closely connected with Messiah's work in this world were intimately familiar with the prophecies and persons that pointed to and culminated in Christ's life, ministry, and reparative work in this world. We should point out that Psalm 110 has always been considered a messianic text, even in ancient Jewish literature. The *Targum of Psalms* exchanges the term "priest" (*kōhēn*) for the more indicative term "leader, teacher" (*rbʾ*), which points to the eschatological Messiah as Israel's charismatic leader (Ps 110:4).[27]

d. Wisdom: God's Confidant

***Prov 8:30a:** I was beside him as a confidant.*

Wisdom is speaking here, affirming her role as God's confidant.[28] "Confidant," or reliable, trusted, intimate friend, is the meaning of the Hebrew word *ʾāmôn* II, which derives from the root *ʾ-m-n*.[29] However, there is also a homonymous word, *ʾāmôn* I, which denotes a "craftsman." Some translations prefer to render the term in this passage as "craftsman." We have opted for the former meaning, "confidant," because it is supported by poetic parallelism,[30] and by the Septuagint's rendering of the Hebrew as *harmozousa*, "fitting (to him)." The idea reflected in both the Hebrew and Greek versions, is that of a certain intimacy and harmony between God and his Wisdom.

(6) "Son of Man" or "Son of Weakness" (Dan 7:13–14//John 3:13; 5:27; 6:27, 53, 62; Matt 24:30; 26:64; 25:31; Acts 7:56; Rev 1:13; 14:14)

***Dan 7:13–14:** As I looked on, in the night vision, one like a Son of Man was coming with the clouds of heaven; he reached the Everlasting One and was presented to him. Dominion, glory, and kingship were given to him. All peoples and nations of every language must serve him. His dominion is an everlasting dominion that shall not pass away, and his kingship, one that shall not be destroyed.*

In its present form, the Book of Daniel dates to the time of the Jews' persecution by Antiochus IV Epiphanes in the years 167–164 BC. The book was written in Hebrew and Aramaic, and it contains many hints at the events that marked the political, religious, and cultural milieu in Palestine in the second century BC.

The book *1 Enoch*, composed between the fourth century and the turn of the era, is one of the earliest commentaries on Daniel and one of the first evidences that Daniel 7:13–14 was read as a messianic in some Jewish circles of the pre-Christian era. What is even more interesting is that *1 Enoch* raises the "Son of Man" to the same level as God, making him co-eternal with him, "When they see that Son of Man sitting on the throne of his glory…For from the beginning the Son of Man was hidden, and the Most High preserved him in the presence of his might, and revealed him to the elect" (*1 Enoch* 62:5–7); or, "For the Lord of spirits has given (them) to him and has glorified him" (*1 Enoch* 51:5).

That Dan 7:13–14 was read as a messianic prophecy in the Jewish circles in the talmudic period (beginning with the third century) may be seen in the excellent comparison made by one rabbi between two messianic texts, Daniel 7:13 and Zechariah 9:7: "Rabbi Alexandri said, 'Rabbi Joshua opposed two verses, It is written, "And behold, one like the Son of Man came with the clouds of heaven" [Dan 7:13] while [elsewhere] it is written, "[Behold, your king comes to you…] lowly, and riding upon an ass!"' [Zech 9:7]—if they are meritorious, [Messiah will come] with the clouds of heaven; if not, lowly and riding upon an ass. King Shapur [I] said to Samuel, 'You maintain that the Messiah will come upon an ass: I will rather send him a white horse of mine'" (*Sanhedrin* 98a).

Additional Jewish testimony to the messianic character of the text of Daniel 7:13 may be found in the *Zohar*:

> And they [the Israelites] will exercise dominion both on high and here below, as it is written, "And, behold, there came with the clouds of heaven one like unto a Son of Man" (Dan 7:13) alluding to the Messiah, concerning whom it is also written, "And in the days of those kings shall the God of heaven set up a kingdom" (Dan 2:44). Hence Jacob desired that the blessings should be reserved for that future time, and did not take them up immediately. (1:145b)

At the first sight, the Aramaic expression *bar ʾĕnoš*, "Son of Man," seems to be a reiteration of the Hebrew phrase *ben ʾādām*; if this is true, it may be read to designate any human being. This phrase, *ben ʾādām*, appears fourteen times in poetic parallels[31] and ninety-three times in the Book of Ezekiel, where it points to man's humility versus God's majesty. Interestingly, it is found only once in the book of Daniel, and designates the prophet as humble receptacle of divine messages (Dan 8:17). If the Hebrew phrase itself was known to the author of the current form of the book of Daniel, we might wonder what was his intention when he chose rather to include the Aramaic phrase *bar ʾĕnoš* in Daniel 7:13? Perhaps the Aramaic phrase is not simply a calque of the Hebrew phrase. The Hebrew word *ʾādām*, "humanity," is connected to the word *ʾădāmâ*, "ground," and therefore the phrase *ben ʾādām* underscores man's earthly origin.

On the other hand, the etymology of the Aramaic word *ʾĕnoš*, "human being, man," in the Aramaic phrase *bar ʾĕnoš*, is still debated.[32] We suggest relating the Aramaic word *ʾĕnoš* to a homonymous root *ʾ-n-š* I, meaning "to be weak."[33] Relating human being, man, to weakness seems a reasonable and clear path toward solving the etymology of this word. Additionally, while the Hebrew phrase underscores human humility, the result of being taken from the earth, the Aramaic phrase underscores a novel element of this humility, namely, the weakness of the human person when meeting God.[34]

In Daniel 7:13 the Aramaic phrase *bar ʾenoš*, "Son of Man," connotes a very interesting character. First, the Son of Man needs to be introduced to the heavenly king. Second, he is riding on, or with, the clouds of the sky. He does not need a formal introduction to the king, but rather he reaches him[35] at the end of his journey in the sky.

In a nutshell, God's partner, as depicted by Daniel 7, is a complex individual, rejoicing in the condition and privileges of a (semi-)divine being, while remaining human, submissive before the heavenly king. In this humble position, God's partner may be labeled "the Son of Man," or more precisely, "the son of weakness" or "the weak one."

If Daniel 7 deals with the relationship between God the Father and God the Son, as the ancient Christian interpreters argued, then we can assume that the latter has a certain propensity toward weakness, or sharing in human weakness. This is why he was designated to become one of us long before he took flesh and became man. Paul underscores Christ's willingness to share in our weakness, when he writes, "For we do not have a high priest who is unable to sympathize with our weaknesses (*astheneias*), but we have one who in every respect has been tested as we are, yet without sin. Let us therefore approach the throne of grace with boldness, so that we may receive mercy and find grace to help in time of need" (Heb 4:15–16 NRSV). We might complement this Pauline text with a short paragraph from the so-called eschatological discourse of Jesus, "Then the sign of the Son of Man will appear in heaven, and then all the tribes of the earth will mourn, and they will see 'the Son of Man coming on the clouds of heaven' with power and great glory" (Matt 24:30 NRSV). The "sign of the Son of Man" was interpreted by ancient readers as a reference to the sign of the cross, a fair interpretation, if one agrees with the etymology we have advanced above, and the rendition of the Aramaic phrase as "son of weakness." Thus, the sign of the "weak one" cannot be anything other than the cross, and God, as Paul points out, can imbue the symbol of the cross with the character of his divine power, "For the message about the cross is foolishness to those who are perishing, but to us who are being saved it is the power of God" (1 Cor 1:18).

In the New Testament, the phrase "the Son of Man" is frequently on Jesus' lips, and in all cases except one it is a definite reference. Most of the time, Jesus uses this title to contrast his current state of humility and suffering with the glory and dominion he had before, and which he will reveal to the chosen ones at the end of time. The most consistent feature of the New Testament descriptions of "the Son of Man" is the judicial function of the exalted Jesus. The relevant texts speak of an exalted eschatological Son of Man (Matt 24:30; 25:31; 26:24; John 5:27; Acts 7:56; Rev 14:14). Some of the New Testament texts using the phrase focus on the preexistence in glory of the Son of Man: "No one has ascended into heaven except the one who descended from heaven, the Son of Man" (John 3:13 NRSV; cf. 6:27, 62).

According to Daniel 7:13, the divine-human character "was coming" (*ʾātēh hăwâ*), a vague expression that designates the appearance of Messiah as a lasting process. Messiah "was coming" before the great incarnation, and in Daniel's vision, "the Son of Man" was approaching the human observer, Daniel himself, but was unable to reach him at that point in time. On the contrary, he was approaching and "reached" (*mĕṭâ*) "the Everlasting One." The use of the verb *mĕṭâ* suggests that this encounter was a surprising, unexpected event. Since the Messiah "was coming," but was never able to reach Daniel, we can infer that he was moving at that time only within the divine realm and had not yet descended into human history. The quest of "the Son of Man" for "the Everlasting One" will be rewarded with a substantial release of power from the latter to the former (Dan 7:14). This release of power may be a reference to Messiah's eternal glory, about which Jesus spoke before his arrest, "So now, Father, glorify me in your own presence with the glory that I had in your presence before the world existed" (John 17:5 NRSV). However, Daniel 7:14 may also be a prophetic allusion to Christ's glorification after resurrection, "And Jesus came and said to them, 'All authority in heaven and on earth has been given to me'" (Matt 28:18 NRSV).

The "Son of Man," then, is depicted as "coming with [or: upon] the clouds of the sky." In the Old Testament, the cloud is the garment or dwelling place of deity, the symbol of its presence in the midst of the people.[36] Isaiah 19:1 lauds the "Lord riding upon a soft cloud"; at the transfiguration, the cloud was the sign of God's presence on the mountain (Matt 17:5 and parallels); and on the day of his ascension, Jesus was taken up in a cloud, "When he had said this, as they were watching, he was lifted up, and a cloud took him out of their sight" (Acts 1:9 NRSV). Similarly, at the end of time, a cloud will announce Christ's second coming, "Then they will see 'the Son of Man coming in a cloud' with power and great glory" (Luke 21:27 NRSV). The recursive connection between this text and Daniel 7 is obvious and reifies the specificities of Christ's role as Son of Man and Son of God.

Turning to the second character of the passage Daniel 7:13–14, we may make a general observation. "The Ancient of Days," though very popular, is perhaps not the most accurate rendition of the Aramaic phrase *ʿattîq yômayyāʾ*.[37] The basis of this phrase is that God the Father is the One who advances ahead of the passage of days, that he will always be ahead of time. We suggest a revised translation, "the one who goes beyond the days (time)," namely, "the Everlasting One." God is beyond time.

In addition to the specific linguistic criteria, the imagery evoked by the traditional rendering ("Ancient of Days") tends to be misleading and makes many readers think of a white-haired, gray-bearded, aged deity. We must stress that this vision of God is false. A careful reading of Scripture indicates that whenever God the Creator appears, his representation is sonic only: a sound, or a voice.[38] If the author wanted to designate an old person, a white-haired and gray-bearded elderly man, he would have used a different Hebrew term, namely, *zāqēn*, "old man."[39] The portrait of the "Head of Days" (corresponding to *ʿattîq yômayyāʾ* in Dan 7) presented in *1 Enoch* might seem to depict such an aged deity, "And there I saw One who had a head of days, and *his head was white like wool*, and with him was another being whose countenance had the appearance of a man, and his face was full of graciousness, like one of the holy angels" (*1 Enoch* 46:1).

Daniel speaks in chapter 7 of the brutal, chaotic rule of the earthly kings. His attention is drawn by the fourth beast and the blasphemies uttered by its eleventh horn (Dan 7:7–8). But the rule of the fourth beast, alluding to the reign of Antiochus IV Epiphanes, comes to an end when *ʿattîq yômayyāʾ*, "the Everlasting One," makes his appearance along with his celestial court in order to bring his judgment upon the earth. The beast is condemned and slain, and the "Son of Man" comes, is introduced to God, and receives his dominion on earth. The "Son of Man" is depicted here as the heavenly patron of the suffering people; the one who can and does suffer along with Israel (a true son of weakness). The "Son of Man" thus appears very similar to Michael, the patron (guardian angel) of suffering but righteous Israel (Dan 10:13, 21). This "son of weakness," who rides with the clouds in divine fashion, may be seen as the mediator, destined to build a bridge between God and humans, which has been so long awaited and longed for by the suffering Job (Job 9:33).

Because of the eschatological dimension of Daniel 7, the Aramaic expression *māran ʾătāʾ*, "Our Lord is coming!"[40] was used in the apostolic church as a refrain in the liturgical assemblies (1 Cor 16:22), and a reflection of the first Christians' longing for the *parousia*, "(second) coming," of Christ (1 Thess 5:1; Rev 22:17).

2. God's Propensities toward Incarnation

Having listed some of the most significant biblical texts on the preexistence of Messiah in the bosom of the Godhead, we are going to consider now the evidence regarding Messiah's presence at specific moments in time, as part of the plan of salvation history. All these pre-incarnate appearances of Messiah reflect a certain propensity of God's partner of dialogue toward incarnation. As Daniel (7:13) makes clear, the "Son of Man," the divine-human character, "was coming" repeatedly in the realm of man's history as a rehearsal of the future embodiment.

(1) The "Angel of Yahweh" (Gen 32:25, 27; Hos 12:4–5 [Eng. 3–4]; Exod 3:2–4; Josh 5:13–15; Judg 2:1–5, 13:17–20)

> ***Gen 32:25, 27:*** *Jacob was left alone. And a man wrestled with him until the break of dawn.... Then he [the man] said, "Let me go, for dawn is breaking." But he answered, "I will not let you go, unless you bless me."*

As Jacob returns from Haran in Mesopotamia, on his way back home, he is under tremendous stress generated by the imminent meeting with his brother Esau (Gen 32:7). Having his family and possessions sent to the other side of the Yabbok ford, Jacob "remained alone" or "was left alone." He was in all likelihood reluctant to cross the river and meet the brother he deprived years ago of his firstborn right. The scene is quite evocative: Jacob was left alone, abandoned by all, while awaiting an unpleasant encounter in the dark of night. Suddenly, the mysterious character makes his appearance. Genesis 32:25 characterizes this figure as a "man" or "someone" (*ʾîš*). From the syntax, we can ascertain that this "man," rather than Jacob, began the wrestling session. To add more ambiguity to this already mysterious story, Genesis 32:2 mentions that angels "fell upon Jacob."[41] The wrestling ends at dawn with the victory of Jacob and the defeat of the mysterious man. Based on Genesis 32:29,[42] and 32:31,[43] we may identify the "man" (*ʾîš*) who wrestled with Jacob with *ʾēl*, or *ʾĕlōhîm*, "God, divine being, angel." The theological significance of this passage is that the theophany and the combat itself were meant to strengthen a fearful fugitive, Jacob, for the next day's meeting. We can also deduce a certain condescension of the divine messenger toward Jacob. It is as if the divine messenger willingly accepted defeat by Jacob in order for the latter to regain his confidence in both God and himself. This could be catalogued as an act of divine *synkatabasis*, "condescension."

> ***Hos 12:4–5 [Eng. 3–4]:*** *In the womb he tried to supplant his brother, and in his strength, he strove with God; he wrestled with an angel and prevailed; he wept and implored him. He found him at Bethel and there he spoke to us.*

Based on the assumption that the mysterious "man" could be a divine being, Hosea, a prophet of the eighth century BC, offers what may be the earliest interpretation of the text of Genesis 32, equating the "man" (v. 25) or the supposed "divine being" (vv. 29, 31) with an "angel" (Hos 12:4–5 [Eng. 3–4]).[44] In addition, Hosea made some theological modifications within the story itself. If, in Genesis 32, Jacob prevails over the man, in Hosea 12, Jacob is the defeated one and the angel is the victor. This exegetical shift may be explained by the religious-ethical demise of Israel (Jacob) in the eighth century BC. Hosea's contemporaries, the descendants of Jacob, surpassed their ancestor in terms of wickedness. Thus they were not worthy to prevail, as Jacob did, over an angel.

A similar interpretation is found in the *Targum Pseudo-Jonathan* on Genesis 32:25, "And Jacob remained alone beyond the Jubeka; and *an angel* contended with him in the likeness of a man." In other Targumim, the word "God" in Genesis 32:29 was considered to be an abbreviation of the phrase "angels of God." For instance, in the *Targum Neophyti* we read, "He said, 'Your name shall no more be called Jacob, but Israel, for you have made yourself great with angels of God and with men and you have overcome them'" (Gen 32:29).

Cyril of Alexandria interprets the angel as an allusion to Messiah before incarnation:

> For an angel in the form of God wrestled with him; then his thigh grew numb. However, the divine Jacob confessed such a great grace in the wrestling. For he says, "For I saw God face to face, and my soul was saved" [Gen 32:30]. Therefore, the mystery about Christ was predicted through the wrestling with the angel. The descendants of Jacob continued to oppose Christ, whom the prophets called "angel of great council" [Isa 9:6; cf. LXX]. For instance, some do not accept the numbness, that is his redemption. Others do not want to confess that they saw in him face to face the one who is, in nature, and truly God. For in himself Emmanuel showed us the Father, saying, "Whoever has seen me, has seen the Father" [John 14:9].[45]

Exod 3:2–4: *An angel of Yahweh appeared to him in a flame of fire out of a bush. He gazed, and there was a bush all aflame, yet the bush was not consumed. Moses said, "I must turn aside to look at this great sight. Why does not the bush burn up?" When Yahweh saw that he had turned aside to look, God called to him from the midst of the bush, "Moses! Moses!" He answered, "Here I am."*

This text is part of Moses' call, divulged within a tremendous theophany that occurred "at the mountain of God, at Horeb." Horeb is the name of the mountain of legislation in Elohist and Deuteronomist, while its correlate mountain, Sinai, plays the same role in Yahwist, Priestly sources.[46] The place-name Sinai (*sînay*) is probably related to the Hebrew common noun *sĕneh,* "bush." This etymology is supported by the later identification of Horeb, the site of the wondrous bush (Exod 3:1–2) with Sinai. At this place, God reveals himself to Moses in a strange way, namely, in a flaming bush that burned with no consummation. It is interesting to note that the name of the place-name Horeb (*ḥōrēb*) means "destruction, site of ruins,"[47] which probably points to an abandoned Midianite place of worship. The other name of the place, "mountain of God" (i.e., holy mountain), suggests such a place of worship. The *Targum Onkelos*, in an exegesis of Exod 3:1, replaces "the mountain of God" with "the mountain on which was revealed the glory of the Lord," in an attempt to erase any pagan trace from the story. Appearing in a non-Hebrew place of worship, God means to say that even this place belongs to him and that it may become holy through his presence. Similar instances of Yahwistic adoption of non-Hebrew places of worship occur in Bethel (Gen 28) and Mamre (Gen 18), both Canaanite places, out of use at the time of theophany, yet chosen by "God of the fathers" as loci of his saving interventions.

The historical meaning of this passage can be encapsulated in the following idea: "God of the fathers" is willing to come down to the level of his people. Moreover, he is willing to share with Israel the bitterness of slavery in Egypt. In this we see the significance of the divine voice crying out of the middle of a burning bush: God descends into the middle of the fire, namely, Israel's suffering. He is not philosophizing from heaven, but enters into the midst of affliction. As on the sixth day, when he descended, took dust of the ground, and fashioned humanity, he is now coming down again, showing deference toward his creature fashioned in his image. God of Israel is understood, therefore, as supremely compassionate, co-suffering with people in the midst of all tribulations. Another element of the significance of the burning bush focuses on Israel's endurance of Egypt's exploitation, "Why did God show Moses such a symbol? Because he [Moses] had thought to himself that the Egyptians might consume Israel; hence did God show him a fire which burnt but did not consume, saying to him, 'Just as the thorn-bush is burning and is not consumed, so the Egyptians will not be able to destroy Israel'" (*Exodus Rabbah* 2:5).

For Christians, the episode of the burning bush is more than merely a theophany. It represents one of the rarest Old Testament glimpses into the unfathomable mystery of the Trinity. Conventional interpretation holds that the revelation and teaching of the God of the Scriptures as a triune divinity belongs to the New Testament, and this is one of the most important tenets of the Christian faith. In the episode of the burning bush, however, we have indicators of the three persons of the Trinity. God the Father, as always, manifests himself as a sound, as the voice that emanates from within the flame, conversing with Moses about the sacredness of the place and other issues, including Moses' commission to Egypt and the revelation of the divine Name, *Yahweh*.[48] This whole conversation unfolds throughout the third chapter of Exodus. The fire in this theophany can be understood to symbolize the presence of the Spirit, defined as a person in at least two Old Testament texts (Ps 51:11; Isa 63:10). We should add at this point that it was a "pillar of fire" that led Israel through the wilderness after the exodus (Num 14:14), while "tongues of fire" announced the presence of the Holy Spirit on Pentecost (Acts 2:3). As for "the angel of Yahweh" (*malʾak Yahweh*), this is one of the most common titles of Messiah prior to his incarnation. The role of Messiah here is of intermediary between God, speaking out of the bush, and Moses: "At first an angel acted as intermediary and stood in the center of the fire, and afterwards the Shechinah [i.e., God's presence] descended and spoke with him from the midst of the thorn-bush" (*Exodus Rabbah* 2:5).

> *Josh 5:13–15: Once, when Joshua was near Jericho, he looked up and saw a man standing before him, drawn sword in hand. Joshua went to him and asked him, "Are you one of us or of our enemies?" He replied, "Neither, but I am captain of Yahweh's host. Now I have come!" Joshua threw himself face down to the ground and, prostrating himself, said to him, "What does my lord say to his servant?" The captain of Yahweh's host said to Joshua, "Remove your sandals from your feet, for the place where you stand is holy." And Joshua did so.*

The text of Joshua 5:13–15 represents a lost tradition that probably contained instructions given to Joshua. There are some parallels with other theophanies, such as the commissioning of Moses at the burning bush (Exod 3), or the angel's admonition of Israel at Bochim (Judg 2). The "captain of Yahweh's host"[49] is another messianic title that falls under the all-encompassing rubric of "angel of Yahweh." The *Targum Jonathan* explains the phrase as follows, "I am the angel who was sent from the presence of Yahweh." In Joshua 5:13–15, a "man" (*ʾîš*) appears suddenly in front of Joshua asking him to remove his sandals, for the land on which he is standing is "holy" (*qādôš*). This wording is reminiscent of Exodus 3, the theophany at the burning bush. The significance of such a parallel is to show that the God of Israel is always in motion and that places and objects are holy not owing to intrinsic qualities or magical acts attached to them but rather because of God's dynamic presence. Similarly, the appearances of the "angel of Yahweh" differ from one moment to another, from one place to another. That this "captain of Yahweh's host" is a special divine emissary (angel) can be seen from the fact that Joshua addresses him as "my lord." In addition, Joshua falls to the ground as a sign of respect, and the angel accepts this veneration without hesitation. In the same vein, one of the Midrashim explains, "He cried out from his very toe-nails, 'I am captain of the host of the Lord; I am a prince of the celestial host, and wherever I appear the Holy One, blessed be He, appears'" (*Genesis Rabbah* 97:3).

> ***Judg 2:1, 4–5:*** *The angel of Yahweh came up from Gilgal to Bochim and said, "I brought you up from Egypt and I led you into the land which I had promised to your fathers...." When the angel of Yahweh spoke these words to all the Israelites, the people lifted up their voices and wept. So they named that place Bochim, and they offered sacrifices there to Yahweh.*

At Bochim ("Weepers"), the "angel of Yahweh" (*malʾak Yahweh*) appears to rebuke Israel for falling into the sin of idolatry. The divine messenger is depicted here as equivalent to Yahweh (cf. Gen 16:7), and he moves with as much authority as Yahweh from a well-known place, Gilgal,[50] to an unknown place, later named Bochim by the Israelites, on account of their penitence triggered by the appearance of the angel. Moreover, in his discourse, the angel identifies himself with Yahweh, stating that he, namely, the angel, brought Israel out of Egypt according to the promise he (the angel, again) had made to the patriarchs.

The *Targum Jonathan* is representative of ancient Jewish interpretations and sees in the "angel of Yahweh" a title for the prophets and priests of Israel, "And Pinhas, the prophet, went up, the one who is compared to the angel of Yahweh..." (Judg 2:1). According to Numbers 25:7, Pinhas, the priest and Aaron's grandson, was well known for his strong, almost violent, way of defending mainstream Israelite tradition. One of the episodes where Pinhas's role of defender of the Yahwistic worship became manifest is the incident concerning Baal-peor (Num 25:1–3). It was here that the Israelites tried to replace Yahweh with Baal-peor. The anti-idolatry attitude demonstrated by the priest was probably the decisive reason for the Targum to insert the name of Pinhas in Judges 2:1,[51] who appeared in front of the people as an "angel of Yahweh." In the same hermeneutical environment, one of the Midrashim equates the angel at Bochim not with Yahweh, as found in the text of Judges 2:1–5, but rather with one of his prophets, following in the footsteps of Moses, "Was it not Moses who brought them out [of Egypt]? Certainly; but you can infer from this that prophets are compared to angels. Similarly it says, 'And the angel of the Lord came up from Gilgal to Bochim.' And he said, 'I made you go up out of Egypt' (Judg 2:1)" (*Numbers Rabbah* 16:1).

Returning to the text of Judges 2:1, 4–5, we may add another proof that the angel who appeared at Bochim was a special kind of angel. We base this on the result of his rebuke, which was, namely, the general and public repentance of the people. But what may be most surprising is the further reaction of the Israelites after the angel's departure. They do not stop at a simple act of repentance. Rather, they bring a sacrifice to Yahweh, who revealed himself as the "angel of Yahweh." In the Old Testament, common angels never receive worship or sacrifices from men. Only the "angel of Yahweh," referring to Messiah in his pre-incarnation appearances, is treated with such deference and respect by the people, who are willing to "prostrate themselves" (cf. Josh 5:14) or "bring sacrifices" (cf. Judg 2:5; 13:17–20; see below).

> ***Judg 13:17–20:*** *So Manoah said to the angel of Yahweh, "What is your name, that we may honor you when your words come true?" The angel of Yahweh said to him, "Why ask my name? It is (a name) of wonder." Manoah took the kid and the meal offering and offered them up on the rock to Yahweh; and a wonderful thing happened while Manoah and his wife looked on. As the flame went up from the altar toward the sky, the angel of Yahweh ascended in the flame of the altar, while Manoah and his wife looked on; and they fell on their faces to the ground.*

The text of Judges 13, part of the Samson's cycle, contains the story of Manoah and his wife, Samson's parents, and their encounter with the "angel of Yahweh." The latter announces to Manoah's barren wife that she will become the mother of a Nazirite son.

Manoah's request to know the name of the angel can be easily understood if we take into account the belief of the ancient Hebrews (Semites) that knowing one's name means having control over that person.[52] The angel's reply is quite ambiguous; he says that his name is *pilʾî,* meaning "wonderful, secret, unknowable."[53] This adjective is related to the noun *peleʾ* found in the messianic title, *peleʾ yôʿēṣ,* "wonder-counselor" (Isa 9:5). Both forms derive from a root *p-l-ʾ*, meaning "to be different, curious." This root defines the moment when an act initiated by a performer becomes effective. Therefore, in Isaiah 9:5, the Messiah, named "wonder-counselor," is one who can surprise his king with his wise advice. But what does "wonderful" mean in Judges 13:18? Recall Genesis 32:30 and Jacob's inquiry about the name of the man who wrestled with him all night. His adversary answered with a question ("Why do you ask my name?"), followed by sheer silence. The episode narrated in Judges 13 represents a step forward from both Genesis and Isaiah. We must remember here that the name of God, *YHWH* (*Yahweh*), has already been revealed to Moses (Exod 3:13–15).[54] Given this, reluctance on the part of the angel to reveal his name in Judges 13:18 seems quite unlikely. The question is whether the adjective *pilʾî,* "wonderful," refers to the angel's name or to the mystery surrounding the divine messenger's appearance. Since in the angel's answer the word *šēm,* "name," is missing, we are inclined to opt for the latter variant. So the angel wants to convey a paradox: that not knowing his name is a wonderful thing, because this will always allow room for further surprising interventions. Knowing the name of a colleague in dialogue equates not only with obtaining power over that individual, but it also diminishes the potential for future surprise. An interesting explanation of this may be found in one of the Midrashim:

> The angel said to him [Manoah], "I am not able to tell you my name for the Holy One, blessed be he, gives us a name to accord with the errand on which he sends us." Thus "Such knowledge is a mystery (*pĕlîʿâ*)" [Ps 139:6] means: "in accordance with each particular wonder which he performs through us he gives us a different name." (*Numbers Rabbah* 10:5)

Manoah wants to know the angel's name in order to honor him when his promise will be fulfilled. The root *k-b-d* in the Piel (intensive) conjugation means "to honor," and it may have both God and people as object. By choosing this polyvalent root,[55] the author of this fragment meant to underscore the peculiar role of the messenger, who is worthy of veneration similar to that due to God. This interpretation is further supported by the ascension of the angel in flames climbing from the altar (Judg 13:20). This spectacular departure of the angel was labeled with a related term, *maplîʾ,* "wonderful, surprising" (v. 19). What was so "wonderful" in this angel's disappearance? Probably the fact that the divine messenger uses the flame of the sacrifice as a way to return to heaven. Moreover, the angel functions in the same role as any sacrifice: a bridge between humans and their Creator. Thus, the angel of Yahweh fulfills the same role as Messiah. When the angel ascended using the flame of the sacrifice as a stairway to heaven, Manoah and his wife "fell on their faces" to the ground in a sign of worship. A common angel would never accept such a great veneration.[56] Finally, Manoah and his wife offered a sacrifice, along with a meal offering, upon the rock "to Yahweh," thus equating the angel who appeared in front of them with Yahweh.

Other Occurrences of the "Angel of Yahweh"

In all the following examples, the "angel of Yahweh" shows an obvious willingness to share in the suffering of those he encounters. This characteristic runs throughout the whole spectrum of angelic appearances, making this character look very similar to the "Son of Man" or the "son of weakness," with his well-known eternal propensity for "emptying" himself (Phil 2:7: *ekenōsen*) and "sympathizing (*sympatheō*) with our weaknesses" (Heb 4:15).

Here are some of the most important occurrences of the "angel of Yahweh," who made his appearances in the key moments of salvation history.

(1) The angel who appeared to Hagar (Sarah's maiden), promising her, "I will multiply your seed exceedingly" [as if he were the Lord] (Gen 16:10); and, "And the angel of the Lord said to her, 'Now you have conceived and shall bear a son; you shall call him Ishmael, for the Lord has given heed to your affliction" [identifying himself with God] (Gen 16:11 NRSV). One of the roles of this angel was to comfort the fugitive Hagar, who found herself in a state of dire solitude and confusion.

(2) The angel who prevented Abraham from offering Isaac as a sacrifice: "He said, 'Do not lay your hand on the boy or do anything to him; for now I know that you fear God, since you have not withheld your son, your only son, from me'" (Gen 22:12 NRSV). This angel explicitly identifies himself with God, the Provider.

(3) The "angel of God" (*malʾak hāʾĕlōhîm*), another name for the "angel of Yahweh," who appeared to Jacob in Mesopotamia: "Then the angel of God said to me in the dream, 'Jacob,' and I said, 'Here I am!'...'I am the God of Bethel, where you anointed a pillar and made a vow to me. Now leave this land at once and return to the land of your birth'" (Gen 31:11, 13 NRSV). The angel identifies himself with God, who appeared to Jacob at Bethel (cf. Gen 28:13: "I, Yahweh, am the God of Abraham your father, and the God of Isaac...."). Jacob's dream about a "raised structure, stairway, ladder" (*sullām*) linking heaven to earth (Gen 28:10–17) will be fulfilled when the Son of Man will be "lifted up" (John 3:14), a hint to crucifixion and ascension. If one takes into account Jesus' words recorded by John 1:51, then (the angel of) Yahweh who appeared to Jacob at Bethel was the pre-incarnate Christ functioning as intermediary between heaven and earth.

(4) The angel of the Exodus: "The angel of God who was going before the Israelite army moved and went behind them" (Exod 14:19 NRSV); "And when we cried to the Lord, he heard our voice, and sent an angel and brought us out of Egypt; and here we are in Kadesh, a town on the edge of your territory" (Num 20:16 NRSV).

(5) The angel who led Israel toward the promised land: "But now go, lead the people to the place about which I have spoken to you; see, my angel shall go in front of you" (Exod 32:34 NRSV) and, "Yahweh then said, 'My Face shall go with you and I shall give you rest'" (Exod 33:14). Here Yahweh identifies himself with his angel, as the pre-incarnate Messiah.

(6) The angel speaking to Balaam: "The angel of the Lord said to Balaam, 'Go with the men; but speak only what I tell you to speak'" (Num 22:35 NRSV), and, "The Lord met Balaam, put a word into his mouth, and said, 'Return to Balak, and this is what you shall say'" (Num 23:16 NRSV).

(7) The angel who appeared to judge Gideon: "Then Gideon perceived that it was the angel of the Lord; and Gideon said, 'Help me, Lord God! For I have seen the angel of the Lord face to face.' But the Lord said to him, 'Peace be to you; do not fear, you shall not die"' (Judg 6:22–23 NRSV).

(2) *Yahweh*, a Name for All Seasons (Exod 3:13–15)

Exod 3:13–15: *Moses said to God, "When I come to the Israelites and say to them, 'The God of your fathers has sent me to you,' and they ask me, 'What is his name?' what shall I say to them?" And God said to Moses, "I am who I am"* (ʾehyeh ʾăšer ʾehyeh). *He continued, "Thus shall you say to the Israelites, 'I am'* (ʾehyeh) *sent me to you." And God said further to Moses, "Thus shall you speak to the Israelites: 'He is* (YHWH [Yahweh]), *the God of your fathers, the God of Abraham, the God of Isaac, and the God of Jacob, has sent me to you. This is my name forever; this is my appellation for all generations.'"*

In Exodus 3:13–15, one of the most important texts of the entire Old Testament, Moses receives the revelation of the personal name of God. We would point out here that, according to Genesis 4:26, the personal name of God was already invoked during the time of Enosh, Adam's grandson. In light of our text from the Book of Exodus, the revelation of the name mentioned in chapter 3 could only have been a reiteration of God's personal name revealed at the dawn of human history, which must have fallen into oblivion. This divine appellation was then restated in Moses' time, along with the disclosure of its eternal significance. The fragment above is part of Moses' call to be God's messenger to Pharaoh, aimed at Israel's liberation from Egyptian slavery. At Moses' pertinent question, God reveals his name.

The meaning of the explicative phrase *ʾehyeh ʾăšer ʾehyeh* (Exod 3:14a) is disputed. This phrase can be translated "I am what I am," which would mean that God is entirely reluctant to reveal his name;[57] but in fact God is offering his name for practical purposes. This is the name to be invoked by the faithful. The Hebrew can also be translated literally, "I am who I am." According to the rules of Hebrew syntax this corresponds to "I am *he who is*," or "I am *the one who exists*," and this is how the translators of the

Septuagint understood it, *egō eimi ho ōn,* "I am *the Being*" (Exod 3:14a).[58] God is the only genuinely unconditioned and noncontingent Being. Note the use in the Septuagint, starting with Exodus 3:15 and throughout the Old Testament, of *kyrios,* "Lord," as substitute for *YHWH.* This was done out of reverence for the divine name, which, according to the Decalogue (Exod 20:7), should "not be taken in vain."[59] When the Masoretes (i.e., the "traditionalists") introduced vowels into the consonantal text of the Hebrew Bible, between AD 500 and 700, they vocalized the tetragrammaton YHWH (the "four-letter" word) with the vowels of the Hebrew common noun *ʾădōnāy,* "lord, master." Since then the Jews have read the name *YHWH* as *ʾădōnāy,* "Lord," *haššēm,* "the Name," or the like. Likewise, most modern Bibles continue the tradition, and use the word "LORD" (usually printed in small caps) to render the Hebrew tetragrammaton.

In addition to its textual importance, the revelation of the personal name of God is also one of the most important moments in salvation history. God demonstrates that he is willing to share his name, that his precious name may be reverentially invoked in perpetuity. One should not read the tetragrammaton YHWH the way this was vocalized by the Masoretes.[60] On the contrary, the scholarly reconstruction of *Yahweh*[61] is much closer to its reality, "He is...." This effects that intended meaning that God is whatever one needs God to be. The divine name shows God's condescension: He is willing to share with us his attributes. We are called to identify what or, rather, who God could be for us in various moments of our lifetimes. Yahweh is an open tableau offered to humanity, awaiting our invocations of need: for an orphan, *He is...my father*; for a widow, *He is...my spouse*; for a sick person, *He is...my healer*, and so on.

The Septuagint understood Exodus 3:14–15 as a statement about God's *being*, as the following quotation from the deuterocanonical book Wisdom of Solomon suggests, "For all people who were ignorant of God were foolish by nature; and they were unable from the good things that are seen to know *the one who exists*[62] from the good things that are visible" (Wis 13:1 NRSV). However odd they may seem, statements on such abstract notions as *eternity* and *being* are not absent from the Hebrew Bible. In another text, taken from the Book of Deutero-Isaiah, we read the following, "You are my witnesses, says the Lord, and my servant whom I have chosen, so that you may know and believe me and understand that *I am he* (*ʾănî hûʾ*)" (Isa 43:10). The term "servant" (*ʿebed*) in Isaiah (especially, Isa 53) is a messianic title.[63] In the present text, the "servant" (or Messiah) identifies himself with *hûʾ,* "he," which may hint at the name Yahweh. God "has chosen"[64] his Messiah before his historical birth. The fact that Messiah is a witness to Yahweh in the Old Testament seems also to hint at his preexistence.

The name Yahweh points out that the God of the Bible is neither a god of philosophy, nor an abstract idea, nor a cold essence, nor a god of so-called natural religions (Baal, Zeus, etc.) who behaves as a mortal, whose name can define his persona. On the one hand, Yahweh is *the Being* (*ho ōn*), but not a cold philosophical entity.[65] On the other hand, he is a *person*, but not totally predictable or knowable. He is a person, but his deeds are unlike man's deeds. His deeds are God's. Yahweh, as a person, represents a bridge between philosophy and the natural, extrabiblical religions. So interpretations such as the Bible does not deal with the idea of *being* or that the God of the Holy Writ does change at all are narrow, reductionist views that ignore the paradoxical language of the Holy Book and the complex deity beyond this language.

What does the revelation (or rather, reiteration) of the divine name have to do with biblical evidence of the preexistence of Messiah in the realm of history? As demonstrated by the reluctance of the angel to reveal his name (Gen 32), or by his strange remark, "It is a wonderful thing [not to know my name]" (Judg 13), the revelation of God's unfinished name ("He is...") keeps that element of surprise intact, so that God (or more precisely, the Son of God, the Messiah) may appear in manifold forms, without letting himself get locked into particular names, concepts, or doctrines, until his historical incarnation. Paul speaks of this variety when he refers to the "many times and ways" chosen by God for his appearances in the Old Testament period (Heb 1:1). Interestingly, on the one hand, God is willing to reveal his name in order to be invoked and worshiped, because he is a God of the covenant, of relationship, and of dialogue; on the other hand, in his omniscience, he is aware of the magical inclinations of humans to attempt to turn everything, even God himself, into toys to be manipulated. For this reason, he reveals an unfinished appellation.[66] God is willing to disclose only what is *stricto sensu* needful for human longing after personal communion with the Creator. All humanity needs to know is that God exists and that his existence is both dynamic and personal, yet not consumed in its various manifestations. Specifics about who God is, or what form his next manifestation will take, or when he will appear again remain the exclusive prerogative of this revealing, awesome God, who is always in motion, never attached to a single place, person, or moment in time. Thus, the very name Yahweh has a messianic dimension owing to the lack of specific identifiers: *He is*...the Messiah in his various comings toward humanity. *He is*...the angel who appeared to Abraham, Hagar, Jacob, Moses, Israel in the wilderness, Balaam, and so many others chosen by God to be receptacles of the pre-incarnation theophanies. Yves Congar was right on point when he made this neat evaluation of the name Yahweh:

> "I will be who I will be." You will see it by my acts. Finally, in the fullness of time, at the end of so many comings, of which none was total or definitive,

> I will be he who comes to you in person, who dwells among you, bodily. I myself will be your Pascha, I myself will be the passage through the Red Sea, I will be the true manna, the true bread of life, the true serpent raised in the desert, the true liberator, the true ransom for your sins, I myself will be the covenant with my people. *I will be Jesus Christ.*[67]

Because of the messianic dimension, or garb, of the name Yahweh, all the brief statements such as, "I am (he)" (John 8:24, 28, 58; 9:9) or the nominal clauses such as, "I am the bread, the light, the door..." (John 6:41; 8:12; 10:9), uttered by Jesus and recorded in the Gospel of John, allude to the first-person variant of the tetragrammaton YHWH, that is, *ʾehyeh,* "I am" (Exod 3:14).

(3) Two Yahwehs? (Gen 18:33; 19:1, 24; cf. Exod 34:5–6; Ps 22:2 [Eng. 22:1])

> *Gen 18:33; 19:1, 24: When Yahweh had finished speaking to Abraham, he departed; and Abraham returned to his place....The two angels arrived in Sodom in the evening, as Lot was sitting in the gate of Sodom. When Lot saw them, he rose to greet them and, bowing low with his face to the ground....Then Yahweh rained brimstone and fire on Sodom and Gomorrah, from the Yahweh out of the heavens.*

The text of Genesis 19:24 is one of the most difficult texts of the Hebrew Bible, since it seems to indicate more than one *Yahweh.* This text is part of a long pericope (Gen 18–19) that narrates the visit of three men to Abraham. The three heavenly messengers bring the news of God's intention to investigate the case of Sodom and Gomorrah, followed by the destruction itself of the wicked cities. These three visitors are defined as *ʾănāšîm,* "men" (Gen 18:2), and, interestingly, Abraham uses the title *ʾădōnāy,* "Lord," as appropriate to address the three visitors. This suggests that Abraham recognizes a divine being among the three men. According to Genesis 19:1, two of the three men sent to Sodom are labeled *šĕnê(y) ham-malʾākîm,* "the two angels." Reading the above quoted texts together, one may draw the conclusion that Abraham received as visitors two angels accompanied by God, or more precisely, the Son of God or Messiah in a pre-incarnation phase.

In Genesis 19:24, the one Yahweh, whom Abraham greeted as *ʾădōnāy,* "Lord," makes the fire and brimstone rain down on Sodom and Gomorrah, "from (*mēʾēt*) Yahweh, out of heaven."[68] Therefore, the basic idea in Genesis 19:24 is that Yahweh on earth is in agreement and cooperating with Yahweh in heaven, in whatever he is doing. According to the authors of the Targumim, always in search of language cleansed of every anthropomorphic trace, the fire and brimstone do not come directly from Yahweh in heaven,[69] but rather *mn-qdm* "from (his) presence." The Talmud finds the twofold mention of Yahweh disturbing and tries to explain it as an idiom, "from Yahweh" should stand for "from him," "Rabbi Ishmael bar Jose said, 'It is written, "Then the Lord caused to rain upon Sodom and Gomorrah brimstone and fire *from the Lord*"; but *from him* should have been written! This is a scriptural idiom'" (*Sanhedrin* 38b). The fact that fire and brimstone descended from heaven seemed odd for some ancient Jewish interpreters: "Rabbi Hanina bar Pazzi said, 'Nothing evil descends from above'" (*Genesis Rabbah* 51:3). That is why Rashi, in his commentary on the Pentateuch, explains that the extreme wickedness of the Sodomites caused a change in natural phenomena, and God caused ordinary rain to descend, which turned into fire and brimstone when it reached the earth.

There are two additional texts that might hint at the plurality of persons within the divinity: Exodus 34:5–6 and Psalm 22:1.

> ***Exod 34:5–6:*** *Yahweh came down in a cloud; he stood with him [i.e., Moses] there, and proclaimed the name Yahweh. Yahweh passed before him and proclaimed, "Yahweh! Yahweh! a God compassionate and gracious, slow to anger, abounding in long-suffering love and faithfulness."*

This text narrates one of God's appearances in front of Moses during Israel's wandering through the wilderness. This theophany occurred at the Tent of Meeting, the customary place where Yahweh used "to meet" Moses and the people. God reveals himself, descending in a cloud. This might remind us of an earlier statement, "When Moses entered the tent, the pillar of cloud would descend and stand at the entrance of the tent, and the Lord would speak with Moses" (Exod 33:9 NRSV). In the Hebrew Bible, the cloud usually signals a theophany, an appearance of the preincarnate Son of God. In addition to the manifestations at the Tent of Meeting, there is also the pillar of cloud in which Yahweh was present, leading Israel through the wilderness (Exod 16:10; 19:9; 20:21; 24:16); the cloud that filled the temple of Solomon on the day of its dedication, announcing God's glory, his presence, in the holy place (1 Kgs 8:10–12); and the cloud with which the "Son of Man" was "coming," and upon which he eventually reached the "Everlasting One" (Dan 7:13–14). So intimately was the cloud related to the notion of God that the author of Exodus 40:38 speaks of *ʿănan Yahweh,* the "cloud of Yahweh." Likewise, in the New Testament the cloud is one of the signs of Jesus' appearances in glory: at the transfiguration (Matt 17:5); the ascension (Acts 1:9); and the second coming (Luke 21:27; Rev 14:14). We might also mention that, according to *Exodus Rabbah* 50:5, the cloud represents one of the defining marks of the messianic age.

The *Targum Pseudo-Jonathan*, in its exegesis of Exodus 34:5–6 reads, "And the Lord revealed himself in the cloud of the glory of his Shekinah, and Moses stood with him there; and Moses called on the Name of the Word of the Lord. And the Lord made his Shekinah to pass by before his face, and proclaimed, the Lord, the Lord God, merciful and gracious, long-suffering, and nigh in mercies...." One may notice, as is usual, the tendency of the Targum to eliminate any anthropomorphic language from the Hebrew Bible by inserting terms such as Shekinah, "glory," "word." But the main difference between the Hebrew text and the *Targum Pseudo-Jonathan* lies in the question: Who is the person proclaiming the name of Yahweh? If, in the Hebrew text, Yahweh himself proclaims the name of Yahweh, in the Targum it is Moses who "calls on the Name of the Word of the Lord." Moreover, the *Targum Neophyti* offers a quite different reading of Exodus 34:6, "...And Moses prayed saying, 'Lord, Lord, a God gracious and compassionate....'" Thus, Moses is the one who calls on the name of Yahweh and who invokes him, "Lord, Lord...." These examples taken from the Targumim show the kind of struggle the ancient interpreters had with the text of Exodus 34:5–6, more precisely, with respect to Yahweh's invocation of his own name not once, but twice. If we rely solely on the Hebrew text, this twofold mention of Yahweh, by none other than Yahweh, may be interpreted in the light of our previous text, Exodus 19:24. In that text, we saw the allusion to two *Yahwehs*, one on earth, visiting Abraham, and another in heaven, pouring his wrath over the wicked cities. Thus, the twofold mention of Yahweh in Exodus 34:5–6 may be a hint of a plurality of persons within the Godhead, as implied by other texts of the Hebrew Bible, such as Genesis 1:26–27 or Isaiah 6:8. Further, if the appearances of God on earth are in fact the appearances of Messiah (i.e., the Son of God), then Exodus 34:5–6 may be read as a reference to one of the pre-incarnation appearances of the Son calling on the Father and the Holy Spirit, the other persons of the triune God. This invocation suggests harmony and cooperation between the persons of the Trinity in fundamental works, such as creation, salvation, and sanctification. One should also read the text of Psalm 22:1 in the same light of the dynamic unity that exists between the two Testaments.

Ps 22:2: My God, my God, why have you forsaken me? Far from my salvation are the words of my roaring.

The suffering Messiah begins his conversation with God with the sound of despair arising from a profound sense of God's abandonment. Since this text, and most likely the entire psalm, was recited by Jesus on the cross in his last moments (Matt 27:46), one may draw the conclusion that this psalm is messianic par excellence. Unlike other Old Testament texts that are typologically interpreted,[70] the typological dimension of Psalm 22 was obviously underscored by Jesus' appropriation of it. Thus, Messiah, or the incarnate Logos, in his solitude calls on the other two persons of the Trinity so that they may share with him in the work of redemption, made possible by his sacrifice, which he willingly accepted. The divine character of the suffering Messiah in Psalm 22 is suggested by the image of a "roaring"[71] lion, an image used in the Hebrew Bible to describe Yahweh, especially in his role as king (Prov 19:12), gathering his people (Amos 3:8; Hos 11:10).

(4) Walking To and Fro (Gen 5:21–24; 6:9; 24:40)

> ***Gen 5:21–24:*** *At the age of 65, Enoch begot Methuselah. After the birth of Methuselah, Enoch walked to and fro with God 300 years; and he begot sons and daughters. All the days of Enoch were 365 years. Enoch walked to and fro with God; then he was not, for God took him.*

> ***Gen 6:9:*** *These are the generations of Noah. Noah was a righteous man; he was blameless in his generation; it was with God that Noah walked to and fro.*

Although Enoch did not live a life as long as his predecessors, his life span paralleled the solar year and hence was a perfect age. While scarcely mentioned in the Hebrew Bible, Enoch occupies a very important place in subsequent Jewish tradition; he was always seen as a model of piety and faith (Sir 44:16; 49:14; Heb 11:5), and several apocryphal writings carry his name (cf. Jude 14–15).

Enoch lived 365 years, but the text is silent about the first 65 years of his life. What it does say is that Enoch lived with God for 300 years after Methuselah's birth. In Noah's case, we are told that he was "righteous (*ṣaddîq*) and blameless (*tāmîm*)," and a consequence, or rather a sign, of Noah's righteousness was his walking to and fro with God.[72] The important element of these passages is to assure us that God descends to the level of his special creatures and allows us to walk side by side with him. Both Enoch and Noah were walking by the side of God, the same way a man does with his friend. This can be understood as a foreshadowing of the great act of divine "condescension" (*synkatabasis*) that was the incarnation of the Logos. God comes down to the level of the human person, so that the latter may rise with God's help to the level of the deity. In patristic literature this process is called *theōsis,* "deification," and Enoch's translation into the heavens by God may be considered an anticipation of this process made possible by Christ's incarnation and humanity's ultimate restoration.

The Septuagint, in its own attempt to eliminate anthropomorphic language, renders the Hebrew verb *way-yithallēk,* "he walked to and fro" (Gen 5:24), with the Greek verb *euērestēsen,* "he was well-pleasing to (God)."[73] The Targumim follow the same interpretative way as the Greek version and read, "And Enoch walked in fear after God the Lord" (*Targum Onkelos*); or, "And Enoch served in honesty in the presence of the Lord" (*Targum Pseudo-Jonathan*). Given the uniqueness of Enoch's fate, one may assume that "he walked to and fro" is more than simply anthropomorphic language. It seems to be the proof of the divine "condescension" (*synkatabasis*) when Messiah, the Son of God in his pre-incarnate stage, descended to the level of understanding of humans and took visible form, walking with the righteous Enoch.[74]

The phrase *ʾênennû,* "he was not," as in "And he was not, for God took him" (Gen 5:24b), has been interpreted in a surprising way by the Midrashim, as a reference to Enoch being taken from the book of the righteous:

> ["And he was not" means] that he was not inscribed in the roll of the righteous but in the roll of the wicked. Rabbi Aibu said, "Enoch was a hypocrite, acting sometimes as a righteous, sometimes as a wicked man. Therefore the Holy One, blessed be he, said, 'While he is righteous I will remove him.' Rabbi Aibu also said, 'He judged [i.e. condemned] him on the New Year, when he judges the whole world.'" (*Genesis Rabbah* 25:1)

Regarding the phrase "For God took him," the Hebrew text has the verb *lāqaḥ,* "he took," while the Septuagint uses a passive form, *metethēken,* meaning "he was translated."[75] There is a very interesting interpretation in the *Zohar* on this topic, "Tradition further tells us that Enoch also had a book, which came from the same place as the book of the generations of Adam.... This is the source of the book known as the *Book of Enoch.* When God took him, he showed him all supernatural mysteries, and the tree of life in the midst of the garden and its leaves and branches, all of which can be found in his book" (*Zohar* I.37b). Or, in another passage, the *Zohar* explains the rapture of Enoch as a sign of God's omniscience and mercy, "When God sees that a man who cleaves to him and with whom he abides will one day degenerate, he takes him from the world prematurely, culling, as it were, the odor while it is still sweet" (*Zohar* I.56b).

> **Gen 24:40:** *And he replied to me, "Yahweh, in whose presence I have walked to and fro, will send his angel with you and make your journey successful; and you will choose a wife for my son from my own family, from my father's house."*

In this paragraph, it is Abraham's servant, Eleazar of Damascus, who speaks, quoting his master on the journey to Mesopotamia to find a wife for Isaac. In Abraham's case, as he himself testifies, he "walked to and fro" not with God but only "in the presence of" or "before" (*lipnê[y]*) Yahweh, a phrase that is not as anthropomorphic as that found in Genesis 5:22, 24; 6:9, "along with" (*ʾēt*). By consequence, it implies only that Abraham acted according to God's will. Another difference between this text and the two others quoted and discussed above is the aspect of the verb. The text of Genesis 24:40[76] points to a complete action in the past, while that used in Genesis 5 and 6[77] alludes to repetitive action undertaken by Enoch and Noah, indicative of their attitudes toward God: they were walking to and fro with God for a long period of time.

In Genesis 24:40, "his [i.e., God's] angel" is the "angel of Yahweh," a well-known messianic title, frequently used in the Hebrew Bible, which we have discussed at length above. Thus, Abraham states an important idea: that he walked to and fro in God's presence. The underlying meaning of this idiom is that Abraham implemented God's precepts in his own life, and he is therefore hopeful that God will reward him by sending his angel to his servant, Eleazar of Damascus. What will the role of the "angel of Yahweh" be? The text that quotes Abraham's response states that he (the angel) will be "with" Abraham's servant. The same particle is used here as in the previous Genesis texts mentioned above.[78] This imputes to our text a similar connotation, namely, that the angel of Yahweh is to share in the weakness of human nature, to comfort those in distress, such as Hagar (Gen 16), or in need, as was the case of Eleazar seeking assistance in a unknown land (Gen 24).

The imagery of walking as a man and talking as a man triggers the assumption that God came down from above. But who could this God be, walking side by side with a person as one friend walks with another? As in many instances in the Hebrew Bible, this person is no other than the Son of God. In order to walk with a human being, a human face is necessary. As we have seen already in this work, the Son of God has the propensity to appear in history at the level of humans, as a human being, and hence we discern one of his best defining titles, the "Son of Man" or "son of weakness." In summary, the one with whom Enoch and Noah used to walk to and fro was likely another anthropomorphic manifestation of the Son of God, the Messiah before his incarnation as Christ. He demonstrated his willingness to come closer to humans, to treat them as his friends. This kind of attitude on the part of pre-incarnate Messiah resonates in Jesus' revelation at the Last Supper, "I shall no longer call you servants, because a servant does not know the master's business; I call you friends, because I have made known to you everything I have learnt from my Father" (John 15:15). The cases of Enoch and Noah represent the anticipation of this friendship that Jesus made available to humanity via his disciples. Even before Messiah's incarnation, God showed us that he is willing, even eager, to walk with us and to talk with us.

(5) The Tabernacling Glory (Exod 33:18–23; Num 12:8a; Isa 6:1–3//John 1:14)

> ***Exod 33:18–23:*** *He then said, "Please, show me your glory!" And he answered, "I will make all my goodness pass before you, and I will proclaim before you the name Yahweh, and I am gracious to those to whom I am gracious and I show (maternal) love to those to whom I show (maternal) love. But," he said, "you cannot see my face, for the humans may not see me and live." And Yahweh said, "See, there is a place near me. Station yourself on the rock and, as my glory passes by, I will put you in a cleft of the rock and shield you with my palm until I have passed by. Then I will take my palm away and you will see my back; but my face cannot be seen."*
>
> ***Num 12:8a:*** *With him I speak mouth to mouth, plainly and not in riddles; and it is the form of Yahweh he can behold.*

There are three terms that we must examine in the Exodus passage quoted above: *glory*, *face*, and *back*.

(a) The Hebrew term *kābôd*, "glory, splendor," derives from the root *k-b-d* meaning "to be heavy" and usually designates the manifestation of God's presence (see Exod 33:18–23; Isa 6:3). In Exodus 33:22, "glory" is a brilliant light that needs no storm for its appearance (Exod 19:16) and later leaves its glow on Moses' face (Exod 34:29). The glory may appear "in"[79] the cloud (Exod 16:10), inside (Num 14:10) and outside the Tent (Lev 9:23), during Israel's wandering through wilderness, and later, inside the temple built by King Solomon (1 Kgs 8:10–11). According to Exodus 24:17, the glory of God looked as a "consuming fire." During Israel's stay in the wilderness, the entire people, not only its charismatic leaders, such as Moses and Aaron, were able to behold God's glory (Lev 9:23). All these instances reflect God's will to make his transcendental glory cohabitate with immanent entities. They also foreshadow the time of Messiah's incarnation when the divine glory dwelt in human flesh among humans (John 1:14).

(b) Approaching the end of his mission, Moses asks God to let him behold his glory. God's answer may be understood as striking a sign of equality between the "glory" and the "face" (*pāneh*) of God, or as making a clear distinction between the "glory" (which may be better understood as God's "back") and God's "face," which might be a term for the divine essence, the mystery of his existence, into which no one is able to take a glimpse. Set in the larger context, or in light of the examples given above, we opt to stay with the second explanation. Thus, "face" refers to God's essence, his being, which surpasses all human understanding.

(c) The term *ʾāḥôr,* "back," may be a hint at God's concrete manifestations, including the natural phenomena through which God made himself known to his people, including the pillars of cloud and fire (Exod 13:21), smoke (Exod 19:18), lightning and thunder (Exod 19:16), and so on. The Exodus passage is silent with respect to what God's "back" refers to, but if we compare Moses' case to one similar, namely, Elijah's *pilgrimage* to Mount Horeb (1 Kgs 19:1ff.), which occurred later in the history of Israel, then we may draw the conclusion that in Moses' case and time, God's "back" connotes a "great and mighty wind" (1 Kgs 19:11). Summing up the Exodus passage quoted above, we must point out that, to Moses' request to contemplate God's "glory," God makes the distinction between "glory" and "face" by stating that no mortal, including his good servant Moses, can see his face and yet live. Thus, what Moses saw was God's glory, or his back. In other words, Moses was enabled to discern the presence of God in one of the natural phenomena already described, quite likely in a "great and mighty wind" (cf. 1 Kgs 19:11).

The text of Numbers 12:8a adds the detail that Moses was able to contemplate the "form of Yahweh." The word *tĕmûnâ* was translated in the passages cited above as "form" or "shape."[80] The same word, *tĕmûnâ,* is found in a quite strange text (Job 4:16), in the context of a night vision but with a meaning slightly different from the sense of "shape"—"It halted; its appearance was strange to me; a shape (*tĕmûnâ*) loomed before my eyes; I heard a murmur, a voice...." The "shape" that stood before Job during that night vision can hardly be identified with God. Thus, the word *tĕmûnâ,* "form," found in the Numbers passage is probably equivalent to *kābôd,* "glory," as we find it in Exodus 33:18–23.

> ***Isa 6:1–3:*** *In the year of King Uzziah's death, I beheld my Lord sitting on a throne, high and lifted up; and the skirts of his robe filled the Temple. Seraphs were standing above him. Each of them had six wings: with two he covered his face, with two he covered his legs, and with two he would fly about. And one would call to the other, "Holy, holy, holy! Yahweh of Hosts! The whole earth is full of his glory."*

The eighth-century BC prophet Isaiah of Jerusalem[81] had a vision in the year of King Uzziah's death. This vision occurred inside the Jerusalem temple; at the moment of the vision, Isaiah was most likely located in the "porch" (*ʾûlām*) of the temple. This space corresponds to the nave of a Christian church and was later called the "Holy Place." The most sacred part of the temple was the "back room" (*dĕbîr*) later called the "Holy of Holies." This area was cube-shaped, as was typical of Syrian temples. This second part, somewhat higher than the level of the *ʾûlām*, was reserved to God and the ark of covenant; the Holy Place was separated from the Holy of Holies by a veil (Exod 26:33). The phrase a "throne high and lifted up" (Isa 6:1) probably designates the *kappōret*, the "mercy-seat," which was the cover of the ark of covenant, flanked by the two wooden figures of cherubim plated with gold and attached to the ark. Thus, in Isaiah's vision, the Lord was sitting in the *dĕbîr*, or more precisely, upon the *kappōret* of the ark of covenant.

The skirts of God's robe filled the temple,[82] namely, the Holy Place, where Isaiah was probably standing. God is depicted here as a king, sitting on his high throne, while the skirts of his mantle filled the Holy Place.

"Seraphs"[83] were standing *mimmaʿal*, "above," God the King. The *Targum Jonathan* reads this slightly differently, "in the height, in front of him (*brwma qdwmhy*)," thus moving the seraphs out of the earthly temple to the heavenly court and making them stand "in front" (not "above") of God, listening to his commands. The *Targum Jonathan* replaces the word "seraphs" with the phrase *šmšyn qdyšyn*, "holy servants." The seraphs were probably arrayed in a circle above the heavenly king while intoning a majestic hymn in honor of their master. This hymn focuses on the paradox of God's personality. On the one hand, the God of Israel is *qādôš*, "holy,"[84] namely, transcendental, separated from the earthly realm; his face, hidden beyond the veil, cannot be seen. The threefold mention of "holy" was seen by ancient Christian interpreters as a hint to the three persons of the Trinity. On the other hand, the hymn underscores God's active presence in the world. God's "glory" filling the earth is a reflection of God's willingness to come closer to the human person, to *tabernacle* among humans. In Isaiah's passage, God's title is "Yahweh of the hosts (*ṣĕbāʾôt*)," an allusion to the host of angels populating the heavenly court. Note that the image of the heavenly court may also be discerned in the title of the angel who appeared to Joshua during the conquest of Canaan. The heavenly messenger introduces himself as "the captain or prince (*śar*) of Yahweh's army (*ṣābāʾ*)" (Josh 5:14).[85]

The text of John 12:41 reads, "Isaiah said this because he saw his glory, and spoke of him [Jesus]." This may be seen as an interpretation of Isaiah 6:1–3. In fact, Isaiah beheld the glory of God speaking prophetically of the preexistent Messiah. According to the prophet Haggai, God's "glory," which is the same as that seen by Isaiah, will fill the second temple, and its brilliance will be greater than that which belonged to the first temple, and this will be due to the presence of Messiah. "The glory of this latter Temple will surpass that of the former, says Yahweh Sabaoth, and in this place I shall give peace—Yahweh Sabaoth declares" (Hag 2:9).

> ***John 1:14:*** *And the Word became flesh and tabernacled among us, and we beheld his glory, the glory as of the only begotten of the Father, full of grace and truth.*

John refers in his prologue to the concrete, historical appearance of Messiah, the Logos, who by his incarnation "tabernacled"[86] among humans and, by consequence, made God's glory accessible to the human eye. The word *doxa,* "glory," in this context refers to two of Messiah's features, namely, eternal generation from the Father, and the communion of love[87] and trustworthiness[88] between God the Father and his Messiah. At the Logos's incarnation these two transcendental features of Messiah's profile began to intertwine and cohabit with the historical, temporal features of his profile, such as being born of a woman and living as a human being, with all the consequences pertaining to human nature. The eternal glory of Messiah was allowed to be sheltered by the tabernacle of human flesh.

(6) Vibrant Silence: From Thunder to a Soft Whisper (1 Kgs 19:11–12; cf. Exod 19:16, 18–19)

> ***1 Kgs 19:11–12:*** *He said, "Come out and stand on the mountain before Yahweh." And lo, Yahweh passed by. There was a great and mighty wind, splitting mountains and shattering rocks before Yahweh; but Yahweh was not in the wind. After the wind, an earthquake; but Yahweh was not in the earthquake. After the earthquake, fire; but Yahweh was not in the fire. And after the fire, a soft whispering sound.*

> ***Exod 19:16, 18–19:*** *On the third day, in the morning, there were thunders and lightnings, and a thick cloud upon the mountain, and a very loud blast of the horn; and all the people who were in the camp trembled.... Now Mount Sinai was all in smoke, for Yahweh had come down upon it in fire; the smoke rose like the smoke of a kiln, and the whole mountain shook violently. The sound of the horn became longer, and louder and louder. Moses spoke and God answered him in thunder.*

The text in 1 Kings narrates the encounter between the fugitive Elijah and Yahweh. Elijah, one of Israel's prophets and the champion of the monotheistic religion in the ninth century BC, was persecuted by Jezebel, an idolatrous Phoenician princess married to Ahab, king of Israel. That is why Elijah was running for his life, heading for Mount Horeb, the same mountain where Moses asked God to show his glory (Exod 33:18). The text is silent with respect to the purpose of Elijah's journey; he probably intended to find some comfort from the same God who revealed his glory to Moses. He wanted to see him, to see the One whom he alone was serving. The name of Elijah is quite significant within the historical-religious context of ninth-century-BC Israel. "Elijah" (*ʾēlîyāhû*) means "Yahweh is my God." His encounter took place at Horeb, the holy mountain, also called Mount Sinai, where Moses received the tablets of the law.

The importance of 1 Kings 19 lies with the interesting theophany Elijah attended. This theophany indicates a certain progress, or crescendo, in the way Yahweh chose to manifest himself to his people: from the heavy, concrete, obvious natural phenomena such as thunder, pillars of fire or cloud, strong wind, and earthquake, so common during the period of the exodus (see Exod 19), to a softer way, namely, the human voice. The Hebrew phrase *qôl dĕmāmâ daqqâ* can be rendered literally "a sound of soft murmuring" or "soft whisper." The first meaning, "murmuring," is supported by the Arabic cognate *damdama,* "to murmur." The second meaning, "whisper," is attested in the Book of Job, where a mysterious "form" (*tĕmûnâ*; cf. Num 12:8) standing in front of Job at night produced a soft sound, a kind of whisper, "A form loomed before my eyes; I heard a whisper (*dĕmāmâ*), a voice" (Job 4:16). The presence of the term *qôl* "sound" in both 1 Kings 19 and Job 4 compels us to opt for the second meaning, that of the whispering sound. The editors of *HALOT* mention another interesting meaning for the phrase we are considering, namely, "vibrant silence," which relies on the basic connotation of the verbal root *d-m-m* I, "to be silent." "Vibrant silence" is a strange kind of silence, similar to that uncommon silence triggered by an earthquake, auguring the cessation of that terrifying event, but stirring more fear in one's heart, and hence its ambiguous character. The Septuagint reads interpretatively *auras leptēs,* "soft breeze," struggling to stay in the realm of natural phenomena rather than turning to an anthropomorphic depiction of God. The *Targum Jonathan* goes even further in this attempt to dispel any anthropomorphic tendency in the Hebrew Bible and reads, "the sound of those who praise." What is the significance of 1 Kings 19? God wants to say that now, in the time of Elijah, another phase of divine revelation has begun. God does not want any longer to reveal himself via natural phenomena, such as wind, earthquake, or fire. He chooses a new way, that of a whisper, a human voice speaking to human ears. The theophany in 1 Kings 19 can be seen as another example of God's propensity toward incarnation, by choosing the human voice as a more elevated way of manifestation.

(7) The Occurrence of God's Word (Hos 1:1; *et passim* in prophetic books)

Hos 1:1: The word of Yahweh that occurred to Hosea son of Beeri, in the days of kings Uzziah, Jotham, Ahaz, and Hezekiah of Judah, and in the days of king Jeroboam son of Joash of Israel.[89]

From the outset, a caveat is necessary. The prophetic formula *dĕbar Yahweh ʾăšer hāyâ ʾel* should not be rendered "The word of Yahweh that was...." Using forms of the verb "to be" is inadequate, since the verbs found in both the Hebrew and Greek versions to convey the image of the "word of Yahweh" have much richer meanings than the abstract "to be." Thus, the Hebrew verb *hāyâ* means "to come to pass, to happen, to occur, to become," while its Greek counterpart in the Septuagint, *ginomai,* may be rendered by a wide range of English verbal phrases such as "to come into being *through birth or natural production*, to come into being as an event, phenomenon, to occur as process." As can be seen, both verbs connote such ideas as "occurring," "happening," or "coming" of an event or phenomenon. Far from indicating a simple, abstract state of being or existence, these verbs have the semantic potential to emphasize the dynamic and concrete aspects of the word of God. In this light, Hosea and other prophets using similar formulae want to convey more than the simple statement that the word of God was addressed to them, or that they possess the word of God and are to share it with God's people. In fact, these formulae are meant to underscore a quite important theological idea, namely, that the word of God is coming to the prophet as a dynamic person, and the coming of this word is understood and embraced as an event, with a well-defined place in salvation history. That this coming, or occurring, of the word of God was perceived as an event can be seen in the historical details attached to the prophetic formula. In the above illustration, taken from the Book of Hosea, we are told that the word of God came to Hosea, and that this event *occurred* when a number of individuals were exercising their kingship in Judah and Israel. Though its origin is beyond this physical world, the word of God has nothing to do with the mythical realm. On the contrary, the transcendental word comes down to a concrete human being, Hosea son of Beeri, or any other prophet, a man among men, living in a society with kings and subjects, at a certain moment in time. The word of God occurs, happens, comes. In other words, it is not an abstract or mythical entity; rather it is a personal, dynamic partner in dialogue. In summary, the prophetic formulae underscore two important ideas: (a) the word of God is a dynamic, personal entity; and (b) its coming to a prophet is regarded as an event. Thus, the word of God coming, or occurring to any prophet may be considered a type of Messiah in his pre-incarnate phase.

This eventful coming of the word of Yahweh is another proof of God's willingness to descend to the level of the human person, and to engage in a dynamic, personal, concrete dialogue with his creature. We may add here that the word is not simply a means by which God inspires his prophets. Contrary, there is an intrinsic unity between God and his word, and this unity is underscored in the Hebrew Bible by the construct phrase *dĕbar Yahweh*. Note that the *Targum Jonathan,* in its tendency to exclude anything that might diminish God's holiness, his transcendence, focuses on the separation between God and his word, "The prophetic word that is before Yahweh...." According to this Targum's reading, the word is not simply God's, but rather the "word of the prophecy," a prophetic word, that comes not directly from Yahweh but from the presence of Yahweh, or from before him. In the same vein of thought should be understood the statement, "'The word of the Lord' means prophecy" (*Shabbath* 138b).

In short, we may say that the "condescension" (*synkatabasis*) of God through his word foreshadows the time of the great coming of the Logos, the incarnation. The repeated *comings* of the word of God to Israel's prophets have prepared the way for this great coming. We might mention at this juncture that these comings were in different degrees expressions of the relationship between the divine word and the human receptacle. They were, metaphorically speaking, *small incarnations* of God's word. Hosea is perhaps the best illustration of such an idea. Among the Old Testament prophets, Hosea is the one who was chosen to experience God's bitterness and long-suffering love for Israel in the fabric of his life, in his very flesh. His prophetic message was a living message; it was his own life. It is difficult, if not impossible, to strike a line between the human word and God's word in any prophet's case, much more so in the case of Hosea, where the interplay between various words is so vivid, fluid, and nearly unbreakable. We may say that the word of God came to Hosea and dwelt inside his personal life. Hosea's drama foreshadows quite well both the incarnation of the Logos and the suffering of Christ, abandoned by his own, rejected by his listeners, yet loving his own, and praying for his enemies.

(8) Melchizedek (Gen 14:17–24; Ps 110:4//Heb 7:1–3)

> ***Gen 14:17–24:*** *After his [Abram's] return from defeating Chedorlaomer and the kings with him, the king of Sodom came out to meet him in the Valley of Shaveh, which is the Valley of the King. And Melchizedek, king of Salem, brought out bread and wine; he was the priest of God Most High. He blessed him, saying, "Blessed be Abram of God Most High, Possessor of heaven and earth. And blessed be God Most*

> *High, who has delivered your foes into your hand." And he (Abram) gave him a tenth of everything. Then the king of Sodom said to Abram, "Give me the persons, and take the goods for yourself." But Abram said to the king of Sodom, "I have raised my hand to Yahweh, God Most High, Possessor of heaven and earth: I will not take so much as a thread or a sandal strap of what is yours, lest you should say, 'It is I who made Abram rich.' Except only what the young men have eaten; and the share of the men who went with me—Aner, Eshkol, and Mamre—let them take their share."*

The text of Genesis 14 represents the unique example of a foreign political episode to be found in the entire second section of Genesis (chapters 12–50), which deals mainly with family stories centered on figures such as Abram (Abraham), Isaac, Jacob, and Joseph. The brief note on Melchizedek (Gen 14:18–20) is an abrupt break within the context of Genesis 14, which narrates a battle between two coalitions of kings: one coalition of five Palestinian kings, led by the king of Sodom, and another of four foreign kings headed by Chedorlaomer, king of Elam. The foreign coalition defeats the Palestinian kings and keeps them under submission for fourteen years. At the end of this period, the Palestinian kings rebelled against Chedorlaomer. The rebellion is immediately crushed and captives are taken from the defeated city-states. Lot of Sodom, Abram's nephew, is one of these captives. At the hearing of the sad news that his nephew was in the enemy's hands, Abram gathers his trained men and joins the Palestinian coalition. This time the victory will be on the Palestinians' side.

We quoted above a rather long passage from Genesis 14 in order to show with clarity how the brief insertion on Melchizedek (Gen 14:18–20) is flanked by two passages pertaining to the meeting between Abram and the king of Sodom (Gen 14:17 and Gen 14:21–24). Genesis 14:17 states that the king of Sodom went out to meet Abram at the Valley of Sheva, which is the Valley of the King. Then, suddenly, with no introduction, for three verses (18–20), the author of this passage deals with the mysterious character Melchizedek. The text of Genesis 14:21–24 retakes the story concerning the king of Sodom interrupted in v. 17, and reproduces a conversation between Abram and the king of Sodom in which the latter asks Abram to give him the captives.

What, then, is the content and the significance, both historical and theological, of the inclusion of verses 18–20? Note that in the Hebrew text the name Melchizedek is written as two separate words, *malkî*, "king of," and *ṣedeq*, "righteousness." Hence, one possible rendition of the name Melchizedek, is "righteous king." This etymology is found in Hebrews 7:2 and in the writings of the Alexandrian Jew Josephus, "The first founder (of

Jerusalem) was a leader of the Canaanites, called in his native tongue 'righteous king'—for indeed he was" (*Jewish Wars* 6:438). We are told that Melchizedek is a king of Salem, related perhaps to *šālôm*.[90] Salem was identified very early with Jerusalem, "And Melchizedek, the king of Jerusalem...was a priest serving in the high priesthood before God Most High" (*Targums Onkelos* and *Neophyti*). Note also that the Amarna Tablets, dated in the fourteenth century BC, mention the name of one of the Canaanite city-states, Urusalim, "city of Salim," which was identified with the biblical Jerusalem (*EA* 287:5; 289:14). We are also told in Genesis 14:18–20 that Melchizedek is a priest of the "Most High God" (*ʾēl ʾelyôn*), which is the name of the chief god of the Canaanite pantheon. He "brought out" (*hôṣîʾ*) gifts, wine and bread, but the text is completely silent concerning the recipient of these gifts. Apparently these were for Abram's men. In addition, Melchizedek blesses Abram and his God, who is identified with the "Most High God." What role does this inclusion play, then? In all likelihood, the author's intention was to create a contrast between the king of Sodom, who, instead of thanking Abram for his support, pursues the spoils of war, and Melchizedek, the ideal king and priest, who does not ask anything, but rather offers gifts and blessings to a courageous Abram. And what better place to have a parade of kings, leaders, than in the Valley of the King! The term used to describe Melchizedek as a priest is *kōhēn*, which is commonly employed to designate the Israelite priest, and is distinct from *kōmer*, which designates the idolatrous priest (2 Kgs 23:5). Thus, Melchizedek is portrayed as an Israelite priest prior to the historical inception of this institution.

As we can see, there is a great difference between these two figures, the king of Sodom and King Melchizedek. One emerges empty-handed; the other brings gifts. One comes out to meet Abram (representing the Hebrews); the other brings out gifts with no specific addressee.[91] One is an earthly king, coming out only to take advantage of his subjects or neighbors; the other is the heavenly king, who comes out to bring gifts. One is only the king of an infamous city, Sodom, born to dominate; the other is both king of peace and priest of the Most High God, born to serve others. Melchizedek's profile fits quite well in Jesus' view of serving leadership that should prevail among Christians (see Mark 10:42–45). As priest, Melchizedek intercedes for his people beside his God. If there is any feature to define this mysterious character, then self-offering would be the most appropriate description: Melchizedek comes across as the self-offering king and priest. Seen from this perspective, Melchizedek may be considered a type of the Messiah. For both God the Creator (Prov 8:24) and his Messiah, or his Wisdom (Prov 8:23; Ps 2:6; the "Son of Man" or "son of weakness" in Dan 7:13–14), have a genuine propensity for self-offering to others.

> ***Ps 110:4:*** *Yahweh has sworn and will not relent, "You are a priest forever with respect to Melchizedek."*
>
> ***Heb 7:1–3:*** *For this Melchizedek, king of Salem, a priest of God Most High, who met Abraham returning from the slaughter of the kings, and blessed him; and Abraham gave him a tenth part of everything. By the interpretation of his name, he is, first, "king of righteousness," and also king of Salem, that is, "king of peace"; without father, without mother, without genealogy, having neither beginning of days, nor end of life, but made like the Son of God, he remains a priest in perpetuity.*

The text of Psalm 110, which received a very early christological reading in the history of the church, represents the bridge between Genesis 14:18–20 and the Letter to the Hebrews. According to Psalm 110:1, David depicts Yahweh, the Lord in heaven, addressing "my Lord," and inviting him to sit at God's right side until God, the Master of the universe, will defeat all his enemies. In light of verse 1, we may read verse 4 in the same way as we have described above. Thus, God addresses the king of Israel as a potential candidate for the title of Messiah, "You are a priest forever, with respect to Melchizedek." The *Targum Onkelos* reads, "The Lord has sworn and will not *turn aside*, that you are *appointed leader* for the age *to come*, because of *the merit that you were* a righteous king." This reading probably reflects a polemic with the proponents of the christological interpretation, because the use of *kōhēn,* "priest," in the Hebrew text has been replaced with *mtmny rabʾ,* "appointed leader [teacher]." Interestingly, the *Targum Onkelos* reads this psalm as a messianic text, yet the messianic agent is appointed for a remote future, not an imminent one. That is, the ancient Jewish interpretation looks "for the age to come" (*lʿlmʾ dʾty*), and the messianic agent is a righteous king by his own "merit" (*zkwtʾ*), with no divine decree or type (standard) of comparison.

Note also that the Hebrew phrase *ʿal-dibrātî* may be rendered in either of two ways: "after the manner of," or "with respect to." In either case, the basic idea of Psalm 110:4 is that the main criterion for distinguishing the King-Messiah from any other king is his similarity to Melchizedek. And that similarity lies not in the royal role of Melchizedek but rather in his priestly function. The King-Messiah will be a priest, but not just any priest. He will be a priest according to the type of Melchizedek. We have seen above that Melchizedek in Genesis 14 was depicted as a self-offering priest who brought forward gifts of bread and wine. Likewise, the King-Messiah will follow Melchizedek's example, offering himself as the redemptive sacrifice.

Melchizedek has been interpreted from an early point in the history of the church as a type of the Son of God, of Messiah. This interpretation is based on the Septuagint reading of Psalm 109:3 [Hebrew 110:3], "From the *womb,* before the *bringer of morn* (*heōsphorou*) *I have begotten you.*" Melchizedek is depicted as the Son of God, whose existence goes beyond the time when the "bringer of morn" was brought into being. The emphasis falls on *begetting* and *womb*, which make us think of Melchizedek as one who enjoys a special relationship with God, one who is not created but rather begotten by the Almighty. The "bringer of morn" may be a hint of Lucifer, the "dawn" (Hebrew *šaḥar*), a term designating the fallen star (archangel) of God (Isa 14:12ff.). This reading, underscoring the birth of Melchizedek from God, inspired Paul's statement in Hebrews 7:3 about this enigmatic profile, "Without father, without mother, without genealogy, having neither beginning of days, nor end of life, but made like the Son of God, he remains a priest in perpetuity."

In light of the passages quoted above, we should perceive Jesus as a priest forever, as is demonstrated by Old Testament foreshadowing. As with Melchizedek, he is a self-offering priest. More precisely, he is at one and the same time priest and sacrifice. He brings forward as gifts his own body and blood, symbolized in Genesis 14 by bread and wine, offered by Melchizedek, and fulfilled in the church as the Eucharist. Interestingly, the relation between Melchizedek and his redemptive self-offering, emphasized by the christological interpretations, is hinted at in the *Zohar,* which juxtaposes Melchizedek with Yom Kippur, "This [primary harmony of the created world] is alluded to in the words 'Melchizedek (king of righteousness) king of Salem' (completeness), the king who rules with complete sovereignty. When is he completely king? On the Day of Atonement, when all faces are illumined" (*Zohar* I.87a).

Notes

1. In the Niphal (passive) conjugation, the rendering of *nāsak* should be "to be poured out" or "to be appointed/made leader" (by a libation).

2. Literally *mē-ʿôlām* means "from what is hidden, concealed," from a root *ʿ-l-m,* "to conceal, hide."

3. Literally *mē-rō(ʾ)š* means "from the head."

4. Literally *miq-qadmê ʾāreṣ* should be rendered "prior to the foundations of the earth."

5. The basic meaning of the verb *nāsak* is, as we saw above, "to pour out," and the Niphal form used in the MT is best translated as "to be poured out" or "to be consecrated leader" (with a libation).

6. We should add that Psalm 2:6 reads quite differently in the Masoretic Text than in the Septuagint. Specifically, the way it is vocalized, the Masoretic Text of Psalm 2:6 reads, "I appointed my king on Mount Sion." However, in v. 6, God is speaking, while in v. 7 the speaker is Messiah. As one can notice, the transition in

this textual context is quite cumbersome. With the assistance of the Septuagint, the pre-Masoretic textual tradition may be reconstructed by a simple modification in vocalization. In the MT the verbal root *n-s-k* is vocalized as a Qal (active conjugation) perfective form, *nāsaktî,* meaning "I poured out (appointed)," while the Septuagint presupposes a *Vorlage* (an original Hebrew text) with a Niphal (passive conjugation) perfective form, *nissaktî,* "I was poured out (appointed)." This is one good example of the Septuagint's preservation of the original reading, and thus it may help to reconstruct the pre-Masoretic stage of the Hebrew text.

7. In Phoenician and Neo-Punic inscriptions, the root **q-n-y* (Hebrew *qānâ*) designates "to create, produce," as in the phrase [*ʾl qn*] *ʾrṣ,* "El, creator (possessor) of the earth." The Ugaritic verb *qny* means: (1) "to acquire, possess"; (2) "to forge, plot"; (3) "to create" (cf. *qnyt ilm* "[female] creator of gods"—an epithet of goddess Athirat). The Akkadian verb *qanûm* means "to acquire, buy" as in Eblaite personal names, e.g., *Iqna* (*iq-na,* "[the god] acquired"). Here we might list other Semitic cognates: Syriac *qna,* "to acquire property"; Old South Arabic *qny,* "to acquire, to possess"; Ethiopic *qanaya,* "to acquire, buy"; Arabic *qana,* "to acquire" (rarely "to create").

8. The three second-century Greek translations (Aquila, Symmachus, Theodotion) chose the verb *ktaomai,* "to acquire."

9. We should add that Hebrew *qānâ,* "to acquire," is preferable to Greek *ktizō,* "to create," because it preserves the parallelism of the members, a quite important device of Hebrew poetry. Thus, the verb *qānâ,* "to acquire" (v. 22), parallels quite well the verb *ḥ-w-l,* "to give birth in great labor pains" (v. 24); note that the idea of birthing is closer to the idea of acquiring than to the idea of creating, as proposed by the Septuagint reading (*ktizō*). On the meanings of the root **q-n-y,* see J. de Savignac, "Note sur le sens du verset 8, 22 des Proverbes," *Vetus Testamentum* 4 (1954): 429–32. With the rare meaning of "to create" the verb *qānā* appears only in Psalm 139:13. Note also that in Genesis 14:19b we have a phrase and imagery similar to that found in the Ugaritic texts, hence the rendition, "God, the Creator (*qōnēh*) of heaven and earth." But here, based on the context of Genesis 14 centered on the ideas of possessing and power, we can propose a different translation, namely, "God, the Possessor of heaven and earth."

10. What Eve also meant to say, perhaps, was that the newborn child was not less than her, but rather equal to her, a human being (literally, *ʾîš,* "man") like her.

11. Literally, his "journey" (*derek,* "way, road, journey, manner"). On the imagery of God setting out on a journey, see the parable of the evil tenants in Matthew 21:33, *apedēmēsen,* "he [God] left (home) on a journey"; the word *rēʾšît* may be rendered as a complement, "as the beginning."

12. The Polal conjugation means "to be brought forth (through labor pains)" (Pss 8:24; 51:7; 90:2; Job 15:7).

13. Hebrew has a common term for "begetting" or "giving birth," namely, *yālad.*

14. Literally, *tĕhōmôt,* "depths" (cf. Prov 8:28), plural of *tĕhōm,* which is to be related to the Akkadian *tiamtum,* "sea" or "(goddess) Tiamat." Note that Tiamat, the mother-goddess, next to the god Apsu, is quite active in the Babylonian cosmogony, as attested by the epic *Enuma elish* (*When above*).

15. The text is silent concerning the way these came into being.

16. Isaiah 14:12–15 tells us in metaphoric language how Lucifer rebelled against God and eventually how he was punished by being hurled into the "pit (cistern)." Hebrew *bôr*, "pit (cistern)," is another term, besides *tĕhôm*, designating the primeval "deep," which through the free will of the rebellious Lucifer, came to be seen as the locus of the fallen angels.

17. The word *šaʿăšuʿîm*, "delight," derives from the root *š-ʿ-ʿ* II, meaning "to be amused, to take delight," and thus it can convey the idea of amusement a child may provoke by his playing. In parallel, in Jeremiah 31:20, "Ephraim," another name for the people of Israel, is labeled a "pleasing child" (*yeled šaʿăšuʿîm*) of God, that is, a child who pleases God.

18. The Qal verb (active conjugation) means "to laugh"; the Piel (intensive conjugation) form of the root conveys the meaning "to be merry, to play, to make sport."

19. Note *bĕnê(y) hā-ʾĕlōhîm*, "sons of God" (Gen 6:2).

20. For further details pertaining to this text, see above, "The Fallen Messiah. 1. The First Step: Humanity as a Reflection, or Image, of the Triune God. (1) Unity in Diversity."

21. While parts of the *Targum Jonathan* go back to pre-Christian times, its redaction was made later, around the fourth to fifth centuries in Babylonia.

22. The term *peleʾ*, "wonder," derives from the root *p-l-ʾ*, denoting the idea of "being unable to understand."

23. The term *geber*, "male," derives from the root *g-b-r*, "to be strong, to be superior."

24. The word *ʿāmît* means "community, association of people" (see Arabic *ʿāmmat*, "people," and perhaps Akkadian *emūtu*, "family" < *emu* "father-in-law"); hence, the whole phrase *geber ʿămîtî* may be rendered "my partner" or "my fellow man."

25. For further details regarding this text, see below, "The Rising Messiah. III. The Suffering, Death, and Resurrection of Messiah. 2. The Passion. (1) Forsaken by His Disciples (Zech 13:7//Mark 14:27)."

26. This term is comparable to the Akkadian direct speech marker *umma*.

27. For more details on Psalm 110 and the identity of Melchizedek, see below, "2. God's Propensities toward Incarnation. (8) Melchizedek (Gen 14:17–24; Ps 110:4//Heb 7:1–3)."

28. The presence of the verb "to be" as a converted imperfect (*wā-ʾehyeh*) points to a certain moment in the past; this moment was probably the point at which God began to create the cosmos.

29. Literally, the root *ʾ-m-n* means "to be firm, reliable."

30. That is, "confidant" parallels quite well *šaʿăšuʿîm*, "source/object of delight," found in the second member (v. 30b).

31. See Numbers 23:19; Isaiah 51:12, where the human being is compared to God, but note Psalm 8:5, where the same phrase designates a human being very close to God, a man who is crowned as king by God.

32. The editors of *HALOT* connect this word to the Semitic root *ʾ-n-š* II, "to be intimate" (Ugaritic *anš*, "to be intimate"; Arabic *ʾanīs*, "close friend").

33. Akkadian *enēšu*, "to be weak." Unlike the root *ʾ-n-š* II, the root *ʾ-n-š* I is attested elsewhere in the Hebrew Bible, e.g., "to be sickly" (2 Sam 12:15). The

parallel use of the two phrases (Hebrew *ben ʾādām* and Aramaic *bar ʾĕnoš*) brings support to the latter etymology. Both phrases underscore the humbleness of human condition in contrast to the majesty of God.

34. This contrast is even stronger if we take into account that the word *ʾēl*, "god," derives from the root *ʾ-w-l* II, meaning "to be in front, to be strong."

35. The Aramaic verb *mĕṭāʾ* (cf. Hebrew *māṣāʾ*) means "to reach."

36. For example, the "pillar of cloud" (*ʿammûd ʿānān*) in Exod 13:21; 14:19; 33:9; Num 12:5; the "cloud" (*ʿānān*) in Exod 16:10; 24:16; 34:5; Lev 16:2; Num 19:8; 1 Kgs 8:10–11; Job 26:9; Ps 105:39.

37. The Aramaic word *ʿattîq* appears only in three places in the Old Testament, all of these are found in the Book of Daniel (7:9, 13, 22); usually translated as "ancient," it is derived from a Semitic root *ʿ-t-q* whose history goes back to the Akkadian verb *etēqum*, meaning "to pass by, advance" (cf. Ugaritic *ʿtq*, "to go past, to become old").

38. For instance, the thunder on Mount Sinai in Exodus 19:19, during the covenantal theophany, "Moses spoke, and God answered him in thunder."

39. The word *zāqēn*, "old," is related to *zāqān*, "beard."

40. This expression includes the same verb as in the text under consideration, *ʾātâ*, "to come," referring to the "Son of Man" coming with/on the clouds of the sky.

41. The root used here, *p-g-ʿ*, also means "to attack"; hence, Jacob names the strange place "God's camp" (*maḥănēh ʾĕlōhîm*).

42. In Genesis 32:29 the mysterious "man" (Hebrew *ʾîš*) explains the new name of Jacob, "Israel" (*yiśrāʾēl*), as the "one who fought with God"; the name "Israel" is made of two parts, the imperfective form of a root *ś-r-h* I, "to strive, to fight," and *ʾēl*, the generic name for "God." In fact, the original meaning of the name "Israel" was slightly different, having *ʾēl*, "god; El" as subject: "(God) El fights" (Otto Eissfeldt); or "May El prevail!" from a different root *ś-r-h* II, "to rule" (Martin Noth).

43. According to Genesis 32:31, Jacob names the place Peniel (*pĕnîʾēl*), "God's face"; this place-name consists of two elements, **pĕnê* (*pĕnî*: old oblique case), "face," and *ʾēl*, "God," as a remembrance that the fugitive patriarch was found worthy to see the face of God.

44. The Hebrew term *malʾāk*, "messenger, angel," derives from a root **l-ʾ-k*, "to send."

45. PG 71:284A–B.

46. We may reiterate at this juncture that according to the *documentary hypothesis*, there are four sources or documents behind the Pentateuch's current form: Yahwist (ninth century BC), Elohist (750–700 BC), Deuteronomist (622 BC), and Priestly source (sixth century BC).

47. From the root *ḥ-r-b* I, "to be desolate, to devastate."

48. This is the scholarly vocalization of the tetragrammaton YHWH.

49. In Hebrew *śar-ṣĕbāʾ-Yahweh*; the term *śar* (in the Septuagint, *archistratēgos*, "chief captain") designates "prince, leader, captain."

50. Joshua's base (see Josh 4–10).

51. The context of Judges 2 is dominated by Israel's idolatry.

52. For example, see Genesis 2:19, where Adam, in naming the animals, exercises his role of representative on earth of God the King.

53. The Septuagint text of Judges 13:18 rendered the Hebrew adjective *pilʾî* with *thaumaston,* "wonderful"; the *Targum Jonathan* reads *mprš,* "distinctive, diverse."

54. The revelation of the Name (Exod 3:13–15) may simply be a repetition, if we take into account the note found in Genesis 4:26 that the name YHWH was for the first time invoked in the days of Enosh, Adam's grandson.

55. And not, for instance, a more specialized one, like *h-w-h,* which, in the Hishtapel, means "to bow down, to prostrate," as attested in a similar narrative, Joshua 5:14.

56. See, for instance, the refusal of the angel in Revelation 22:8–9.

57. For instance, something like, "Mind your own business."

58. *Ho ōn,* "the Being" or, more precisely, "the One Who Is" (for Hebrew *ʾehyeh,* "I am") in v. 14b.

59. That is, employed for no serious reason.

60. That is, *Yehowah* (or *Jehowah,* following the German spelling), which is in fact a grammatical hybrid. The consonants reflect a finite form of an archaic root **h-w-h* (*h-y-h,* "to be," is the attested root in the Hebrew Bible), while the vowels mirror the word *ʾădōnāy,* "lord."

61. Imperfective, third person masculine singular, from the root *h-y-h*, meaning "He is."

62. In Greek *ton onta,* in the accusative case.

63. See also Isaiah 53.

64. The verb in the Deutero-Isaiah passage appears in the perfective aspect, *bāḥārtî,* "I have chosen."

65. The Septuagint noticed quite well this distinction when it chose the masculine rather than the neuter form of the participle, *ho ōn* (masculine), instead of **to on* (neuter), to express the idea of "being," a personified being, that is.

66. That is, in syntactical terms, a nominal clause with no predicate.

67. Yves Congar, *Jesus Christ,* trans. Luke O'Neill (New York: Herder & Herder, 1966), 38–39.

68. The phrase *mēʾēt* is usually translated "from, out of" (cf. the Septuagint *para*; Vulgate *a*[*b*]); yet alone, without *min,* "from," the particle *ʾēt* means "along with."

69. As is the case in the Masoretic Text.

70. That is, as references or allusions to Jesus' life and ministry, with no clear validation from the one who was seen as their antitype.

71. From the root *š-ʾ-g,* "to roar."

72. The imperfective Hithpael (iterative and reciprocal) conjugation of the root *h-l-k, yithallēk,* defines a repetitive motion, "walking to and fro," or going about with no precise destination. The particle *ʾet* may be rendered "together with" or "besides, by the side of." The idea underscored by this particle is that "walking *with* God" suggests an intimate relationship between God and his human companion.

73. Note that the same verb, *euērestēsen,* is found in Sir 44:16; cf. Heb 11:5, where Enoch is mentioned as an example of faith and piety.

74. The name *Enoch* ("dedication") derives from the root *ḥ-n-k,* meaning "to dedicate"; cf. Arabic *ḥanaka,* "to train," "to dedicate" [II].

75. See Sir 44:16; Heb 11:5; but note Sir 49:11, *anelēmphthē,* "he was taken up," probably as a parallel to Elijah's translation to heaven, described with the same verb, *analambanō,* "to go up" (2 Kgs 2:11).

76. The verbal form used in Genesis 24:40 is *hithallaktî*, the perfective Hithpael of the root *h-l-k,* "to walk, go."

77. The form of the root *h-l-k,* "to walk, go," used in Genesis 5 and 6 is the imperfective.

78. That is, *ʾet*, meaning "along with," fits quite well with the role of the "angel of Yahweh" (pre-incarnate Messiah).

79. The preposition "in" underscores the protective function of the cloud; see Exod 24:16.

80. Perhaps the Hebrew word *tĕmûnâ* should be connected with the Ugaritic term *tmn*, meaning "form." We may add that the editors of *HALOT* suggest a relationship between *tĕmûnâ* and another Hebrew term, *mîn,* "kind, type, species," which both derive from a common Semitic root **m-y-n*, still attested in Arabic *myn,* with the meaning "to invent, to fabricate."

81. Also called the Proto-Isaiah. We may mention that modern biblical scholars divide the Book of Isaiah into three sections: Proto-Isaiah (Isa 1–39) written by a Jerusalem prophet, Isaiah, who lived in eighth century BC; Deutero-Isaiah (Isa 40–55), composed by one of Isaiah's spiritual disciples sometime during the Babylonian captivity (586–539 BC); and Trito-Isaiah (Isa 56–66), put in writing at a postexilic date, most likely around 520 BC.

82. The word *hêkāl*, meaning "palace" and "temple," is another term for *ʾûlām,* "porch" or "Holy Place."

83. The word *śārāp,* "seraph," deriving from the root *ś-r-p,* "to burn up, to set a fire," designates beings (of flames?) attending in the heavenly court of Yahweh.

84. From the root *q-d-š,* "to separate."

85. Also see above, "The Angel of Yahweh."

86. The verbal form *eskēnōsen,* "he tabernacled," is related to the noun *skēnē,* "tent, tabernacle," which is the common Septuagint rendition of the Hebrew word *ʾōhel,* "tent," designating the Tent of Meeting in the Pentateuch texts (e.g., Exod 30:36; Num 18:2).

87. The term *charis,* "grace," renders quite well the Hebrew notion of *ḥesed,* "long-suffering, unconditional love."

88. The term *alētheia,* "truth," matches the Hebrew term *ʾemet,* "truth," deriving from a root *ʾ-m-n,* "to be firm, strong," hence the idea of trustworthiness that permeates both nouns.

89. The introductory formula *dĕbar Yahweh hāyâ ʾăšer ʾel-,* "The word of Yahweh that occurred to Hosea, son of Beeri…" (Hos 1:1) is found, with minor variations, in the titles of other prophetic books (e.g., Ezek 1:3; Joel 1:1; Jonah 1:1; Mic 1:1; Zeph 1:1; Hag 1:1; Zech 1:1; Mal 1:1).

90. The word *šālôm,* "peace," derives from the root *š-l-m,* whose basic meaning is "to be complete, to finish"; the verbal root conveys the idea of fulfillment, of entering a state of wholeness and harmony, of restored relationship, of reconciliation.

91. "He produced the appropriate food for the whole world, and did not withhold blessing from all the worlds" (*Zohar* I.87b).

II

The Birth of Messiah

THIS SECOND SECTION WILL CARRY US from the texts alluding to the preexistence of Messiah, his place and role within the bosom of the Godhead, and his repeated manifestations in the world before the great coming, to those texts of the Hebrew Bible pertaining to the birth of Messiah. We are going to dwell on some of the most important messianic prophecies that allude to aspects of the birth of Messiah, such as the profile of the mother of Messiah; the virginal conception and birth; the time and place of birth; and the star of Jacob, the forerunner of Messiah. Our final point will be to consider the lineage of Messiah.

The birth of Messiah, as prophesied in the Hebrew Bible, appears to be a mysterious, almost hidden moment, which takes place away from the curious eyes of the world, a barely observable event, and thus difficult to record. It is an event wrapped not in shining glory, like the promulgation of the law on Mount Sinai (Exod 19), but rather in deep humility, known only to a small group of attendees chosen from various walks of life to bear witness to the birth of the long-waited Messiah. What distinguishes most of the texts on the birth is great emphasis on the place and role of Messiah's mother. She is described as a virgin, and as "veiled" during the conception. The mother of Messiah plays a unique role in the messianic saga. As for the time and place of the birth, the prophecies tend to be quite detailed including the place-names related to postpartum moments. Since the genealogies played an important role in Israel's religious life, it is necessary for us to study the lineage of Messiah, namely, his ties with other important figures in the history of salvation.

1. THE MOTHER OF MESSIAH

In Psalm 22, a suffering, desolate, nearly dying Messiah mentions his "mother" twice (vv. 10, 11). He does refer to "our fathers"[1] (v. 5), but does not refer at all to his physical father. In Messiah's agonized words, it was God, rather than his physical father, who helped him to emerge from his mother's womb (v. 10). This uncommon situation, on the one hand, emphasizes the role of the mother in protecting her son; on the other hand, the historical absence of the physical father from the sufferer's perspective points to God as the primary and effective cause of Messiah's conception and birth. But above all it underlines God's reliability in critical moments of one's life.

With respect to the mother of Messiah, we notice an interesting crescendo throughout salvation history, a crescendo underscored by the unfolding of the main attributes of the one chosen by God to become the mother of Messiah. First, we learn that "the woman," a providential female, will become the mother of the messianic agent; then we are told that the woman is actually "the veiled one" at the time of Messiah's conception; then we find out that the woman, the veiled one, is in fact "the queen" of the human race, the best representative of humanity, who is to become the vessel of incarnation.

(1) The Woman (Gen 3:15)

> ***Gen 3:15:*** *I will set harassment between you and the woman, and between your seed and her seed; he shall strike at your head, and you shall strike at his heel.*

Former "partners" in dialogue, though only temporarily and for the satisfaction of immediate interests, the woman (Eve) and the serpent are told by God, after the humans disobeyed the divine commandment, that they will be in a conspicuous, reciprocal, continuous, ambiguous harassment. Yet this harassment is willed as a punishment and brought into reality—initiated, that is, by none other than God himself. Thus, the harassment is not simply a continuation or consequence of the misdirected dialogue between a cunning serpent and a defensive Eve, who has been in search of security in a garden haunted by a unnamed, unknown, enemy. As we have pointed out already in this work, Genesis 3:15 is rather quiet with respect to the outcome of this harassment. The key to final victory lies with God, the initiator of the enmity and the ultimate redeemer of the relationships involved.[2]

Interestingly, a woman let herself be tempted by the serpent, and a woman is prophesied to become the channel by which the final and lasting victory will turn into reality. Eve is the one through whom disobedience entered the world; the new Eve will be the mother of the one obedient to God, the messianic agent. The faith in a providential woman, a new Eve fashioned after the pattern of the first Eve and able to remedy the mistakes of her forebear, is dealt with in one passage of the *Zohar:*

> Here is a proof. When the serpent had subverted Adam and his wife, and infected her with impurity, the world fell thereby in a state of defilement, and was laid under a curse, and death was brought into it. So the world had to be punished through him until the tree of life came and made atonement for man and prevented the serpent from ever again having dominion over the seed of Jacob. For each time the Israelites offered up a he-goat the serpent was subdued and led captive, as already said. Hence Jacob brought his father two he-goats (*śĕᶜîrîm*), one to subdue Esau, who was hairy (*śāᶜîr*), and the other to subdue the grade to which Esau was beholden and to which he adhered, as has been said already. And it is through this that the world will be preserved until a woman will appear after the pattern of Eve and a man after the pattern of Adam, who will circumvent and out-maneuver the evil serpent and him who rides on him, as explained elsewhere. (*Zohar* I.145b)

"The woman" (*hā-ʾiššâ*) and the "seed" (*zeraᶜ*) make for an odd association. As we have already noted in this work, in at least two instances (Gen 3:15 and 4:25), the term *zeraᶜ* should be rendered "seed." This is especially apparent in Genesis 4:25, in which the Hebrew term *zeraᶜ* refers to an individual rather than a collective offspring. There is strong evidence supporting this meaning (individual) in the Targumim, where the word *zeraᶜ*, "seed," was replaced with *br*, "son."[3] Note the definite article on the noun "the woman": Messiah is the son of "the woman." Thus Messiah's mother is a certain, providential woman, designed and prepared to become *the* new Eve.

With respect to the seed, offspring, the Hebrew text uses *hûʾ*, "he, it," meaning the seed of a male individual. The Septuagint reads *autos,* "he," alluding to a male descendant of Eve, rather than "seed," which is a neuter noun in Greek (*to sperma*). Therefore, the Septuagint identifies the seed with a man—hence the messianic interpretation. "He" (*autos*) equates with Messiah, with Jesus Christ. This is a tenet of interpretation held by most of the fathers. The Latin version of the Bible (Vulgate) chooses the feminine pronoun *ipsa,* "she herself," and in so doing shifts the focus from a male to a female figure, namely, the providential woman, or the new Eve. It is through her that Messiah will enter the world. This particular article of faith has gained its greatest currency in Roman Catholic theology and spirituality.

Eve probably believed that she would be "the woman" to give birth to the messianic agent, and thus be the one to fulfill the prophecy of Genesis 3:15. This is reflected at least in two instances, Genesis 4:1 and 4:25, namely, the births of Cain and Seth. In Genesis 4:1, Eve's statement, *qānîtî ʾîšʾet-Yahweh,* "I acquired a man with *the help of* Yahweh," may be also read

"I acquired a man, *namely*, Yahweh." This last rendition is possible because of the ambiguity of the Hebrew particle *ʾēt*, which can be either the sign of the accusative case[4] or of a preposition, in this case, "with *the help of*." The Midrashim offer an interesting explanation of Genesis 4:1:

> Rabbi Ishmael asked Rabbi Akiba, "Since you have served Nahum of Gimzo for twenty-two years, [and he taught], every *ak* and *rak* is a limitation, while every *eth* and *gam* is an extension, tell me what is the purpose of the *eth* written here?" "If it said, 'I have gotten a man, the Lord,'" he replied, "it would have been difficult [to interpret]; hence *eth* ['with the help of'] the Lord' is required." Thereupon he quoted to him: "For it is no empty thing from you (Deut 32:47), and if it is empty, it is so on your account, because you do not know how to interpret it. Rather, *eth the Lord* [teaches this]: In the past, Adam was created from the ground, and Eve from Adam; but henceforth it shall be, in our image, after our likeness (Gen 1:26): neither man without woman nor woman without man, nor both of them without the Shekinah." (*Genesis Rabbah* 22:2)

That Eve believed she could be "the woman" mentioned in Genesis 3:15 may also be assumed from a careful reading of Genesis 4:25, where, at the birth of Seth, Eve states, "For God has set (appointed) another seed for me." In Genesis 4:1, Eve hoped she would give birth to "a man,"[5] perhaps to an incarnate Yahweh.[6] After the episode of Cain's murder, and more precisely at Seth's birth, Eve thought that God replaced the unworthy seed (Cain) with a new seed (Seth)—hence her almost exuberant statement underlying the idea already hinted at in Genesis 3:15 that the seed was "hers." (In Genesis 4:25, Eve speaks of "another seed for me," which may be rendered in a slightly different way, "another seed belonging to me.")[7] This assumption with respect to Eve's messianic hope is supported by Genesis 5:3, "When Adam had lived 130 years, he begot a son in his likeness, after his image, and he named him Seth." Seth was considered a better candidate for the title "the seed of the woman" or messianic agent, because he was born "in the likeness, after the image" of Adam.

(2) The Royal Consort (Ps 45:8–10)

> ***Ps 45:8–10:*** *You love righteousness and hate wickedness. That is why, God, your God, has anointed you with oil of gladness above your friends. All your robes* are fragrant *with myrrh, aloes, and cassia. From ivory palaces lutes entertain you. Kings' daughters* are *among your noble women. At your right hand stands the royal consort in gold from Ophir.*

Psalm 45 is the only *profane lyric* in the Psalter.[8] This psalm is also the only text in the entire Hebrew Bible equating the king of Israel with God,

"Your throne, O God, is everlasting" (Ps 45:6). Apparently this statement goes a step further than the balanced royal ideology of Psalm 2:7, where the king is an adopted son of God. In this last text, Yahweh addresses the king of Zion from heaven with the following words, "You are my son, today I have begotten you" (NRSV). The use of "today" points to the day of coronation when Israel's king was officially adopted by God as his son. In any event, the deification of the king as it occurs in Egypt and Babylon is completely absent in Israel. Moreover, Psalm 45:8[9] suggests that between God and humanity there is an unsurpassable chasm.

This psalm was composed to celebrate a royal wedding.[10] Marriage was used by classical prophets, beginning with Hosea,[11] as a metaphor to describe the intricate relationship between God and his people, and this metaphor was employed extensively in the New Testament with respect to Christ, the bridegroom of the church (cf. Matt 9:15; Eph 5:22–33; Rev 19:7–9). Psalm 45 is the lyrical version of the same metaphor, with the queen representing Israel, or humanity, and the king pointing to Yahweh. Ancient Christian interpreters saw in this psalm a poem about the love between Christ and his church. During the exile, when the Israelite monarchy ceased to exist, Psalm 45 was read by some as a messianic text.[12] Thus, the Targum of Psalm 45:2 reads, "Your beauty, O King *Messiah,* is greater than that of the children of men." Following the tradition of the ancient synagogue, the Epistle to the Hebrews (1:8–9) takes another interpretive step, stating that the king who is mentioned in the psalm is Christ, the Son of God.

If Genesis 3:15 depicts *the* providential woman as Messiah's mother, Psalm 45 insists on her position in the messianic saga as the "royal consort," namely, God's "bride." The queen[13] stands[14] to the right of the bridegroom. The choice of the rarely used term *šēgal*, rather than the more common word *malkâ,* "queen" (king's wife), was obviously intentional. The ambiguity of the word *šēgal* fits quite well in the context of Psalm 45, where both God, the King in heaven, and Messiah, the king on earth, hold roles of priority. The woman of the palace also plays here a double role, that of Messiah's mother, and the heavenly king's spouse. Thus, the word *šēgal,* "the royal consort," was auspiciously chosen to depict her in this double hypostasis.

We might mention that in the renditions of the Targum on Psalm 45, verse 10 is quite different from the Hebrew text (and the Septuagint): instead of "royal consort,"[15] the Targum reads freely *ʾwryytʾ,* "Torah." If, in the Hebrew text, the royal consort is dressed in the gold of Ophir, in the Targum, it is the Torah that, we are told, is "written"[16] in the gold of Ophir. According to one of the Midrashim, the queen dressed in the gold of Ophir alludes to Sarai, Abraham's wife (*Genesis Rabbah* 45:1).

(3) The Veiled One (Isa 7:14//Matt 1:18, 22–23; Luke 1:26–27, 30–31)

> *Isa 7:14: Therefore my Lord himself will give you a sign. Look, the veiled one shall conceive and bear a son, and shall call his name Immanuel.*

The historical context of this important prophecy—actually, one of the most popular messianic texts—may be summarized in a few words. Isaiah of Jerusalem, the eighth-century BC prophet, approaches King Ahaz of Judah on the eve of the so-called Syro-Ephraimite war (733–732 BC). The king of Israel, Pekah, had joined Rezin of Damascus in his revolt against Assyria, and together they were heading to Jerusalem in order to depose Ahaz, a client of Assyria, and replace him with a certain *ben ṭābĕʾal*, "son of Tabeel" (Isa 7:6; cf. 2 Kgs 15:37; 16:5). Isaiah's message to Ahaz was quite simple: Trust God rather than all weaponry and any measure of defense because all man-made remedies are meant to fail. Yet, instead of listening to Isaiah's warning (Isa 7:4f.), Ahaz appeals to the Assyrian king Tiglath-pileser III, sending him gifts from the temple in order to remain a king (2 Kgs 16:7–8). Assyria intervenes promptly. Damascus and Samaria are attacked and territorially diminished, while Ahaz's Judah was reduced to vassalage.

The text to be discussed, Isaiah 7:14, is part of the so-called Book of Immanuel (Isa 6:1–12:6), which gathers prophecies of Isaiah pertaining to the Syro-Ephraimite war. In his approach to King Ahaz, Isaiah gives him the chance to ask God for a "sign" as a warranty that divine protection is an immediate, concrete reality: "Do ask a sign from Yahweh your God, as deep as Sheol or as high as above" (Isa 7:11). In the context of his meticulous preparations for war, Ahaz's refusal to ask God for a sign sounds rather hypocritical: "I will not ask. I will not test Yahweh" (Isa 7:12). In spite of the refusal, the sign is revealed, namely, in the above-quoted messianic prophecy. The sign refers to the birth of a child whose prophetic name *Immanuel* ("God [is] with us") signifies that Yahweh is still with his people and that he will protect Judah. The close relationship between Isaiah and God whom he serves is underscored by the title *ʾădōnāy*, "my Lord," used by the prophet (Isa 7:14), and throughout the Book of Immanuel Isaiah is more detailed and precise with respect to God's blessings upon Judah via this wonderful child (see Isa 9:1–6; 11:1–9). These prophecies may be listed under the rubric *royal messianism* already found in Nathan's prophecy (2 Sam 7) and subsequently reworked by Ezekiel (34:23), Micah (4:14–5:1), and Haggai (2:23). The center of the so-called royal messianism is occupied by the belief in the permanence of the Davidic dynasty.

The text of Isaiah 7:14 opens with the interjection *hinnēh,* "behold, look," which announces something out of the ordinary, a new moment in the unfolding story (cf. Gen 29:6; Num 25:6), or which calls attention to the following noun or phrase (cf. Gen 15:17; 31:51). In the context of Isaiah 7, the second function seems more likely. Thus, the emphasis falls on the noun following the interjection, namely, on *hā-ʿalmâ,* "the veiled one." The divine initiative in offering a sign of Yahweh's willingness to protect and bless Judah is emphasized by the personal pronoun *hûʾ,* "he, himself," in the phrase "my Lord himself."

With respect to the Hebrew noun *ʿalmâ*, the editors of *HALOT* list among its meanings "marriageable girl," "a girl who is able to be married," and "a young woman" (until the birth of her first child). The basic meaning is a woman (the age is less important) ready (able) to be married. The span of life covered by this term is poorly defined and quite long, ranging from the onset of puberty to the birth of a woman's first child.[17]

We propose a different etymology, namely, to derive the noun *ʿalmâ* from the root *ʿ-l-m* I, "to be concealed, hidden," well attested in Hebrew. If this etymology proves to be correct, *ʿālēm* (masculine) and *ʿalmâ* (feminine) would designate an engaged couple, which would accordingly be rendered as "the concealed ones." During the period of betrothal, the engaged parties used to live in their parents' homes, separated, secluded, forbidden from seeing one another. The feminine form, *ʿalmâ*, may also be rendered "the veiled one." This rendition would reflect the custom of engaged women wearing veils over their faces as a sign of seclusion or concealment, during the time of betrothal. We may mention that, given the ethical standards of the ancient Israelite society, the idea of virginity, though not distinctly stated, is nevertheless implied in the term *ʿalmâ.* As is the case concerning the providential woman from Genesis 3:15 (*hā-ʾiššâ,* "*the* woman"), the noun *hā-ʿalmâ,* "*the* veiled one," from Isaiah 7:14 has the definite article attached, which points to a special female character, chosen by God from the very beginning to become the mother of Messiah.[18]

The word *ʾôt* designates a "sign" confirming the truth of an earlier statement (Exod 3:12; Judg 16:17; 1 Sam 2:34). In Isaiah's case, the prophecy is a sign of confirmation of Isaiah's claims in 7:7–9 regarding the fate of Judah's enemies. Interestingly, the pregnancy and birth are described by means of an adjective (*hārâ,* "pregnant") and an active participle (*yōledet,* "the one who gives birth"), both forms being quite loose in terms of timing. The prophecy is intentionally ambiguous and evasive with respect to the precise time when these events will occur. Everything is wrapped in mystery and cautiously disclosed.

According to the Hebrew text, it is the mother who names her son ("she will call"), while the Septuagint reads "you shall call," which refers to King Ahaz's invitation to name the child. The Hebrew version underscores the role of the mother in giving a name to her son, while hinting at the absence of the physical father.[19] Regarding the identity of the child Immanuel, we assert that the modern hypothesis that assumes that Isaiah had in mind a son of King Ahaz (e.g., the future king Hezekiah) seems unlikely from a chronological (and linguistic) point of view.

The name Immanuel encapsulates a similar theology as the tetragrammaton YHWH (Yahweh) revealed to Moses (Exod 3:13–15). Yet more than the unfinished name YHWH ("He is..."), which emphasizes God's unconditioned, mysterious, always dynamic being and his perpetual openness to human concerns, the name Immanuel[20] points to a one-to-one, personal relationship between God and his people. The latter name also underscores God's willingness to descend to a place among us, to share our human destiny with us, to be one of us. This name is a step forward in the gradual unfolding of the mystery of the "One who is" on the path toward incarnation.

> ***Matt 1:18, 22–23:*** *Now the birth of Jesus the Messiah took place in this way. When his mother Mary had been engaged to Joseph, but before they lived together, she was found to be with child from the Holy Spirit....All this took place to fulfill what had been spoken by the Lord through the prophet, "Look, the virgin shall conceive and bear a son, and they shall name him Emmanuel," which means, "God is with us." (NRSV)*

> ***Luke 1:26–27, 30–31:*** *In the sixth month the angel Gabriel was sent by God to a town in Galilee called Nazareth, to a virgin engaged to a man whose name was Joseph, of the house of David. The virgin's name was Mary....The angel said to her, "Do not be afraid, Mary, for you have found favor with God. And now, you will conceive in your womb and bear a son, and you will name him Jesus." (NRSV)*

Matthew states that Mary was engaged to Joseph when she conceived her son. Then, he cites the Septuagint's version of the Isaianic text, with a slight modification, "they shall call," instead of "you shall call." He also provides a translation of the name Immanuel. Note that the same Matthew cites the Hebrew text of Hosea 11:1 when he speaks of the return of the infant Jesus from Egypt after Herod's death (Matt 2:15). The Hebrew text of Hosea 11:1 has the singular "my [i.e., God's] son (*bĕnî*)," which fits quite well in Matthew's christological application of this text, whereas the Septuagint version reads "his [i.e., Israel's] children (*ta tekna autou*)," with explicit reference to Israel. As one can notice, Matthew was at ease with both Hebrew and Greek versions of Scripture. Why, then, does he not cite the Hebrew version (*hā-ʿalmâ,* "the veiled one") in Matthew 1:23, which would have made more sense in the context of his story about a betrothed Mary? One explanation may be that the quotation from the Septuagint of Isaiah 7:14 (*hē parthenos,* "the virgin") was inserted later into the Gospel of Matthew. Another explanation might be that initially Matthew wrote the Gospel in Aramaic, with Isaiah 7:14 in Hebrew or Aramaic translation, and a later disciple translating Matthew's Gospel into Greek automatically used the Septuagint version without paying attention to his master's emphasis on Mary's betrothal to Joseph, and without mention of Mary's virginity. It is interesting to note that the word "virgin" (*parthenos*) with respect to Mary appears in Luke 1:27, perhaps under the Septuagint's influence, but not in Matthew, while the brief note "betrothed" appears in both Gospels. One may deduce that the most common feature of Jesus' birth tradition was Mary's betrothal to Joseph, and that the miracle of Jesus' conception occurred during this betrothal period. We might add that Luke 1:31 cites freely from Isaiah 7:14 replacing *Immanuel,* the prophetic name of Messiah, with *Jesus,* its historical counterpart.

If the Hebrew text of Isaiah 7:14 would have had the word *bĕtûlâ,* "virgin,"[21] then it would have been a quite general reference: Jesus' conception will occur in the life of a grown-up girl with no sexual experience, most likely not yet engaged (cf. Exod 22:15). This cannot be the case if we try to understand the entirety of the Christian tradition of Christ's birth as a fulfillment of Isaiah's prophecy. On the contrary, if we consider the Hebrew text to be the closest to the autograph, then the miracle of conception will happen to *ʾalmâ*, an unmarried woman prior to her first birth, thus including the period of engagement. Assuming that our proposed etymology is correct,[22] the unmarried woman mentioned in Isaiah 7:14 might have been a woman betrothed at the moment of her child's conception. The Hebrew version corresponds much better to what Matthew 1:18 and Luke 1:27 had to say about Mary; namely, that she was "betrothed" to a man named Joseph when the annunciation, or the conception, occurred. We might mention at this juncture that Matthew's characterization of Joseph as the "husband" (*anēr*) of Mary should be understood in terms of Joseph as the "fiancé." Given the holiness of the betrothal institution, he should be considered *de iure* Mary's husband (Matt 1:19).

Finally, we should also mention that there is important theological significance to be extracted from both evangelists' observation that Jesus' conception occurred during the betrothal period. In ancient Israel, betrothal was considered a sacred institution that existed only as a free covenant between a man and a woman. The Hebrew text of Isaiah 7:14

alludes prophetically to the fact that God's intervention will break the betrothal covenant so that Immanuel will be born. Hence the use of the interjection *hinnēh,* "behold," which calls attention to the word *hā-ʿalmâ,* "the veiled one," and thus signals a miracle or an uncommon event. Symbolically, with the birth of Immanuel, a covenant was broken so that a new covenant (between God and his people) could be initiated.

2. Virginal Conception and Birth (Isa 7:14 [LXX]; Ezek 44:1–3; Jer 31:22; Exod 3:2; Isa 49:1, 5//Luke 1:34–35)

> *Isa 7:14: That is why the Lord himself will give you a sign: Look, the virgin shall conceive and bear a son, and you shall call his name Emmanuel.*

The Septuagint, here as in other instances, proves to be rather an interpretation of the Hebrew text, although the reading proposed by the Greek version, *hē parthenos,* "the virgin," does not conflict with the Hebrew text, for the meaning "virgin" is implied in the Hebrew term *hā-ʿalmâ,* "the veiled one" (betrothed). As an example of early Jewish interpretation, the Septuagint has its own merit, because it offers new readings and nuances of Hebrew words unknown to today's readers of the Hebrew lexicon but familiar to Hebrew speakers in the pre-Christian era. A good illustration is the term *ʿalmâ*, which designates a marriageable woman, someone who could have been engaged but was not yet married. As we pointed out in the previous discussion, given the high moral standards regarding marital issues in ancient Israelite society, we may rightly assume that for a fiancée (*ʿalmâ*) it was a common thing to be a virgin. Thus the Septuagint's reading (*hē parthenos,* "the virgin") is quite plausible on social-ethical and perhaps lexical grounds. Given its use and authority since the time of the apostles, and then throughout patristic period, the Septuagint was seen by Christians as an almost inspired version of the Scripture. Within this pious context, the text of Isaiah 7:14 has always been read as a reference to the virginal conception and birth of Christ. In our opinion, in order to gain a complete profile of the one who conceived and gave birth to Immanuel, we should take a closer look at both venerable biblical versions, namely, the Hebrew text and the Septuagint. The conclusion drawn from a linguistic investigation of Isaiah 7:14 is that Messiah's mother will be a "virgin" (*parthenos*), and the birth of Messiah will occur during her betrothal period, when she will either wear a veil (*ʿalmâ,* "veiled one") or be "concealed" (from her future husband).

According to Luke, the fulfillment of Isaiah's prophecy is announced by the angel Gabriel to a virgin by the name of Mary, betrothed to a man, Joseph, and living in Nazareth of Galilee at the time of the announcement. Gabriel gives Mary the good news that she will conceive and give birth to a son, who will be named Jesus.[23] This son will be both the son of the Most High and the son of David, whose throne he will occupy (Luke 1:30–33). The dialogue between Mary and Gabriel, according to the evangelist Luke, finishes by pointing to the virginal conception and birth of Jesus, made possible exclusively by God's wonderful power.

> ***Luke 1:34–35:*** *Mary said to the angel, "How can this be, since I do not know a man?" The angel said to her, "The Holy Spirit will come upon you, and the power of the Most High will overshadow you; therefore the child to be born will be holy; he will be called Son of God."* (NRSV)

Mary's reply to the angel's news, "I do not know a man," refers to the absence of any intimate relationship with a man and thus marks the betrothal period during which time the engaged ones were living in separate homes. It does not imply any "monastic" vow to spend one's life in absolute chastity, and, in fact, ancient Israelite society did not know such an institution.[24] The brief note on Mary being betrothed to Joseph supports this interpretation. We may note that the conception of Jesus is described in terms of a new creation—hence the imagery of the Holy Spirit coming upon Mary, which parallels the Spirit's manifestation in the beginning as hovering over the primordial watery deep, keeping a vigilant eye on the possible enemies of the Creator (Gen 1:2).

The title "Most High"[25] mentioned by Gabriel is a famous name for God used in the Hebrew Bible, which is found in texts dealing with themes such as creation and royalty (e.g., Gen 14:18; Num 24:16; Isa 14:14). Majesty, power, universalism, and transcendence are the main characteristics of God Most High, of which Psalm 97:9 may offer a good illustration, "For you are Yahweh, Most High over all the earth; you are exalted far above all gods." In the biblical tradition, this, possibly Canaanite, god *ʾēl ʿelyôn*, "God Most High," was equated with Yahweh (see Gen 14:22; Ps 47:2). The use of the name "Most High" in Luke's narrative of annunciation fits quite well with this understanding, for the angel's emphasis is on God's powerful intervention. Messiah's incarnation is an act of power and is due exclusively to God. Interestingly, as with other events in the history of salvation recorded in the Scriptures, the cooperation between the persons of the Trinity is a distinguishing mark. The incarnation of Messiah (Son of God) will occur, according to Gabriel's testimony, by the work of the two other persons of the triune God, namely, the Father ("Most High") and the Holy Spirit.

Ezek 44:1–3: *Then he led me back to the outer gate of the sanctuary facing eastward, but it was shut. And Yahweh said to me, "This gate will be shut; it will not to be opened! No one shall enter by it because Yahweh, the God of Israel, has entered by it, and it shall be shut. As for the prince, he may sit in it to eat bread before Yahweh, since he is a prince; he shall enter by way of the vestibule of the gate, and shall depart by the same way."*

This short passage points symbolically to the *perpetual virginity* of the mother of Messiah, before, during, and after delivery. The text of Ezekiel 44:1–3, which is quite similar to 46:1–2, belongs to the prophet Ezekiel, active during the period of the Babylonian exile (586–539 BC). The historical background of this text takes us to the beginning of the exile. Ezekiel was among those eight thousand Judean exiles brought to Babylon after 598 BC (Ezek 1:2; 2 Kgs 24:16), and thus prior to the destruction of the Jerusalem temple in 586 BC. His last dated prophecy occurred in 571 BC (Ezek 29:17). The passage quoted above is embedded in a larger section pertaining to regulations for worship (Ezek 43:13–46:24), most of which are modeled after the cultic regulations found in the Book of Leviticus. In the subsection devoted to the official ministers (Ezek 44:1–31) is a brief note to a *nāśîʾ*, "prince," attending a communion sacrifice (Lev 2–3), in the portico of the eastern gate.

With respect to the eastern gate mentioned in the Ezekiel passage, there are many traditions, but nothing certain about its precise location. For instance, *Mishnah Middot* 1:3 mentions the eastern gate of the temple facing the Mount of Olives. The eastern gate was always identified—incorrectly, we may add—with the Golden Gate (or the Double Gate) of the temple. The architecture of the Golden Gate belongs to the end of the Byzantine period (seventh century), even though Herodian elements have been detected in its structure.[26] The Golden Gate was built perhaps in honor of emperor Heraclius in AD 631, when he brought back the holy cross, which had been captured by Muslims in AD 614. In the same century, the Muslims closed this gate to stop nonbelievers from approaching the Temple Mount area.[27] Since Ezekiel 44:1–3 was read by the early Christians in parallel with Jesus' entrance in Jerusalem on Palm Sunday, a tradition was quickly spread that the gate will remain forever shut. Since Jesus entered this gate once, he alone will reopen it at the end of time, when he will come again in glory. A text from the prophet Zechariah is employed in support of this tradition, "On that day, he will set his feet on the Mount of Olives, near Jerusalem on the east; and the Mount of Olives shall split across from east to west, and one part of the Mount shall shift to the north and the other to the south, a huge gorge" (Zech 14:4). Thus, Jesus will come down to the Mount of Olives, as also predicted on the ascension day (Acts 1:12), and, headed for the city of Jerusalem, he will reopen this gate which has been shut.

The word *nāśîʾ*, "prince, leader,"[28] is, in Ezekiel, an epithet of the new David; a *David redivivus*, or a royal Messiah (Ezek 34:24; 37:25). The term was replaced in the *Targum Jonathan* of Ezekiel 44:1–3 with *rbʾ*, "teacher, master." It is interesting to note that, in Ezekiel, the enemy of Messiah, prince Gog, bears the same title as the new David (Ezek 38:2–3; 39:1). Thus, the *nāśîʾ*, "prince," in Ezekiel 44:3, is the royal Messiah, whose first responsibility is to bring salvation in the last days. The eating of bread can be seen as an allusion referring to king David, the type of Messiah, and more precisely to that episode where the fugitive David took the shewbread from the sanctuary and ate it along with his soldiers (1 Sam 21:1–9). It is important to remember, however, that David has never been described as *nāśîʾ*, "prince"; throughout the Hebrew Bible, this term refers in most cases to tribal leaders or chieftains (e.g., Num 13:2; 34:25).

The term *ʾûlām*[29] designates the "portico, porch" of either a palace (1 Kgs 7:6) or a temple (1 Kgs 6:3; 7:12; Ezek 8:16; Joel 2:17). Since this brief passage is about sanctuary and "bread" (*leḥem*) as a reference to the sacred meal following the community sacrifice (Lev 7:15; Deut 12:7), we may assume that this portico belongs to the temple rather than to the palace. In this case, the mother of Messiah is symbolically portrayed as a sanctuary with her son eating bread inside, that is, feeding himself with his mother's food. He enters and goes out of the portico of the sanctuary of Mary's body, the symbolic temple.

Jer 31:22: How long will you waver, O rebellious daughter? For Yahweh has created something new on earth: A woman shall encompass a man.

Most of the so-called Book of Consolation (Jer 30:1–31:22), which contains promises of recovery for Israel, was written between the finding of the Book of the Law (Deuteronomy) in 622 BC and the death of King Josiah in 609 BC. The reform initiated by Josiah (2 Kgs 22:3–23:24) was centered on cultic purgation and a rapid rise of nationalistic aspirations. The latter aspect should be considered in light of Assyria's decline, paired with Josiah's northern campaigns to conquer Samaria and Galilee (2 Kgs 23:15, 19). Within this historical framework we have to read the hope, exuding from the promises of Jeremiah 30–31, that the northern exiles, outliving Samaria's fall in 722/721 BC, will return to a new, restored kingdom of David, consisting of both Judah and Israel. The messianic character of such a hope lies with their emphasis on unity between the two former kingdoms, serving "Yahweh their God, and David their king" (Jer 30:9).[30]

This text uses a rather graphic word for "woman," *nĕqēbâ*.[31] The same word is found in Genesis 1:27 and describes the only distinction permitted by God with respect to humans, the gender distinction. The term used here for "man," *geber*, derives from the root *g-b-r*, meaning "to be strong," and hence the contrast between "woman" and "man."[32] This prophecy, found in the Book of Jeremiah, precedes the famous statement about the "new covenant" inscribed in hearts (Jer 31:31–34), which also has been connected with the messianic hope.

As for the notion of "encompassing," the root *s-b-b* (Polel conjugation) conveys the basic idea of "going around" or "moving around protectively" (Deut 32:10), "sheltering, encompassing" (Jer 31:22). The Septuagint has the plural form *perieleusontai,* "they shall go about," referring to the Israelites, while the Vulgate reads *circumdabit,* "she shall encompass." The *Targum Jonathan* on Jeremiah 31:22 distinctively sees Israel's return from captivity as a genuine longing for instruction; hence its peculiar reading, "The people of the House of Israel will long for instruction." The Targum's reading generated the talmudic interpretation that Torah ("instruction") could function as a protecting wall for its industrious students, "In the West it was stated, 'Without Torah' and without a [protecting] wall. 'Without Torah,' for it is written. Is it that I have no help in me, and that sound wisdom is driven quite from me. 'Without a [protecting] wall,' for it is written, 'A woman shall encompass a man'" (*Yevamoth* 62b). Also the phrase "a woman shall encompass a man" may lie at the basis of the statement "A man's home is his wife" (*Yoma* 1:1). Specifically, a woman becomes man's tabernacle and shelter. Thus read, the text of Jeremiah 31:22 may be a prophetic variant of Adam's statement in Genesis 2:24 about a man's leaving his parents to cling to his wife. With respect to the root *s-b-b* found in Jeremiah, one may assume that it connotes the idea of protection or shelter, "You are my shelter; you preserve me from distress; you surround me with the joyous shouts of deliverance" (Ps 32:7). Conversely, at its return from captivity, Israel will shelter Yahweh, her "man," as her most precious treasure. This is an image of tender love similar to the embracing love between a woman and a man.

Jerome, in his commentary on Jeremiah, understood this verse, and especially the phrase "a woman shall encompass a man," as a prophecy of Mary's virginal conception of Christ, "The Lord has created a new thing on earth; without seed of man, without carnal union and conception, 'a woman will encompass a man' within her womb, one who, though he will later appear to advance in wisdom and age through the stages of infancy and childhood, yet, while confined for the usual number of months in his mother's womb, will already be perfect man."[33] Thus, a woman will become the tabernacle, or the shelter, of God's "fellow-man" (Zech 13:7), the incarnate Logos. The profound theological meaning of this passage, read in light of the gospel, is that a female human will be able to encompass the almighty God, whom the heavens are unble to encompass, whose dwelling place is above heavens.

The conception of Messiah, that is, his incarnation, is seen as a *new creation*, as something absolutely new (*ḥădāšâ*, "a new thing")—hence the use of the verb *bārāʾ*, "to create," in our passage from Jeremiah. The Septuagint offers a reading different from the Hebrew text, "because the Lord has created salvation (*sōtēria*) for a new plantation." This rendition emphasizes the soteriological aspect of Israel's return from exile. According to the Greek text, God's salvation will dawn over a "new plantation" (*katathyteusin kainē*), which is a new Israel. Note that the verb *bārāʾ* in the Hebrew Bible appears only a few times, always with God as subject, connoting a powerful action.[34] The use of the verb *bārāʾ*, "to create," in Jeremiah points to the relationship between the first Adam, created in the image of God (Gen 1:27) and the "last Adam" (1 Cor 15:45). The restoration of humanity worked by Christ is therefore seen as a new creation. Yet the "new thing" (*ḥădāšâ*) of which Jeremiah speaks may also refer to the unity of the two natures of Christ.

> ***Exod 3:2:*** *An angel of Yahweh appeared to him in a flame of fire out of a bush. He gazed, and there was a bush all aflame, yet the bush was not consumed.*

For details regarding this passage, part of the call of Moses, and its meanings (historical, theological), see the section "The Preexistence of Messiah." What we would like to add here is one specific Christian interpretation; namely, that which is centered on the eternal virginity of the Mother of Messiah, for the burning bush in patristic writings points to just such an aspect of the profile of the *Theotokos* (a Greek term, meaning "birth-giver of God"). We have already said above that fire symbolizes the life-giving, purifying power of the Spirit. According to the annunciation narrative (Luke 1:35), "The angel answered, 'The Holy Spirit will come upon you, and the power of the Most High will overshadow you; therefore the child to be born will be holy; he will be called Son of God'" (NRSV). Thus the angel Gabriel informs Mary that the conception of Jesus will take place through the power of the Spirit. In light of the gospel, the burning bush may be considered a foreshadowing of the Messiah's conception leaving intact his mother's virginity, just as the bush burned but was not consumed by the mysterious fire. As we have pointed out previously, Messiah appears in the scene of the burning bush as an "angel of Yahweh." Gregory of Nyssa compared the burning bush with the Mother of Messiah, whose human nature was not destroyed by God's intervention at the moment of conception, "From this [the burning bush] we learn also the mystery of the Virgin: The light of divinity which through birth shone from her into human life did not consume the burning bush, even as the flower of her virginity was not withered by giving birth."[35]

> ***Isa 49:1, 5:*** *Listen, O coastlands, to me, and give heed, you peoples from afar! Yahweh has called me from the womb; from the bowels of my mother has he mentioned my name....And now Yahweh says, who fashioned me in the womb to be his servant....*

This text is part of the Book of the Consolation of Israel written at the end of the exile (587–539 BC) by a prophet known as Second Isaiah, or Deutero-Isaiah. The central theme of this book (Isa 40–55) is that of a new exodus under God's leadership, a theme that is solemnly restated at the end of the book (Isa 55:12–13). A distinguishing feature of Second Isaiah is that it contains four lyrical passages, the Songs of the Servant of Yahweh.[36] These songs depict the "Servant of Yahweh" (*ʿebed Yahweh*) as one who regathers his people while being the light of all nations; as one who proclaims the monotheistic faith; as one who, by his suffering and death, is able to forgive the people's sins and who at the end of his saving mission is glorified by God. Who was this Servant? There are three main answers to this question. Some interpreters argue that the Servant was in reality the community of Israel about to return to its homeland. According to other authors, the Servant was a historical person, possibly the prophet himself (that is, the Deutero-Isaiah). It seems to us that a synthesis of these two explanations would be the most reasonable answer to the question. Thus, the Servant of Yahweh was a historical person, possibly the prophet, who represented the people of Israel. As the majority of Isaiah's interpreters notice, an understanding that is limited to a sixth-century BC "servant," whether it be an individual, a community, or a combination of the two, does not take into account all the details furnished by the texts themselves. This is an especially important point, considering that the Servant is the mediator of a future salvation. This detail justifies the third answer pertaining to the Servant's identity, namely, the messianic interpretation of the songs of the Servant of Yahweh, an interpretation encountered in both Jewish and Christian communities of faith. We may add that among Jewish interpreters, the suffering aspect of the Servant's mission has been persistently overlooked, while the Christian kerygma from the beginning has emphasized this aspect with respect to Jesus' mission to procure humanity's salvation through his suffering and death (Mark 10:45; Luke 22:19–20; cf. Matt 12:17–21).

The text of Isaiah 49:1, 5 quoted above belongs to the second song of the Servant (Isa 49:1–6). This song underscores a few aspects of the Servant's mission: his election from his mother's womb, his new teaching, his double role as gatherer of Israel and light to the nations. Yahweh appears in the second song as the only father of the Servant. There is no mention of a physical father, although the "maternal womb" (*beṭen*) is twice mentioned. Therefore, the call of the Servant coincides with his conception in the womb. Like Jeremiah (1:5), the Servant in Isaiah has been called from the very beginning of his life. Significantly, the conception is depicted as a direct divine intervention and, more precisely, as an act of creation: it is Yahweh who *fashioned* the Servant. The verb used here, *yāṣar,* "to fashion, form," is found also in the Yahwist narrative of humanity's creation (Gen 2:7), which suggests that the Servant of Yahweh is the "last Adam" (1 Cor 15:45), fashioned by Yahweh in his mother's womb.

3. Time of Birth (Gen 49:10; Num 24:17; Dan 9:24–27; Mal 3:1; Hag 2:6–9; Ps 118:25–27)

Messiah's time of birth is gradually gaining clearer contours: from a general statement regarding an ideal ruler, originally from the tribe of Judah (Gen 49:10), whose coming will be heralded by a mysterious star (Num 24:17); through prophecies pointing to the temple as *terminus a quo* (Mal 3:1; Hag 2:6–9; Ps 118:25–27); to an apocalyptic estimation of Messiah's time of birth and ministry (Dan 9:24–27).

> ***Gen 49:10:*** *The scepter shall not depart from Judah, nor a ruler's staff from between his feet, until* Shiloh *comes; and the obedience of the peoples shall be his.*

This brief passage comes from the so-called Blessings of Jacob or Jacob's Testament (Gen 49:1–28). The patriarch Jacob foretells the future of his sons—or, more precisely, of the tribes bearing their names. The prophecies found in Genesis 49 deal with events of the patriarchal age,[37] while pointing to later situations and events. Since Judah plays an important role in Jacob's blessing, the general opinion today is that the final form of this section dates back to David's time. We say final form, because Jacob's testament is replete with a considerable number of archaic features.[38] The text of Genesis 49:10 records Jacob's prophetic statement regarding Judah (vv. 8–12). It alludes obviously to king David, of Judah's tribe, as the founder of the unified kingdom, yet it remains an open text for messianic applications.

The term *šēbeṭ*, translated here as "scepter," is a shepherd's rod or staff used to guide, chastise, smite, or slay. In the hand of a chief or ruler, *šēbeṭ* becomes a scepter. In the case of the tribal chieftains, *šēbeṭ* is an honorary symbol (cf. Num 21:18; Mic 7:14).[39]

Jacob's prophecy states that the tribal identity of Judah was not to pass away until *Shiloh*[40] comes. In other words, there will be no transfer of power in the historical experience of the tribe of Judah until the reality of that mysterious person, Shiloh, appears. The phrase "until Shiloh comes" means that Judah would exercise a royal or ruling role among the other tribes until Shiloh takes over. The phrase *ʾad kî,* "until," indicates that at a certain point in time a change will take place. This change will, however, occur as a smooth transition, without any sort of radical disjunction.

The focus of Jacob's prophecy of Judah falls on the key term *Shiloh.* There are several interpretations of this difficult term.

(a) Some take *Shiloh* as a place-name, "until he comes to Shiloh," where *he* stands for either David or the tribe of Judah. This was probably the understanding of the Masoretes, as demonstrated by their marginal notes. Yet this explanation seems quite unlikely, because the tabernacle was pitched centuries later at Shiloh (Josh 18:1–10), and in Jacob's time the place-name Shiloh was not significant.

(b) Some suggest that this word relates to the verb *šālaḥ,* "to send." This is in fact the Vulgate's interpretation, *donec veniat qui mittendus est,* "until he who is sent comes." Hence *mittendus est,* "the one who is sent," might hint at Christ, God's messenger on earth. However, such an interpretation cannot be accepted because *šālaḥ,* "to send," and *šîlōh* (*Shiloh*) are two different words; the proof is the third consonant, *ḥ* in *šālaḥ,* and *h* in our term, *šîlōh.*

(c) According to ancient Jewish interpreters, Ezekiel 21:32 would provide the proper answer for the meaning of the word *Shiloh.* The Ezekiel text reads, *ʾad-bōʾ ʾăšer-lô ham-mišpāṭ,* "until the one comes to whom belongs the judgment." How did the phrase *ʾăšer-lô,* "to whom it belongs," from Ezekiel 21:32 turn into our form, *Shiloh* (*šîlōh*)? We may explain the transformation as follows: The first consonant, *aleph* (ʾ), from *ʾăšer-lô,* was dropped, while the consonant *resh* (*r*) was assimilated to the following consonant, *lamedh* (*l*): hence the term *šellô* < *ʾăšer-lô,* "to whom it belongs," quite similar to our form *šîlô* (Qere!). This explanation seems quite attractive, though there is no other biblical evidence for such an assimilation, that is, between *ʾăšer* and *lô.*

(d) The Septuagint's reading, *heōs an elthē ta apokeimena,* "until the things laid up for him come," seems to be in the same line of thought as the rabbinic interpretation based on Ezekiel 21:32, with the additional remark that the Septuagint inserts in Genesis 49:10 the idea of tribute or gifts.[41] We find similar renderings in the *Targum Onkelos* on Genesis 49:10, "whose is the kingdom"; in some manuscripts of the Samaritan Pentateuch; and in the Syriac version (Peshitta), "the one to whom it [authority] belongs." Finally, the Midrashim also echo such an idea, "Until Shiloh comes: he to whom kingship belongs (*shelo*)" (*Genesis Rabbah* 99:8).

(e) Another suggested way of explaining the single appearance in the entire Hebrew Bible[42] of *šîlōh* is to relate this form to the Egyptian word *śr*, "prince."[43] This etymology seems quite likely in the context of Genesis 49:10, which speaks of rulers originating from Judah.

What, then, is the identity of this ideal ruler, or "prince"? According to the *Targum Onkelos* on Genesis 49:10, the term *Shiloh* designates Messiah, "He who exercises dominion shall not pass away from the house of Jehuda, nor the teacher (*spr*ʾ) from his children's children for ever, until the Messiah (*mšyḥ*ʾ) comes, whose is the kingdom, and whom the peoples shall obey." The ancient Jewish teachers follow in the footsteps of the targumic interpretation, seeing in *Shiloh* an allusion to the *royal Messiah* (*Genesis Rabbah* 98:8). One of the Midrashim solemnly declares, "The Messiah's name is *Shiloh*, as it is stated, 'Until Shiloh comes'" (*Lamentations Rabbah* 1:51). But note also the identification of *Shiloh* with Moses, "'Until Shiloh comes,' this is Moses, the numerical value of the two names Shiloh and Moses being the same" (*Zohar* I.25b).

The last part of Genesis 49:10 foresees the time when the one from Judah, the ideal ruler, will gain the obedience of *ʿammîm*, "peoples," irrespective of their ethnic identities.[44] The renderings of the Septuagint (*prosdokia*) and the Vulgate (*expectatio*) presuppose a different Hebrew word, that is, *tiqwâ*, "hope." Both the Septuagint and the Vulgate point to the messianic hope, that is, "he [Messiah] is the peoples' expectation."

To summarize our observations on Genesis 49:10, we may draw the conclusion that Messiah will come after an uninterrupted line of rulers, kings originating from Judah. Moreover, he will be the ideal ruler and the expectation of the nations, which should be understood as the one whom the nations will obey cheerfully. Unlike the frequent changes in dynasty of the northern kingdom, the southern kingdom for its duration enjoyed the stability of one dynasty, that of King David. Jesus, originating from the tribe of Judah, as the son (descendant) of King David (Rom 1:3), fulfilled this prophecy by coming at the end of a line of kings, all of whom belonged to the same tribe.

Num 24:17: *I see him, but not now; I behold him, but not near. A star is emerging from Jacob; a scepter is rising from Israel, and it smashes the brow of Moab and destroys all the sons of Seth.*

This passage is found in the so-called Balaam Cycle (Num 22–24). The narratives that form the framework for the prophecies of Balaam combine

Yahwistic and Elohistic traditions and tend to be later than the prophecies themselves. During Israel's wandering through the wilderness, when the Hebrews came to camp in the Plains of Moab, Balak, the king of Moab, sent a message to Balaam son of Beor, a soothsayer from the banks of the Euphrates, to come over to Moab and curse the Hebrews. Strangely, Balaam recognized Yahweh as his own God (Num 22:18), and therefore, instead of cursing the Hebrews, Balaam began to bless them (Num 23:11–12, 25–26; 24:10). Later traditions depict Balaam in rather somber colors as a prophet hostile to Israel, whom Yahweh forced to bless the Hebrews (Deut 23:5–6), and who moved the people toward idolatry at Peor (Num 31:16). A plaster inscription discovered at *Deir ʿAlla* in Jordan in 1967, dating to approximately 700 BC, mentions the name of a "visionary" (*ḥzy*), "Balaam son of Beor," who could have been the same prophet spoken of in the Book of Numbers. The inscription was probably written originally on a wall or a stela hung on a wall of a sanctuary that collapsed during an earthquake. The script of the inscription is Aramaic; and the dialect in which the text was written is either Aramaic or Canaanite. Interestingly, Balaam in the Hebrew Bible is the worshiper of *ʾēl šaddāy*, "God of the mountain" (Num 24:4, 16),[45] similar or identical to the one worshiped by the Balaam of the inscription. In a nutshell, the plaster inscription of *Deir ʿAlla* supports the historicity of the Balaam cycle. The most striking feature of the whole section on Balaam is that the God of Israel resorts to a non-Hebrew prophet to convey his will to the fugitive tribes wandering through the Plains of Moab, specifically regarding their future vis-à-vis other nations. Moreover, God chooses a non-Hebrew prophet to deliver a prophecy pertaining to the time and circumstances of Messiah's birth.

Balaam's prophecy contains at least three key words. First, the prophet speaks of a "star" (*kôkāb*) emerging from Jacob. As the star in the ancient Near East was used to designate a god or a deified king, the focus of this prophecy seemingly falls on a descendant of Jacob who would have divine qualities. The verb used here to describe the star's movement is *dārak,* "to tread, to walk, to travel." But the Hebrew verb *dārak* may be related to the Ugaritic form *drkt*, meaning "dominion." In this case, Numbers 24:17 should be read as a hint at the royal profile of Jacob's descendant, who will combine divine and royal features in the same person. We might add that the three magi, in the New Testament application of Balaam's prophecy,[46] speak of a "star" (*astēr*) that had "appeared" (*phainomenou*) in the "east" (*anatolē*) (Matt 2:2, 7, 9). This matches quite neatly with the place of Balaam's prophecy, namely, the eastern side of the Jordan River. Second, Balaam mentions a "scepter" (*šēbeṭ*), which commonly signifies royal authority, as we have already discussed above.[47] Third, the son of Beor emphasizes that both star and scepter, or god and king, emerge through a human agent, specifically *Jacob/Israel*. This means that the one who is both divine and royal will also be human. Thus, the one prophesied by Balaam will be at the same time God, king, and human being. Read in the context of the gospel account, this prophecy speaks of Messiah and his triply faceted profile. This was seen prophetically in the gifts offered by the magi to the infant Jesus at his birth. According to Matthew 2:11, the three magi brought gifts of gold, frankincense, and myrrh. Each gift was telling Jesus' fate on earth from a particular viewpoint: Gold indicated that he would be a king; frankincense, that he would be a God; and myrrh, that he would die, emphasizing his humanity.

In Balaam's own words, Messiah was not present at the time when the prophet delivered God's message, nor was he present in the Plains of Moab, when Balaam described what he was seeing. Interestingly, the second verb for seeing used in our text is *š-w-r*.[48] We may picture the prophet Balaam being brought by Balak "on the summit of Peor" (Num 23:28), overlooking the tribes of Israel arrayed for battle, while speaking his prophecy. Balaam was looking down, searching through the Hebrew troops and trying to discern among the thousands of men the figure of Messiah, but finally he had to concede that Messiah was not there at that particular point in time. According to what we can glean from Balaam's prophecy, the time of Messiah's birth should be placed after 1200 BC, the relative date of Israel's entry into Canaan. Within the larger framework of the Israelite monarchy, this should be understood more precisely as following the inception of the monarchy in Israel.

The text of Numbers 24:17 has been read as messianic since early times. The *Targum Onkelos* on Numbers 24:17 is a good illustration of this:

> I shall see him, but not now; I shall behold him, but it is not near. When the mighty King of Jacob's house shall reign, and the Messiah, the Power scepter of Israel, be anointed, he will slay the princes of Moab, and bring to nothing all the children of Seth, the armies of Gog who will do battle against Israel and all their carcasses shall fall before him.

Similarly, the *Zohar* speaks of a royal Messiah, David's descendant, with respect to the same text:

> "There shall come a star out of Jacob" (Num 24:17). This star will shine for forty days and forty nights, and when the Messiah shall be revealed and all the nations of the world shall gather around him, then will the verse of Scripture be fulfilled which says, "And in that day the root of Jesse which stands for an ensign of the peoples, to it shall the Gentiles seek: and his rest shall be glorious (Isa 11:10)." (*Zohar* II.172b)

More evidence that Numbers 24:17 was considered messianic in early Jewish circles comes from those rabbinic sources where Rabbi Akiba, one of the leading Jewish teachers of the second century, appears as an enthusiastic supporter of Bar Kokhba (Koziba), the Jewish insurgent who dared to rebel against the Roman army, and who died at Bethar in the times of Hadrianus (AD 135). Simon received the nickname *Bar Kokhba,* "son of the Star," after he was welcomed with the title *Messiah* by none other than Rabbi Akiba. One of the Midrashim briefly records that episode, among other details pertaining to Bar Kokhba's revolt and his death as a martyr:

> Rabbi Johanan said, "Rabbi used to expound, 'There shall step forth a star (*kokab*) out of Jacob (Num 24:17), thus: read not *kokab* but *kozab* (lie).'" When Rabbi Akiba beheld bar Koziba he exclaimed, "This is the King Messiah!" Rabbi Johanan bar Tortha retorted, "Akiba, grass will grow in your cheeks and he will still not have come!" (*Lamentations Rabbah* 2:4)

The Talmud has a slightly different recollection, "Bar Koziba reigned two and a half years, and then he said to the Rabbis, 'I am the Messiah.' They answered, 'Of Messiah it is written that he smells and judges: let us see whether he [bar Koziba] can do so.' When they saw that he was unable to judge by the scent, they slew him" (*Sanhedrin* 93b).

> ***Dan 9:24–27:*** *Seventy weeks have been determined for your people and your holy city until the measure of transgression is filled and that of sin complete, until iniquity is expiated, and eternal righteousness brought in; and prophetic vision sealed, and the Holy of Holies anointed. You must know and understand: from the issuance of the word to restore and rebuild Jerusalem until Messiah the Leader is seven weeks; and for sixty-two weeks it will be rebuilt, square and moat, but in a time of distress. And after those sixty-two weeks, Messiah shall be cut off, but he has no.... The people of a leader that shall come shall destroy the city and the sanctuary, and its end* shall be *through a flood. Desolation is decreed until the end of war. During one week he will make a firm covenant with many. For half a week, he will put a stop to the sacrifice and the meal offering. On the wing* of the sanctuary *will be an appalling abomination until the decreed destruction will be poured down upon the devastator.*

Chapter 9 of the Book of Daniel concerns Daniel's prayer (vv. 1–19), followed by the angel Gabriel's intervention (vv. 20–27). The text quoted above is a part of Gabriel's intercession and is, in fact, an instance of revelation regarding the end of Jerusalem's desolation.[49] Gabriel begins his rather mysterious discourse by mentioning a "word" (*dābār*) having "gone out" (*yāṣāʾ*) during Daniel's prayer, "At the beginning of your supplications a word went out, and I have come to declare it, for you are greatly beloved. So consider the word and understand the vision" (Dan 9:23 NRSV). Perhaps that word came from the throne of God to be addressed to Daniel, who, in the beginning of the chapter (Dan 9:2), was trying to understand Jeremiah's prophecy regarding the seventy years decreed for the Babylonian captivity. Jeremiah prophesied, "For thus says the Lord, 'Only when Babylon's seventy years are completed will I visit you, and I will fulfill to you my promise and bring you back to this place'" (Jer 29:10 NRSV; cf. 25:11–12). Jeremiah's computation begins with the year 605 BC, when the revelation was made to him, and ends with the decree of Cyrus in 538 BC, by which the Persian king permitted the exiles to return to their homeland and rebuild Jerusalem (2 Chr 36:22–23; Ezra 1:1–2).

Pondering Jeremiah's calculation, Daniel offers an original interpretation of Jeremiah's seventy years, presenting them instead as "seventy weeks" (Dan 9:24), or, more precisely, as seventy weeks of years, namely, 490 years. Daniel's computation is different from that of Jeremiah. It begins with the decree of Cyrus in 538 BC and ends with the coming of Messiah (Dan 9:25). Moreover, Daniel divides the seventy weeks or those 490 years into three subdivisions: seven weeks (49 years) + sixty-two weeks (434 years) + one week (7 years). From Cyrus's decree in 538 BC to the time of "Messiah the Leader" (*māšîaḥ nāgîd*) is sixty-nine weeks, or 483 years (Dan 9:25–26). After these 483 years, Messiah the Leader will be put to death without *fault* by "a leader who is to come" (*nāgîd hab-bāʾ*). In addition, this leader, Messiah's enemy, will destroy the city and sanctuary (Dan 9:26). In the last week of years,[50] Messiah the Leader will strike a firm "covenant" (*bĕrît*) with many. In the middle of the last week of years, adds Daniel, Messiah the Leader will put an end to sacrifice and oblation (Dan 9:27). Then, the "appalling abomination" (*šiqqûṣîm mĕšōmēm*) will appear on the "wing'" (*kĕnap*) of the temple. And this situation will last until the "devastator" (*šōmēm*) will be destroyed.

The interpretation embraced by most modern scholars is that Daniel 9:24–27 hints at the Maccabees' time, when Antiochus IV Epiphanes launched his persecution against the Jews (167–164 BC). It may be useful to recall at this juncture that the Book of Daniel was committed to writing in the middle of the second century BC. According to the modern view, therefore, Messiah, or the anointed one mentioned here, would be the high priest Onias III (2 Macc 4:30–38), deposed and assassinated in 175 BC by the men of Antiochus IV Epiphanes. He could also be the "leader of the covenant" (*nĕgîd bĕrît*) mentioned in Daniel 11:22. The term *šiqqûṣîm* is the plural of *šiqqûṣ*, meaning "horror, monster, abhorrence, object to abhor"; in cultic contexts, this term may designate images and symbols of pagan deities.[51] The term *šiqqûṣ* may be either an allusion to the god Baal[52] or a designation of the god Zeus Olympios, to whom the temple of Jerusalem was rededicated by Antiochus IV Epiphanes (2 Macc 6:2). According to the Talmud, the seventy weeks, or 490 years, of Dan 9:24 refer approximately to the period between the destruction of the First

Temple (586 BC) and the destruction of the Second Temple (AD 70) (*Nazir* 32b).

The classical Christian interpretation of Daniel 9:24–27 sets the beginning of Daniel's reckoning at the twentieth year of the Persian king Artaxerxes, when he allowed his cup-bearer, Nehemiah, to return to Palestine and rebuild the city of his fathers. The year 455 BC was the twentieth regnal year of Artaxerxes, which corresponds to the year 299 AUC.[53] If we add the 483 years predicted by Daniel, we reach the year 782 AUC, which converts to AD 27/28. This was the historical moment when Jesus began his public ministry (Luke 3:1). After three and a half years, which amounts to the middle of the last "week" spoken of by Daniel, the violent death of Messiah occurred.

Thus, taking into account the year when Jesus began his public mission, and based on the evangelist's estimation that Jesus was about thirty years old (Luke 3:23), we may approximate his date of birth. If we subtract thirty years from 782 AUC, we would reach 752 AUC as Jesus' date of birth, which converts to the year AD 1. This was the calculation done by Dionysius Exiguus, which has been proved to be wrong. In reality, Jesus was born earlier, probably in 750 AUC or 4/3 BC.

From the following texts we learn a new detail, that Messiah was to be born in a period when the Second Temple was still standing, namely, prior to its destruction in the year AD 70.

> ***Mal 3:1:*** *Look, I am sending forth my messenger to clear a way before me. And unexpectedly the Lord whom you seek shall come to his Temple. As for the angel of the covenant that you desire, he is already coming, says Yahweh of Hosts.*

The Book of Malachi, thought by modern scholars to be anonymous, since the name of the prophet *malʾākî* means "my messenger," was put into writing after the renewal of worship in the Second Temple (516 BC). This was earlier than the interdiction of mixed marriage promulgated by the religious reformer Nehemiah (445 BC) in the first half of the fifth century BC. Malachi speaks in the passage quoted above of the coming of Messiah while the Second Temple was still standing, hence prior to AD 70, the year in which the Second Temple was destroyed by Roman troops. We should add that the foundation of the Second Temple was laid in the spring of 537 BC.

In Malachi's passage, Messiah is presented from two perspectives. First, he is called "the Lord" (*hā-ʾādôn*), and, more precisely, he is referred to as the long-awaited Lord, the one sought by Israel.[54] Second, Messiah is also called the "angel of the covenant" (*malʾak hab-bĕrît*). The verb used to describe Messiah in this sense means "to delight in,"[55] and thus Messiah is the delight of those who seek him, just as the suffering Messiah is the delight of the Almighty.[56]

The text uses twice the word *malʾāk*, meaning "messenger, angel."[57] The first occurrence designates a servant of God sent to prepare a way for the royal Messiah. This usage indicates a prophet—hence the rendition "my messenger." This was to be the precursor of Messiah (Isa 40:3), the new Elijah (Mal 3:23), whom Matthew identifies as John the Baptist (Matt 11:10). The precursor's role was similar to those royal messengers in the ancient Near East whose duty was "to clear"[58] the way for the coming of their master. The second use of the word has a totally different meaning, namely, the "angel of the covenant," who is identical with "the Lord." Thus, the second angel should not be understood as a precursor of Messiah, because his coming to the temple is simultaneous with that of the Lord (i.e., Yahweh). Rather, the second use of angel should be understood as another messianic title.[59] The coming of the Lord is presented as an unexpected event: He will come *pitʾōm*, "suddenly, unexpectedly." "The covenant" (*hab-bĕrît*) mentioned in Mal 3:1 may be a hint to the "new covenant" (*bĕrît ḥădāšâ*) of Jeremiah's proclamation (Jer 31:31–34), which will be mediated by Messiah, as God's angel, or messenger.

This text was understood as messianic in Jewish circles, as attested by the Midrashim, "In the millennium, likewise, when he [God] will reveal himself, salvation will come to Israel, as it says, 'Behold, I send my messenger, and he shall clear the way before me (Mal 3:1)'" (*Exodus Rabbah* 32:9; cf. *Numbers Rabbah* 16:11).

> ***Hag 2:6–9:*** *For thus said Yahweh of Hosts, "In just a little while, I will shake once again the heavens and the earth, the sea and the dry land. I will shake all the nations, and the precious things of all the nations shall come here, and I will fill this house with glory, said Yahweh of Hosts. Silver is mine and gold is mine—declares Yahweh of Hosts. The glory of this latter house shall be greater than that of the former one, said Yahweh of Hosts; and in this place I will grant prosperity—declares Yahweh of Hosts."*

The last period of Israel's prophecy—that is, the postexilic phase—was inaugurated by the prophet Haggai. If the keyword for the preexilic prophets was *punishment*, and for the exilic prophets it was *consolation*, the keyword for the postexilic prophets was *restoration*. Haggai's activity coincides with the birth of the Jewish community, which lies at the core of Judaism. His prophecies, which amount to brief exhortations, can be easily dated to the period framed by the months August and December of the year 520 BC. The rebuilding of the temple, which began in spring of 537 BC, was in jeopardy, and Zechariah and Haggai were instrumental in their efforts to encourage Prince Zerubbabel and the high priest Joshua to continue their work of rebuilding the temple.

The passage from Haggai quoted above deals with the Second Temple at the midpoint of its construction. Haggai asks his audience to look beyond the present shape of the holy place and to focus on the eschatological momentum, which will culminate with Yahweh's bringing of Israel to salvation. At this time, the glory of the Second Temple will surpass the majesty of the First Temple.

We may mention that the title Yahweh of Hosts (*Yahweh ṣĕbāʾôt*) is repeated five times in this passage. This title depicts Yahweh as surrounded by heavenly powers (Ps 103:21; 148:2), ready to intervene in Israel's favor, as a "mighty hero" (Ps 24:8; cf. Isa 9:5[60]). The basic idea that emanates from the use of this title is that of power and majesty of God, depicted as Lord of both creation and history.

Haggai launched this prophetic word during the reign of Darius I (522–486 BC), in a time of political peace. His audience was thus genuinely puzzled. According to Haggai, although the present seems serene, God will soon intervene in human history, shaking the foundations of the entire world. This shaking up of the human habitat was meant to usher in the messianic age. Not even the cosmic bodies will be excepted from the terrifying tremors that God will induce (cf. Amos 8:9; Matt 24:29). Perhaps Haggai has in mind God's revelation, after the exodus from Egypt, on Mount Sinai, in the midst of powerful natural phenomena including smoke, earthquake, fire, and thunder (Exod 19:16–25). As a result of God's future intervention, remarks Haggai, the "nations" (*gôyîm*) will bring their "precious things" (*ḥemdâ*) to Jerusalem. These precious gifts will be used in adorning the temple. God's intervention will thus mark the beginning of the messianic age, which will have the temple as its center. Beginning with Nathan's prophecy addressed to David and regarding Solomon and his call to build God's house (2 Sam 7:12–14), the temple became one of the most important pillars of the messianic hope. So strong was this belief that Ezekiel, an exilic prophet, after the destruction of the First Temple (586 BC), insisted on the need to rebuild the sanctuary according to the parameters he had received in his visions. In the same vein of thought as Haggai 2:6–9 is Isaiah's view regarding the nations as they gaze on Jerusalem and its temple, "In days to come, the mountain of the Lord's house shall be established as the highest of the mountains, and shall be raised above the hills; all the nations shall stream to it" (Isa 2:2 NRSV).

The second part of the passage quoted above focuses on the Second Temple. God fills this new sanctuary with so much "glory" (*kābôd*), silver, and gold, that the majesty of the postexilic temple will go beyond that of its predecessor. The "glory" indicates God's luminous presence in his sanctuary (Exod 33:18–23; 40:34–35; 1 Kgs 8:10–11; Isa 6:3), yet in our passage, given its juxtaposition with "silver" and "gold," the term "glory" may designate the ornaments and the precious objects in the temple's sacred inventory. This line may be an allusion to the refurbishing of the Second Temple (Ezra 6:8–9; cf. Zech 6:11),[61] and the "prosperity"[62] to be enjoyed expands from the sanctuary to those involved in its building process. The Septuagint's version reflects the difficult and delicate duty of the prophet to convince the exiles to continue the building of the holy place. The temple mentioned in Haggai 2:6–9 is the Second Temple restored by King Herod and visited by Jesus in his teaching endeavors.

The text of Haggai 2:6–9 was explained by the ancient Jewish interpreters as giving a definite date for the advent of Messiah. Thus, Rabbi Akiba suggested that "a little while" in Haggai 2:6[63] refers prophetically to Simeon *bar Kokhba*, the Jewish insurgent who was thought by many, including Rabbi Akiba, to be the long-awaited Messiah, the "Son of the Star" (cf. Num 24:17). Rabbi Akiba wrote of Haggai's time frame as hinting to the short "reign of bar Koziba (or Kokhba) of two and a half years" (*Sanhedrin* 97b).

> ***Ps 118:25–27:*** *We beseech you, Yahweh, save, we beseech you, Yahweh, send prosperity! Blessed* be *he that comes in the name of Yahweh! We have blessed you out of the Temple of Yahweh. Yahweh is God, he gives us light. Bind the festal offering to the horns of the altar with cords.*

Psalm 118 is a *thanksgiving song* comprising two sections (vv. 5–18 and 19–28), framed by hymnic praises (vv. 1–4 and 29). The first section consists of the praises to the Lord, brought by an individual, as testimony in front of the community. The second section is in fact an interplay of voices between the individual of the first section and the community. This section begins with the individual's request to enter the temple and continues with the community's voice acknowledging God's salvation and their praising and asking God for further assistance. The community greets the one coming in the name of Yahweh, then confesses its faith while promising sacrificial worship (vv. 25–27). According to the view of modern scholars,[64] the individual had survived a serious crisis and was about to enter the holy place accompanied by the community of the worshipers in order to give praise to the Lord, the wonder-worker, inside the sacred temple. Apparently, the individual is "the one who comes in the name of Yahweh" (v. 26). The community declares the day in which the individual was recuperated as "the day God made" (v. 24). It was a day of jubilation, worship, and renewal of confession. The individual in Psalm 118 looks quite similar to the anointed king in Psalms 2, 18, 20, and 89. Thus, all four gospels saw the one who comes in the name of the Lord as Jesus the son of David, as he entered Jerusalem on the Sunday prior to his crucifixion (Matt 21:9; Mark 11:9–10; Luke 19:38; John 12:13). The "day" God made (v. 24) was interpreted as a reference to Jesus' resurrection, anticipated by Jesus' entry in Jerusalem astride a donkey. We may mention that the Hebrew phrase *hôšîʿâ nāʾ* means "Please, save!" and entered our liturgical language as *Hosanna*. Whether Psalm 118 alludes to Jesus' entry in Jerusalem or to the Lord's resurrection, we may draw the conclusion from this text that the Second Temple was still standing at the birth of Jesus the Messiah.

The presence of the gloss "David" inside the psalm both in the Targum on Psalm 118 and in the Talmud (*Pesachim* 119a) suggests that Psalm 118 was read as a messianic prophecy pointing to an ideal eschatological king modeled on David. The welcome of Jesus by Jerusalem's inhabitants with the greeting *Hosanna*, "Please, save!" supports this supposition (Matt 21:9 and parallels). Jesus' contemporaries saw in the young teacher from Nazareth an excellent candidate for the title of Messiah, and, indeed, as a son of David, a triumphant royal Messiah.

4. Place of Birth and Other Places in Christ's Itinerary (Mic 5:1 [Eng. 5:2]; Isa 8:23–9:1; 11:1; Hos 11:1)

Bethlehem

> ***Mic 5:1 [Eng. 5:2]:*** *And you, O Bethlehem of Ephrathah, least among the clans of Judah, from you shall come forth to me the one to be ruler in Israel, one whose goings forth are from primeval times, from everlasting.*

The passage Micah 4:14–5:1 [Eng. 5:1–2][65] was probably written in the wake of the invasion of Judah by the Assyrian king Sennacherib in 701 BC, the latter, camped at Lachish (2 Kgs 18:13–16), seeking to besiege Jerusalem. The verse quoted above should be read in conjunction with the preceding verse (Mic 4:14 [Eng. 5:1]), which alludes to the humiliation of Judah's king during the Assyrian campaign. Micah contrasts the pride of the fortified cities, including Jerusalem, with the humble state of sites such as Ephrathah. Interestingly, remarks the prophet, the salvation will arise from Ephrathah, not from the capital.[66]

Micah speaks here of the birth of the Messiah in *Bethlehem of Ephrathah*. The name Ephrathah in patriarchal times was used to designate the territory inhabited by the Judahite clan of the Ephrathites (Gen 35:16, 19; 48:7). King David belonged to this clan (1 Sam 17:12). It is worth noting that Micah considers Bethlehem of Ephrathah as a clan within the tribe of

Judah. It seems that Ephrathah included or was close to Bethlehem. With the rise to power of David from Bethlehem, Ephrathah became more and more equated with Bethlehem until the two place-names were considered synonymous (Gen 35:19; Josh 15:59 LXX; Ruth 4:11).

The village of Bethlehem reached a special status when David, Jesse's son, became king of the united monarchy of Israel with its capital at Jerusalem (2 Sam 5:1–12). Situated six miles south of Jerusalem, Bethlehem lies in the fertile region of Beit-Jalah. The element *bê(y)t,* "house," in the name *bê(y)t-leḥem,* "Bethlehem," matches the Akkadian word *bït-,* "the House of...," found in place-names.[67] As vocalized by the Masoretes, the name *bê(y)t-leḥem* means the "house of the bread," hinting at the agricultural focus of Bethlehem and its environments.

The new king is introduced by Micah as the one who rules for Yahweh or as Yahweh's representative in Israel. This aspect of belonging to Yahweh is underlined by the use of the pronoun *lî,* "to me," with respect to God. Interestingly, Micah does not use the term *melek,* "king," but rather *môšēl,* "ruler." The prophet's reluctance to use the technical term *king* to define Messiah should be understood as a courageous stand against the corrupted monarchy of eighth-century BC Judah. In Micah's view, Messiah will be unlike the contemporary monarchs, who were participating in international political games instead of trusting God and his promises. Thus, says Micah, Messiah will be a ruler rather than a despotic monarch. He will be a model ruler, one interested in the well-being of his people.[68] From this perspective, Micah's ruler will be a leader to whom the people can relate: a man among men, an ideal leader. As the Old Babylonian king Hammurabi used to say about himself, "I am the shepherd of the oppressed,"[69] namely, the caretaker of his subjects. This image of the *shepherd-king* is present also in the Bible (e.g., Ps 23; John 10:1–30), and Micah's ruler will conform to this type. With respect to Jesus, his entrance into Jerusalem a few days before the passion is a good illustration of such an image. Jesus enters the city riding on a donkey, as a humble king, after the model of one of the earlier kings (John 12:12–16). In his life of service to others, Jesus embodied the deep significance of his majestic yet humble entrance into the City of David. Jesus' warning, given to his disciples, may also be brought as an illustration of a responsible leader,

> So Jesus called them and said to them, "You know that among the Gentiles those whom they recognize as their rulers lord it over them, and their great ones are tyrants over them. But it is not so among you; but whoever wishes to become great among you must be your servant, and whoever wishes to be first among you must be slave of all. For the Son of Man came not to be served but to serve, and to give his life a ransom for many." (Mark 10:42–45 NRSV)

Micah depicts Messiah as "coming forth" from Bethlehem, originating from David's place of birth, to be(come) a leader in Israel. This part of Micah's prophecy seems to echo Jesus' very enigmatic answer to Pilate's question, "'Pilate asked him, 'So you are a king?' Jesus answered, 'You say that I am a king. For this I was born, and for this I came into the world, to testify to the truth. Everyone who belongs to the truth listens to my voice'" (John 18:37 NRSV). Upon the coming of Messiah, the old conflict between Yahweh the great King, and the rulers of Israel, initially unwilled by God (cf. 1 Sam 8:5–8; Hos 13:11), will entirely cease. We may mention that Micah uses "Israel" here as the old designation for God's people rather than a mere reference to the northern kingdom, called either Israel or Ephraim.

Yet the one who will go out of Bethlehem to be a ruler in Israel has his origin in eternity. "His goings forth,"[70] commonly rendered "his origin," may hint at Messiah's preexistence and may further hint at his propensity toward incarnation. The linguistic structure of "to come/go forth" in Micah 5:1 [Eng. 5:2] emphasizes the dual origins of Messiah: the eternal origin, and his historical origin from Bethlehem.[71] Hence Messiah's "goings forth" are prior to his birth in Bethlehem of Ephrathah.

With respect to the New Testament application of Micah's prophecy, we may mention Matthew 2:1–12, the pericope on the visit of the magi. In this text, Matthew quotes Micah 5:1 directly, as a prophecy pertaining to the birthplace of Messiah (cf. John 7:42). The answer of the priests and scribes to Herod that Messiah will be born at Bethlehem (Matt 2:6) reflects a very old messianic interpretation of the passage in Micah 5:1. That Micah 5:1 has long been read as a messianic text may be drawn also from the *Targum Jonathan* on this biblical text, "From you, in front of me, Messiah will go out to exercise dominion over Israel."

Modern scholars argue that Mary and Joseph were originally from Bethlehem.[72] They will establish their household later in Nazareth of Galilee, because of the spirit of insecurity caused by Herod's reign (Matt 2). Luke, who informs us that Mary delivered Jesus with Joseph in Bethlehem during a census, was not aware of such a tradition, however (Luke 2:1–7). The proponents of such an interpretation suggest reading Luke 2:7 as, "She laid him in a manger because they had no space in the room," instead of the more conventional rendition, "She laid him in a manger, because there was no place for them in the inn"[73] (NRSV). Joseph's family lived in that room, so Joseph led his fiancée Mary into the back area, normally reserved for the animals, to give birth away from the crowded living space.

Nazareth

> ***Isa 11:1:*** *But a shoot shall come forth from the stump of Jesse, a twig shall sprout from his roots.*

The text of Isaiah 11:1–9 represents a messianic poem that closely defines the features of Messiah. The first feature is Messiah's Davidic origin. Strangely, however, the name of Jesse is mentioned, rather than David. Jesse was the father of King David (1 Sam 16:1; Ruth 4:22) and ancestor of all the kings of Judah, including Messiah (Matt 1:6–16). Why, then, the reference to Jesse, and not to David? Perhaps because of the degenerate condition of the Davidic house at that time. Isaiah was speaking to King Ahaz (cf. Isa 7:14), proclaiming the near destruction of the Davidic dynasty. The royal family was in decline, but the roots and stump of the royal lineage were not dead. The soil was still fertile, and the stump strong enough to produce new fruit. God would not forsake his flora, nor would the descendants of David be cut off completely. A stump or a root will always exist, whence a "shoot" or a "twig" will grow up and bring the coming of Messiah.

The place-name *Nazareth* is not mentioned at all in the Hebrew Bible, and it appears in the New Testament only sixteen times. The brief note in Matthew may be interpreted as hinting at Isaiah 11:1. More precisely, it should be understood to indicate the similarity in sound between the Hebrew word *nēṣer*, "twig, offshoot," and the Greek spelling of the place-name *Nazareth*,[74] "There he made his home in a town called Nazareth, so that what had been spoken through the prophets might be fulfilled, 'He will be called a Nazorean (*Nazoraios*)'" (Matt 2:23 NRSV). Thus, Jesus' family settled in Nazareth in order to fulfill Isaiah's prophecy about Messiah, the "twig" from Jesse's "roots" (Isa 11:1).[75]

The text of Isaiah 11:1 was viewed as a messianic prophecy by the ancient Jewish interpreters. The *Targum Jonathan* interprets it as referring to both the continuity of the Davidic dynasty and Messiah's origin from Jesse's family, "A king will go forth from the son of Jesse, and Messiah will grow up from (his) grandson." The Talmud also sees in Isaiah 11:1–2 a messianic prophecy (*Sanhedrin* 93b; cf. Midrashim *Numbers Rabbah* 13:11; *Ruth Rabbah* 7:2). We may add to these references an enigmatic interpretation of Isaiah 11:1 from the Talmud alluding perhaps to the Messiah as a rejected, and eventually, executed prophet, "When Nezer was brought in, he said, 'Shall Nezer be executed? Is it not written, "And Nezer [a twig] shall grow forth out of his roots?" Yes, they said, Nezer shall be executed, since it is written, "But you are cast forth away from thy grave like Nezer [an abhorred offshoot]"'" (*Sanhedrin* 43a).

Galilee

Isa 8:23–9:1: Yet there will be no more gloom for those who were in distress. At first he brought contempt into the land of Zebulun and the land of Naphtali, but later he made glorious the way of the sea, the land beyond the Jordan, Galilee of the nations. The people walking in darkness have seen a great light; on those dwelling in the land of the shadow of death light has shined.

The historical context of this passage is the same as that of Isaiah 7, namely, the Syro-Ephraimite war (733–732 BC), along with its preliminaries and consequences. Out of fear, King Ahaz of Judah seeks military assistance from Assyria. The text alludes primarily to the Galilean campaign of the Assyrian king Tiglath-pileser III and the deportation of the population in the year 732 BC (2 Kgs 15:29).

Isaiah of Jerusalem suggests a profound shift between the former time, marked by the Assyrian conquest, which led to gloom and distress, and a future time, marked by light and hope. We may mention that "first" (*rî[ʾ]šôn*) in the Hebrew text cannot refer to "time" (*ʿēt*) because the latter form is feminine while the former is masculine. Ancient and modern translators and interpreters have suggested that the phrase be translated as referring to a king, and as early as the time of the Targums we find such an interpretive tendency, "And a strong king will exile what remains of them because they did not remember the prodigy of the sea, the wonders of Jordan, the war of the Gentile fortress" (Targum on Isa 9:1). Note that in this Targum, "king" designates God's means of punishing Israel for forgetting his great works of old. Additional difficulties in the Isaianic text arise from the use of verbs that contradict any expected chronology.[76] This grammatical difficulty is probably apparent only in those texts in which the author wanted to emphasize the ambiguous character of God's intervention, namely, the contrast between divine punishment and grace, rather than a mere unfolding of actions in time.

We may add that the ambiguity produced by the use of masculine adjectives ("former," "last") with a feminine noun ("time") led to the particularity of the New Testament application of this Isaianic text. Thus, Matthew reads Isaiah 8:23–9:1 as a messianic prophecy fulfilled by Jesus' proclamation of the Good News in Galilee of the nations (Matt 4:13–16). The emphasis in Matthew falls on Messiah and the "light" (*phōs*) that will "dawn" or "rise up"[77] as a new beginning in previously ignored territories of the promise land. God will not forget his people dwelling along the Mediterranean shore, the Galilean Sea, and the banks of the upper Jordan.

The ancient Jewish interpretation saw in Isaiah 8:23–9:1 an eschatological prophecy, one to be fulfilled in the future, with the accent falling in this case on God's action:

> Her adversaries are the chief. Rabbah said in Rabbi Johanan's name, "Whoever distresses Israel becomes a chief, as it is written, 'Nevertheless, there shall be no weariness for her that oppressed her. In the former time he

brought into contempt the land of Zebulun and the land of Naphtali, but in the latter time has he made it glorious, by way of the sea, beyond Jordan, the circuit of the nations.'" (*Sanhedrin* 104b)

Egypt

Hos 11:1: When Israel was a child, I loved him; and out of Egypt, I called my son.

The sayings included in Hosea 11:1–11 seem to have been delivered by the prophet himself to the inner circle of his disciples during the first part of the reign of the Assyrian king Shalmaneser (727–722 BC), when Israel was seeking Egypt's assistance against Assyria (2 Kgs 17:4). Using historical evidence, Hosea critiques Israel's pro-Egypt policy, showing that in the past God himself took his son Israel out of Egypt's slavery. Now, remarks the prophet, the same Israel is contemplating the older enemy Egypt as its good friend.

The text of Hosea 11:1 differs among various biblical versions. While the Masoretic Text reads the singular *bĕnî,* "my son,"[78] the Septuagint interprets this verse as a reference to Israel as a people, *ta tekna autou,* "his children." The Septuagint's reading harmonizes "Israel" in verse 1a with "them" in verse 2, while the *Targum Pseudo-Jonathan* offers an original reading, "and since [the time of] Egypt I have called them 'sons.'" The targumic reading may be considered a polemic answer by the ancient Jewish interpreters to the christological interpretation of the early church. Note, though, that the second-century versions of Aquila and Theodotion[79] are identical with the MT (*bĕnî,* "my son").

Matthew read Hosea 11:1 as a prophecy pertaining to the return of Mary, Joseph, and the infant Jesus from Egypt shortly after his birth, "Then Joseph got up, took the child and his mother by night, and went to Egypt, and remained there until the death of Herod. This was to fulfill what had been spoken by the Lord through the prophet, 'Out of Egypt I have called my son'" (Matt 2:14–15 NRSV).

We might mention that Matthew did not use the Septuagint version[80] to apply the Old Testament text to Jesus' return from Egypt, but rather he relied on a Hebrew manuscript that had the singular "my son."[81] Jerome explains, "There is no doubt that in this place Matthew took testimony according to the Hebrew version. Thus, the ones who deride our interpretation neglect the Scripture, from where the evangelist took this testimony and interpreted as referring to the Lord Savior, when he was brought back from Egypt to the land of Israel." Jerome continues, remarking that Matthew saw in Jesus, the Messiah, the new Israel, who fulfilled Hosea

11:1 typologically by recapitulating Israel's history, "In fact this refers to Israel whom he calls from Egypt, whom he loves, who in that time after the error of idolatry is called somewhat like an infant or a child; yet it perfectly refers to Christ."[82]

5. The Forerunner of Messiah's Birth (Isa 40:3; Mal 3:1)

> ***Isa 40:3:*** *A voice cries, "In the wilderness, clear a way for Yahweh! Level in the desert a highway for our God!"*

Isaiah 40 begins the second part of the Book of Isaiah (Isa 40–55), traditionally called the Book of the Consolation of Israel. This designation is inspired by the opening words, "Console my people, console them" (Isa 40:1). We may add that *consolation* is the central theme of Isaiah 40, as distinct from the warnings and menaces that mark the initial segment of the book (Isa 1–39). The author of the second part of the book, known as Deutero-Isaiah, lived sometime toward the end of the Babylonian exile (586–539 BC).

The beginning of Deutero-Isaiah is actually a cantata for several voices, which announces the end of Israel's slavery, depicting it in terms of a new exodus led by God himself. Among these voices, one may distinguish a solitary "voice"[83] in the celestial court, whose identity remains a mystery. According to the reading proposed by the Masoretes, this voice "cries" to the one called "to clear"[84] the way in the wilderness (cf. Mal 3:1). Babylonian texts speak in similar terms of processional ways prepared for a god or a victorious king; this is the road by which Yahweh will lead his people through the desert in a new exodus. Quite contrary to this reading is the Septuagint's rendering,[85] where the "voice is crying in the wilderness."[86] This version indicates that the wilderness is the location of the mysterious voice, rather than the meeting place for God and his people returned from exile.

The evangelists (Matt 3:3; John 1:23) quote Isaiah 40:3 according to the Septuagint and apply this prophecy to John the Baptist, who spent some time in the wilderness of Judea prior to his public mission (Luke 1:80; cf. Matt 3:1). Interestingly, the voice, which might be Isaiah's, is speaking on behalf of Yahweh, but it also calls one's attention to Yahweh.[87] Thus, in the evangelists' interpretations of the passage, Isaiah and, later, John the Baptist may be considered both God's servants and forerunners of Messiah.

In addition, we should note that Deutero-Isaiah introduces the theme of the "way,"[88] connoting a manner of life with respect to Israel (Gen 6:12; Isa 55:7) or to God (Deut 32:4; Exod 18:25). John the Baptist is to announce the "way of the Lord" (Mark 1:3), and Jesus declares that he himself is that way (John 14:6; Heb 10:20). Moreover, Christianity is called simply, "the way" (Acts 9:2; 19:9, 23).

Finally, the universality of the messianic import of this passage can be seen in the Qumran documents, which saw a fulfillment of Isaiah 40:3 in the community's retreat into the wilderness and in their "studying the Torah which he commanded through Moses" (1QS 8:14–15). A similar idea is found in the Targum on Isaiah 40:1, where the emphasis falls on the "people of Yahweh" (*ʿmʾ dywy*) equated with the "assembly of our God" (*knštʾ dʾlhnʾ*) wandering again through the wilderness.

> ***Mal 3:1:*** *Behold, I send forth my messenger to clear a way before me. And suddenly the Lord whom you seek shall come to his Temple. As for the angel of the covenant that you desire, he is already coming, says Yahweh of Hosts.*[89]

6. The Lineage of Messiah (Son of Man: Dan 7:13–14; of Shem: Gen 9:25–27; of Abraham: Gen 12:1–3; of Isaac: Gen 26:4–5; of Judah: Gen 49:10; of Jesse: Isa 11:1; of David: 2 Sam 7:16)

From the outset, we have attempted to underline one of the main features of our reconstruction of the lineage of Jesus the Messiah, namely, the fine crescendo from general to particular, from the whole of humanity to a particular man, in the succession of the messianic seed line. First, Messiah is described as the Son of Man, a man among men, one who from all eternity has been willing to share in our humanity, or rather in our weakness, one who in the bosom of the Godhead has always had a peculiar propensity for incarnation, for becoming human. Later, after the flood, Messiah is introduced as the son of Shem, one of the three sons of Noah who survived the great calamity. At that point in salvation history we learn that Messiah, God's anointed, will be a Semite. Afterwards, the descendants of Shem become a tribe, and Messiah becomes part of a clan, namely, Abraham's family. He can be rightly called the son of Abraham, the great pilgrim, who made his way out of Mesopotamia, to enter Canaan. Because of Abraham's obedience to God, his son Isaac is endowed with a special blessing, that of becoming one of the forefathers of Messiah. Then Messiah is presented as the son of Judah, one of Jacob's sons, and we learn that Messiah will be a leader, a god-like king, coming at the end of a line of leaders, all originating from the same patriarch, Judah. With the rise to power of David, Jesse's son, and as a result of all his great political-religious achievements, Messiah will become known as the son of Jesse and, more importantly, the son of David, the king par excellence.

Son of Man

> ***Dan** 7:13–14: As I looked on, in the night vision, one like a Son of Man was coming with the clouds of heaven; he reached the Everlasting One and was presented to him. Dominion, glory, and kingship were given to him. All peoples and nations of every language must serve him. His dominion is an everlasting dominion that shall not pass away, and his kingship, one that shall not be destroyed.*

The text of Daniel 7:13–14 describes Messiah as *bar ʾĕnôš*, "Son of Man," or "son of weakness"; the word *ʾĕnôš*, "man, human being" might derive from the root *ʾ-n-š*, "to be weak." In light of this text, we may say that one of the first, and most general, descriptions of Messiah is as the "last Adam" (1 Cor 15:45), the final version of humanity, anointed by God to restore the fallen primeval humanity.[90]

Son of Shem

> ***Gen** 9:25–27: And he [Noah] said, "Cursed be Canaan; the lowest of slaves shall he be to his brothers." And he said, "Blessed be Yahweh, the God of Shem. Let Canaan be a slave to him. May God make room for Japheth, and let him dwell in the tents of Shem; and let Canaan be a slave to him."*

This text is part of a larger section, Genesis 9:18–29, dealing with Noah and his sons, Shem, Ham, and Japheth. The order of Noah's sons is fixed by tradition as illustrated in the texts of Genesis 5:32; 6:10; 7:13; and 10:1. The narrative of the three sons (9:20–27) is flanked by Noah's genealogy (9:18–19, 28–29). The gloss "Ham, the father of Canaan" (v. 18) is due perhaps to an editor who wanted to link the traditional presentation of Noah's sons to the narrative in verses 20–27. Seemingly, Canaan was the guilty party in the narrative handed over by the Yahwist, and the list of Noah's sons should have looked quite different, that is, Shem, Japheth, Canaan. This order is supported by verse 24, where the guilty party is labeled as Noah's "youngest son" (*bĕnô haq-qāṭān*). The narrative of the three sons focuses on the difference between Noah's sons, Shem, Japheth, and Ham-Canaan, but the identification of the sons is not a simple task.

While anticipating Israel, Shem can be identified with the Semites; Japheth would stand for the Philistines, although in Noah's blessing he is described as an ally of Shem (Israel) against Canaan.

At first sight, the narrative under discussion (Gen 9:20–27) is as brief and as simple as it might seem. On the one hand, Canaan dishonors the drunk father by looking at his father's nakedness and informing his brothers about this; on the other hand, Shem and Japheth cover their father and thus honor him. Noah's blessing and his curse come as a consequence of the sons' behavior toward their father. The accent of the narrative falls on the blessing of Shem and Japheth, who represent Israel, and the curse of Canaan, who designates the Canaanites. This text reflects the political situation of Israel under the reigns of Saul and David, after the great invasion of the Peoples of the Sea, when the Philistines began to infiltrate Israel's territory,[91] and the Canaanites were still living in the country and fighting for survival. We may mention that the conquest of Canaan initiated by Joshua (circa 1200 BC) lasted for a long while. At the turn of the tenth century BC, David succeeded in capturing one of the last Canaanite fortresses, the Jebusite Jerusalem, and turned it into the capital of his unified kingdom.

Canaan's deed of looking at his father's nakedness does not have anything to do with incestuous sexual relations, even though in Leviticus 20:17–21, "to uncover the nakedness" means to have sexual relations. Rather, Canaan's behavior aims at probing into the mystery of life, which is symbolically represented by father's nakedness. This mirrors the sexual practices of the Canaanites, such as cultic prostitution, which could have led to the breaking of the Creator–creature relationship and the dehumanization that characterized the post-flood creation.[92]

The text under discussion was regarded by the apostolic church as messianic. As evidence, early Christian interpreters looked to the genealogy written by Luke, in which Jesus is called the "son of Shem," among other names (Luke 3:36). Jesus himself hinted at this prophecy in his informal conversation with the Samaritan woman at the well of Jacob, when he stated rather categorically, "Salvation is of the Jews" (John 4:22). We may add here the long section in Romans 9–11 where Paul insists on the place and role of Israel within God's plan for humanity's salvation. Israel is just a part, or a division, of the great branch of Shem, as attested in the Table of Nations, where Shem is described as the begetter of Israel (Gen 10:21–31).

That Genesis 9:25–27 has been regarded as a messianic prophecy from as early as the time of the Targums may be seen from the following ancient Jewish interpretation, "Accursed be Canaan, a working servant shall he be to his brethren. And he said, 'Blessed be the Lord the God of Shem, and Canaan shall be servant unto them. The Lord shall enlarge Yapheth, and he shall make his Shekinah dwell in the tabernacles of Shem, and Canaan shall be servant unto them'" (*Targum Onkelos* on Gen 9:25–27). According to this ancient interpretation, it is not Japheth who will dwell in the tents of Shem, but rather God's Shekinah (*škynh*), namely, the divine Presence.[93]

Another Targum speaks of Japheth (that is, Gentiles) as being proselytized and educated in the Jewish religious schools, "The Lord shall beautify the borders of Japheth, and his sons shall be proselytized, and dwell in the schools[94] of Shem, and Canaan shall be a servant to them" (*Targum Pseudo-Jonathan* on Gen 9:25–27). In the same vein of thought, the Talmud mentions an infusion of Greek language in the Jewish synagogue, namely, through the translations of the Holy Writ, "Scripture says, 'God enlarges Japheth, and he shall dwell in the tents of Shem; [this means] that the words of Japheth shall be in the tents of Shem" (*Megillah* 9b). Similarly, one of the Midrashim remarks, "Our Rabbis have taught thus: Bar Kappara, interpreting the verse, 'God enlarges Japheth, and he shall dwell in the tents of Shem' (Gen 9:27), said, 'This indicates that the words of Shem may be rendered in the languages of Japheth; therefore have [the Rabbis] permitted [sacred books] to be written in Greek'" (*Deuteronomy Rabbah* 1:1). As may be noticed, these ancient Jewish interpretations are close to the christological approach that sees Japheth dwelling in Shem's tents as a hint at the Gentiles joining the Christian church, which originally consisted only of Jewish (Semite) faithful. Also in harmony with the ancient Jewish interpretations mentioned above, Japheth could be a hint at the Greek language of the gospels, which entered the early Christian communities of Semitic background.

Son of Abraham

> ***Gen 12:1–3:*** *Yahweh said to Abram, "Go forth from your land, your kindred and your father's house to the land that I will show you. I will make of you a great nation, and I will bless you; I will make your name great, and you shall be a blessing. I will bless those who bless you and curse those who curse you; and all the families of the earth shall bless themselves by you."*

This text is commonly known as the Call of Abram. With respect to the name of the patriarch, the Scriptures mention two versions, a shorter name *Abram*,[95] which holds until circumcision (Gen 11:26–17:5), and the longer version, *Abraham*,[96] which obtains after the rite has been performed (Gen 17:5–25:12). No similar name is found in the West Semitic onomasticon of the early second millennium BC. The longer name,

Abraham, is given the meaning "father of a multitude" (Gen 17:5), which is perhaps a folk etymology. Abraham may in fact be a dialectal variant with an inserted *-h-*. In any event, no other person in the Hebrew Bible bears the names Abram or Abraham. They were considered special, unique names in the Hebrew tradition and, like the names David and Solomon, were meant to be borne only by those chosen by God for special purposes.

In order to understand Abram's call, we should first summarize the preceding verses in Genesis 11:27–32. These lines introduce Abram's father and his descendants. After the narrative of the Tower of Babel (Gen 11:1–9) we are told that from the three sons of Noah, all nations would arise and eventually fill the earth (Gen 11:10–26). This occurred according to the initial commandment of God given to Adam and Eve (Gen 1:28). The end of Genesis 11 focuses on a single family, that of Terah. We learn that Terah, one of Shem's descendants, had three sons, Abram, Nahor, and Haran. The youngest of Terah's sons begot Lot and then died while Terah's family was still in its native land, in the city of Ur, in Lower Mesopotamia. While still in Ur, Abram married Sarai, and Nahor took Milcah as his wife. Following this, the entire family of Terah was to leave Ur for "the land of Canaan" as their final destination, after stopping for a while in Haran, northwest of Mesopotamia (Gen 11:31). Although the historicity of this migration is still questioned by some modern scholars, the narrative of the event is deeply rooted in Israel's ancient tradition (Gen 15:7), even though by the time these texts of Genesis were edited, Ur had been completely forgotten.

Nevertheless, Ur was an important urban center at the beginning of the second millennium BC, and the migration of Terah's family from Ur to Haran was historically plausible at that time, given the close religious and commercial ties between Ur and Haran. The determinative "of Chaldaeans" attached to the toponym Ur, as found in Genesis 11:28 and 31, was inserted by an editor during the Neo-Babylonian period (626–539 BC).

Abram's call consists of an imperative, five promises, and a commission. Yahweh's imperative to Abram, "Go forth from your land, kindred, and father's house, to the land that I will show you" (Gen 12:1) is as radical and as ambiguous as it might be. It is also harsh, for Abram is not simply requested "to exit"[97] one land and enter another, but rather "to go"[98] from one land to another land entirely. Abram must cut off all the ties with his past, his "land," his "kindred," and his "family," as if none of these had ever existed. He must also focus his attention on a new land on the horizon. The imperative is ambiguous, for God does not say what land Abram should go to. Instead, he merely requires Abram to leave a place familiar to him and journey to an unknown place, the identity of which is to remain secret indefinitely. Under these circumstances, we can visualize the travails of Abram's journey from Ur, through Haran, to Canaan, and we can imagine the patriarch thinking at each stop: Is this the place God intended for me? A similar pattern occurred to Hosea, the eighth-century-BC prophet who lived and worked in the northern kingdom. Yahweh's imperative to Hosea, "Go[99] and marry a woman of fornications"[100] seems quite ambiguous, especially considering that the phrase occurs only once in the Hebrew Bible (i.e., Hos 1:2). As in the case of Abram's new adoptive land, the identity of Hosea's wife, Gomer, the daughter of Diblaim, is revealed only after the human response to God's call (Hos 1:3). This pattern regarding God's dealings with his chosen ones is well attested in Scripture and obtains in the lives of the faithful. Prayers are sometimes intentionally left unanswered, or partially answered, as an invitation to cooperate in God's saving plan. As Abram did, we may ask ourselves: Is this the move God wants from me? This kind of questioning has a certain ethical value attached to it, since it will eventually determine our response to God's call.

God's imperative directed to Abram is followed by five promises, with special emphasis on the first person singular, "I," meaning God alone is both the promise giver and the deliverer (Gen 12:2, 3a). The content of these promises, which Yahweh addressed to Abram prior to his journey to the mysterious land, is as follows: (1) I will make a "great nation" (*gôy gādôl*) of you; (2) "I will bless you" (*ʾăbārekĕkā*); (3) I will make your "name" (*šēm*) great and you are to be a "blessing" (*bĕrākâ*); (4) I will bless those who bless you; (5) I will curse those who curse you. Note that the third statement is distinct from the rest by having an imperative ("Be!") attached to it. The consequence of this nuance is to center all the promises on the movement of Abram to become a blessing for others. This imperative prepares the way for the final commission (Gen 12:3b). We should mention that these promises contrast drastically with the humble beginnings of Abram's pilgrimage of faith from Mesopotamia to Canaan. It was promised that he would become a great nation, but we are told that Sarai, his wife, was barren (Gen 11:30). It was also promised that he would have a great name, but we are told that the Canaanites were in the country at that time, and he, Abram, roamed as a sojourner in a foreign land (Gen 12:6).

Abram's call ends with God's commission to him to become a means through which the promises and blessings directed first to Abram could become part of the destiny of every nation, tribe, clan, and family on earth (Gen 12:3b; cf. 18:18; 22:18; 26:4; 28:14). Although the Masoretic Text conjugates the verb as a reflexive,[101] and hence reads, "And all the families of the earth shall bless themselves by you,"[102] the Septuagint[103] and Sirach 44:21a[104] imply the same verb root, but in a passive construction.[105] The latter two textual witnesses support the christological interpretation of the early church, according to which all the families of the earth will be blessed by or through Christ, the "son of Abraham" (Matt 1:1). As an illustration of such an interpretation, we may incorporate Paul's understanding of Genesis 12:1–3 and 7, "Now the promises were addressed to Abraham and to his seed (*spermati*). The words were not, 'And to his seeds (*spermasin*)' in the plural, but in the singular; 'And to your seed,' which is Christ" (Gal 3:16).

As is the case with Noah's prophecy (Gen 9:25–27), the messianic prophecy of Genesis 12:1–3 may well hint at the reception of the Gentiles as children of Abraham into the Christian church. Through Jesus the Messiah, Abraham's son, the Gentiles may become co-sharers with the Jews in the divine blessings poured initially upon Abram of Ur.

The following ancient Jewish interpretation is noteworthy, for it links one of Abram's blessings: "I will make your name great," to the messianic age, "Said Rabbi Joshua bar Levi, 'In this world, has he given wanderings unto them that fear him; but in the messianic future, will he be ever mindful of his covenant. For what is written of Abram? "And I will bless you, and make your name great" (Gen 12:2)'" (*Genesis Rabbah* 40:2).

Son of Isaac

> ***Gen 26:4–5:*** *I will make your seed as numerous as the stars of heaven, and assign to your seed all these lands, so that all the nations of the earth shall bless themselves by your seed, inasmuch as Abraham listened to my voice and kept what is owed to me: my commandments, my laws, and my instructions.*

Isaac nearly always appears in relation to other biblical characters: either to his father (Gen 21; 22; 24), or to his sons (Gen 25:19–28; 27; 28:1–9; 35:27–29). Only in the text of Genesis 26, which belongs to the Yahwist source,[106] and which is centered on the theme of blessing, is Isaac treated by himself. The brief passage concerning Isaac's blessing (Gen 26:4–5) is novel in that it speaks specifically of a "seed" (*zeraᶜ*) as the mediator of divine blessing, rather than mediation "through you" (*bĕkā*), as was the case with Abram (Gen 12:3b).[107] Once again, the families (i.e., "nations") of the earth are described as the indirect beneficiaries of God's blessings. Nevertheless, in Isaac's case the divine blessings are released through the "seed" of the patriarch. This statement contrasts with that in Genesis 12:1–3, in which Abram is depicted as the mediator of God's blessings for the rest of the world. This peculiarity may be explained by Abram's special status of being, or rather *becoming*, a blessing. Abram is called by God to become a blessing so that after him God's blessings are to be released through, or because of, the patriarch's special status. In fact, Genesis 26:5 makes it clear that Isaac's blessing, as well as its release to the rest of the world through Isaac's seed, is possible only because of Abraham's obedience. God's blessings upon the patriarchs are from this point on given "in return" or "as reward" (*ʿēqeb*) for Abram's obedience.

We might add with respect to Genesis 26:4–5 that the "seed" that carries blessing hints reflexively at the messianic seed promised by God, not to Adam but, entirely unexpectedly, to Eve (Gen 3:15; cf. 4:25). The christological interpretation concerning Isaac's blessing (Gen 26:4–5) is that the seed refers to Christ, through whom the Gentiles have a share in God's blessings, although this blessing was initially addressed only to Abraham's children (Rom 9:4). From this perspective, the genealogy found in Matthew lists Isaac among Jesus' forefathers (Matt 1:2), which is in harmony with Paul's statement, "To them [i.e., the Jews] belong the patriarchs, and from them, according to the flesh, comes the Messiah, who is over all, God blessed forever. Amen" (Rom 9:5 NRSV).

Son of Judah

> ***Gen 49:10:*** *The scepter shall not depart from Judah, nor a ruler's staff from between his feet, until* Shiloh *comes; and the obedience of the peoples shall be his.*

Beginning with Abraham, through Isaac and Jacob, God's blessing comes to hover over the tribe of Judah.[108]

Son of Jesse

> ***Isa 11:1:*** *But a shoot shall come forth from the stump of Jesse, a twig shall sprout from his roots.*

In a period of crisis for the Israelite monarchy, Isaiah of Jerusalem lifts up his eyes to the mountains, musing, like the psalmist, "From where will my help come? My help comes from the Lord, who made heaven and earth" (Ps 121:1–2 NRSV), and God's response to the sad prophet comes as an expedient promise, "From the stump of Jesse, a shoot shall come forth" and turn into an ideal king (Isa 11:1a).[109] The throne of David was so corrupt in the eighth century BC that Isaiah was reluctant to refer to David as the ideal king, out of fear that his contemporaries would look for that king among the members of the extant Davidic dynasty. Such a possibility was out of the question, however. Labeling the ideal king as a "twig" (*nēṣer*) from the roots of Jesse (Isa 11:1b), rather than son of David, Isaiah wants to make a theological point, namely, the ideal king, the King-Messiah, will be like David, a *David redivivus.*[110]

Son of David

> ***2 Sam 7:12–16:*** *When your days are done and you lie with your fathers, I will raise up your seed after you, who shall come forth from your body, and I will establish his kingship. He shall build a house for my name, and I will establish the throne of his kingdom forever. I myself will be a father to him, and he shall be a son to me. When he does wrong, I will chastise him with the rod of men and the affliction of mortals. But I will never withdraw my steadfast love from him as I withdrew it from Saul, whom I removed from before you. Your house and your kingship shall ever be firm before you; your throne shall be established forever.*

This verse is part of Nathan's prophecy (2 Sam 7:1–17), delivered after David had settled into his newly built royal palace. At that time, the king observed, to his genuine surprise, "Look, I am dwelling in a cedar-wood palace, while the ark of God stays in a tent" (2 Sam 7:2). Nathan, in response, showed his unconditional support of the king's decisions (2 Sam 7:3). Yet that very night God's word to David, through Nathan, was fundamentally different from the prophet's own initial, enthusiastic reaction. In his message to the king, who was eager to build a temple, Yahweh states that he has never lived in a house, but always he was on the road, traveling along with his people and revealing his "glory" (*kābôd*) in a tent (2 Sam 7:4–6; cf. Exod 40:34–38). After all, adds Yahweh, he has never asked Israel's leaders to build a temple for him (2 Sam 7:7).

God's message to David via Nathan, similar to some extent to Abraham's call (Gen 12:1–3), may be summarized in five promise statements: (1) I will raise up your son after you; (2) he will build a temple and I will set his throne for ever; (3) I will be a father to him and he will be a son to me; (4) I will chastise him for his wrongs but I will never withdraw my steadfast love from him; (5) David's kingship and throne will be secured for ever. There are three main ideas that permeate God's promise statements. First, David is told that one of his sons will follow him as king over Israel. Second, this son of David will build a temple for Yahweh. Third, as a response to building the temple, Yahweh will establish and preserve the Davidic dynasty for ever. The key term in this prophecy is the Hebrew word *bayit* and its multiple meanings, "house, temple, palace, dynasty," which generated an interesting interplay between David's eagerness to build a temple and God's news that David's son will raise this temple and David's dynasty will be established forever.

As can easily be discerned, Nathan's prophecy is concerned primarily, though not exclusively, with Solomon, David's son and successor. It does not deal exclusively with Solomon because the prophecy speaks of an eternal dynasty. The eternal character of this dynasty does not lie with King Solomon, or with any of his successors, but rather with the unnamed representative of the Davidic royal line, whom God will adopt as his own son (2 Sam 7:14; cf. Ps 2:7). This mysterious figure is identical with the ideal "leader" (*Shiloh*) mentioned in Genesis 49:10 and is destined to come at the end of an uninterrupted line of leaders deriving from the tribe of Judah. We are told, in the text under consideration, that his origin is from David's lineage, namely, one of Judah's families. Later, on the eve of the national tragedy of 587/586 BC, the prophet Jeremiah will allude to Nathan's saying, "The days are surely coming, says the Lord, when I will raise up for David a righteous Branch, and he shall reign as king and deal wisely, and shall execute justice and righteousness in the land" (Jer 23:5 NRSV). The connection between Genesis 49:10 and 2 Samuel 17:12–16, the two central prophecies regarding the King-Messiah, surfaces in the following Midrash:

> Furthermore, the royal Messiah will be descended from the tribe of Judah, as it says, "And it shall come to pass in that day, that the root of Jesse, that stands for an ensign of the peoples, unto him shall the nations seek" (Isa 11:10). Thus from the tribe of Judah were descended Solomon, who built the first Temple, and Zerubbabel who built the second Temple; and [from him will be descended] the royal Messiah, who will rebuild the Temple. (*Genesis Rabbah* 97)

Turning now to the New Testament, we can discern in Gabriel's words, addressed to the virgin Mary of Nazareth, the ideal king, of Davidic origin, the long-awaited King-Messiah. This person is, of course, none other than Jesus, whose birth Gabriel is about to announce, "He will be great, and will be called the Son of the Most High, and the Lord God will give to him the throne of his ancestor David. He will reign over the house of Jacob forever, and of his kingdom there will be no end" (Luke 1:32–33 NRSV). Paul articulates the paradox of the incarnate Logos in a similar way, "This is the gospel concerning his Son, who was descended from David according to the flesh and was declared to be Son of God with power according to the spirit of holiness by resurrection from the dead, Jesus Christ our Lord" (Rom 1:3, 4 NRSV). The Davidic origin of Messiah is underscored in the genealogy of Matthew, "Roll of the genealogy of Jesus Christ, son of David, son of Abraham" (Matt 1:1; cf. Luke 3:31). This theme runs as a golden thread through the Scriptures up to the last book, "It is I, Jesus, who sent my angel to you with this testimony for the churches. I am the root and the descendant of David, the bright morning star" (Rev 22:16 NRSV).

NOTES

1. That is, Israel's ancestors.

2. For more details on this important text, see our discussion in "Part A. The Fallen Messiah. III. Humanity's Fate Revealed."

3. That is, "another son."

4. That is, the direct object marker.

5. Likely identified with the "seed" mentioned in Genesis 3:15.

6. If we read *ʾet* as a direct object marker; see above.

7. The link between Genesis 3:15 and 4:25 is underscored by the use of the same verbal root, *š-y-t*, "to set," with regard to God's initiating the harassment and with regard to God's involvement in Seth's conception and birth. It is God who sets the harassment between serpent's seed and woman's seed; and it is God who sets "another seed" *for* Eve, thus keeping alive the messianic expectancy.

8. Artur Weiser, *The Psalms: A Commentary,* Old Testament Library (Philadelphia: Westminster, 1962), 361.

9. The repetition *ʾĕlōhîm ʾĕlōhe(y)kā,* "God, your God," is meant to underscore the humanness of the king vis-à-vis the divinity of the one who anoints the king as his representative on Zion.

10. Perhaps Joram of Judah with Athaliah; the exhortation addressed to the bride to forget her people fits well with Athaliah's Phoenician origin; Joram is also found in Jesus' genealogy (Matt 1:8).

11. For example, Hosea 1–3; Jeremiah 2; Ezekiel 16; 23.

12. The same reading was frequently applied to Psalm 2.

13. The Hebrew term *šēgal* is a loanword from Akkadian, *ša ekkali,* meaning "the one of the palace, queen" (cf. Neh 2:16, the only other place where this term appears).

14. Note the use of the verbal root *n-ṣ-b,* "to stand, to position oneself," instead of a more common one, *ʿ-m-d,* "to stand." The root chosen here conveys the idea of "attending," with respect to king's court.

15. MT: *šēgal*; cf. LXX: *basilissa.*

16. That is, a copy of the preexistent, semi-divine Torah.

17. As for the etymology, the editors of *HALOT* derive the noun *ʿalmâ* from a root *ʿ-l-m* III, meaning "to be strong," unattested in Hebrew, but found in Ugaritic *ǵlm,* "to be agitated," Jewish Aramaic *ʿlm,* "to be powerful," Arabic *ǵalima,* "to be filled with passionate desire." According to Gesenius's lexicon, this verb is denominative, thus it cannot help much in defining the semantics of the discussed noun.

18. We may also add that the Hebrew language has a specialized term for "virgin," *bĕtûlâ,* which means specifically an adult woman without any sexual experience with men. The root **b-t-l* from which the Hebrew noun *bĕtûlâ* derives, though unattested in Hebrew, is found in Arabic *batala,* meaning "to separate." It

is important to note that in many instances in the Hebrew Bible, *ʿalmâ* is used as a parallel term for *bĕtûlâ*. The Septuagint renders the Hebrew term as *hē parthenos*, "the virgin," but the three second-century Greek translations, Aquila, Symmachus, and Theodotion, read *neanis*, "young woman, girl." The Isaiah Scroll found at Qumran (1QIsa[a]), which was copied in the second century BC, has the same reading as the MT, *ʿlmh*. The *Targum of Jonathan* reads *ʿwlymtʾ*, "young woman, servant," while the Syriac Peshitta, perhaps under the influence of the Septuagint, uses a Hebraism, *btwltʾ*, meaning "virgin."

19. A similar situation obtains with Psalm 22, where Messiah's mother is twice mentioned (vv. 10, 11) in sharp contrast to the absence of any mention of the physical father.

20. Note that in the name *Immanuel* (*ʿimmānûʾēl*), "God [is] with us," the verb "to be" is implied.

21. Corresponding to the Septuagint *parthenos*, "virgin."

22. That is, the derivation of the noun *ʿalmâ* from the root *ʿ-l-m* I, "to be concealed, hidden."

23. From the Hebrew *yēšaʿ*, meaning "salvation."

24. We may mention that Israelite law had provisions for a similar institution—the Nazirite vow (Num 6), but this was only a temporary convention and did not refer at all to sexual abstinence.

25. Hebrew *ʾēl ʿelyôn*, "God Most High"; cf. Greek *hypsistos*, "Most High."

26. See Jerome Murphy-O'Connor, *The Holy Land: An Archaeological Guide from Earliest Times to 1700* (New York: Oxford University Press, 1987), 66.

27. That is, *Haram-esh-Sharif*.

28. Etymologically, this noun derives from the root *n-ś-ʾ*, "to lift up, to raise."

29. Or *ʾê[y]lām*.

30. See Hosea 3:5; note also that the *Targum of Jonathan* on Jeremiah 30:9 inserts the words "Messiah, the son of (David)."

31. This term derives from a root *n-q-b*, "to perforate."

32. The word *geber* is used in Zechariah 13:7, a prophecy that depicts Messiah as the "fellow man" or "neighbor" of God, *geber ʿămîtî*, literally "the man of my community" (in which Yahweh is speaking). Yet the word *geber*, "strong," might also allude to the generic Hebrew name for God, *ʾēl* (*ʾĕlōhîm*), meaning "Almighty," which derives from a root **ʾ-w-l*, "to be in front, be strong" (cf. Arabic *ʾawwal*, "first"). The word *geber* may hint at one of God's specific titles, *ʾēl gibbôr*, "mighty God" (Jer 32:18; Isa 9:5).

33. PL 24:880 D.

34. For instance, the creation of the world and the first man and woman (Gen 1:1, 27; 2:3; 5:1) or the creation of a new heaven and a new earth in a new age (Isa 65:17).

35. *Gregory of Nyssa: The Life of Moses*, trans. Abraham Malherbe (Mahwah, N.J.: Paulist Press, 1979).

36. Isaiah 42:1–4 (and possibly vv. 5–9); 49:1–6; 50:4–9 (and possibly vv. 10–11); and 52:13–53:12.

37. That is, of the period belonging to Reuben, Simeon, Levi, for example.

38. That is, features that predate the monarchy.

39. The second term in Genesis 49:10, *mĕḥōqēq*, derives from the root *ḥ-q-q*,

meaning "to engrave, to inscribe, to decree," and may refer to a "commander, ruler" (literally, "the one who decrees"). Yet, based on the parallel with *šēbeṭ*, we are rendering *mĕḥōqēq* by "ruler's staff" rather than "ruler."

40. Kethib: *šîlōh;* Qere: *šîlô.* We may mention at this juncture that Qere and Kethib are two marginal notes introduced by the Masoretes (beginning with AD 500) in their manuscripts to indicate differences between the way a word was spelled in writing (Kethib) and the way was spelled in reading (Qere).

41. Cf. the Old Latin version of the Old Testament (*Vetus Latina*), *qui reposita sunt.*

42. That is, a *hapax legomenon.*

43. Cf. *šiara* < *šyr(w)* **šyalô.*

44. The word *yiqqĕhat* (**yĕqāhâ*), found here and in Proverbs 30:17, means "obedience." Note as cognates the Arabic *waqiha,* "to be obedient," and the Akkadian *utaqqū,* "to wait, to be obedient."

45. This meaning is based on the connection with the Akkadian word *šadû,* "mountain"; if this etymology holds true, and if this name was in fact pre-Israelite, then the best candidate for the title of *ʾēl šaddāy,* "God of the mountain" will be the Syrian weather god Baal-Hadad, whose dwelling place was on a mountain, Mount Sapon. In Exodus 6:3 *El Shadday* (*ʾēl šaddāy*) is the name of the God worshiped by Moses' ancestors.

46. Balaam's prophecy is actually the only Old Testament text that prophesied the "Star of Bethlehem."

47. See discussion of Genesis 49:10.

48. The root *š-w-r* means "to look at from a bent position" (cf. Gesenius's lexicon: "to look at from a high position"), which should probably be related to Akkadian *šurru(m)* (D conjugation), "to go down, to bend down."

49. The desolation refers specifically to the destruction of the temple and city followed by the Babylonian captivity, 587/586 BC.

50. That is, during the last seven years.

51. The term is to be related to the Shapel conjugation of the root *q-w-ṣ,* "to detest as ceremonially unclean."

52. The use of *mĕšōmēm,* "devastator," may hint at the Phoenician title *baal šamen,* "lord of the heavens," designating Baal.

53. That is, *ab urbe condita,* "since the foundation of the city [Rome]."

54. The root *b-q-š* in Piel conjugation means "to seek" and designates attending cultic services; hence this seeking has a cultic character.

55. Hebrew *ḥāpēṣ.*

56. Psalm 22:9: "He [God] found delight [*ḥāpēṣ*] in him [Messiah]"; cf. Proverbs 8:30, where the preexistent Wisdom is *šaʿăšuʿîm,* "delight," the object of joy, for God the Creator; see our section entitled "The Preexistence of Messiah." 1 (4). The coming of Messiah as "angel of the covenant" is presented as an unfolding event: "he is already coming" (active participle *bāʾ*) as the "coming" (active participle *ʾātēh* [Aramaic]) of the Son of Man on/with the clouds of the sky (Dan 7:13).

57. From a root **l-ʾ-k* (cf. Ugaritic *lʾk*), meaning "to send."

58. Hebrew: *p-n-h* [Piel]; but LXX: *epiblepō,* "to look upon, to supervise."

59. Cf. Isaiah 9:5 [LXX]: *megalēs boulēs angelos,* "angel of great council."

60. *ʾēl gibbôr,* "God, the Hero" or "mighty God."

61. Haggai 2:9 is longer in the Septuagint than in the MT. The additional text reads, "and even peace of soul for a possession to every one that builds, to raise up this temple."

62. Literally, "peace"; note that in Hebrew *šālôm,* "peace," indicates the idea of completeness, harmony, prosperity.

63. "Yet once, it is a little while, and I will shake the heavens, and the earth."

64. James L. Mays, *Psalms,* Interpretation (Louisville: John Knox Press, 1994), 375.

65. Micah 4:14 in the MT's numbering corresponds to 5:1 LXX, and Micah 5:1 MT matches 5:2 LXX.

66. See our discussion of Micah 4:14 [Eng. 5:1], under "Suffering of Messiah" 2. (3).

67. The name appears for the first time in one of the fourteenth-century BC Amarna Tablets (*EA* 290:16), with the spelling *Bīt-NIN.URTA,* where the logogram should probably be read *Bīt-laḫmi* (Lahama). The god Lahmu in the Mesopotamian pantheon is associated with the ocean beneath the ground; yet the name of this deity was entirely unknown in the West.

68. We may add that Hebrew has two homonymous roots, *m-š-l* I (Hiphil), "to compare with" (Akkadian *mašālu,* "to be similar to"), and *m-š-l* II, "to rule." Thus, Micah's lexical choice (*môšēl,* "ruler"—active participle Qal of *m-š-l* II) could be a deliberate hint at the first root.

69. *Code of Hammurabi,* "Prologue."

70. The form *môṣāʾōtā(y)w* derives from *y-ṣ-ʾ,* "to go forth."

71. Note the repetition of the root *y-ṣ-ʾ,* "to come (go) forth," in Micah 5:1 [Eng. 5:2]. The phrase *mî(y)mē ʿôlām* should be rendered "from the days of the eternity" or "from the hidden days" (*ʿôlām,* meaning "eternity," but not in a philosophical sense, derives from the root *ʿ-l-m,* "to conceal, to hide").

72. For example, Jerome Murphy-O'Connor, *inter alia.*

73. The term *katalyma* can designate a "room," rather than "inn" (*pandocheion,* Luke 10:34).

74. For the Aramaic *naṣrat.*

75. The reputed connection between Matthew 2:23 and Numbers 6 [or Judges 13:5, 7] describing the institution of *Nazirite* [*nāzîr*] should be refuted since, from the outset, there is no evidence in the New Testament that Jesus took the Nazirite vow.

76. Specifically, we refer to the use of the perfective aspects of the verbs *hēqal,* "he brought contempt," and *hikbîd,* "he made glorious," aspects that do not indicate the expected passage of time.

77. Cf. *anatellō*; but the Septuagint rendering of Isaiah 9:1 points to verb *lampō,* "to shine."

78. Hence the renderings in the Vulgate, *filium meum*; and in the Peshitta, *bry.*

79. Both read *ton uion mou,* "my son."

80. That is, *ta tekna autou,* "his children."

81. Cf. MT's reading *bĕnî.*

82. Jerome, *In Osee prophetam* (PL 25:915–16).

83. The noun *qôl,* "voice," may connote in plural (*qôlôt*) "voices, thunders" (Exod 19).

84. From the root *p-n-h*, in Piel conjugation.

85. Cf. Vulgate, *vox clamantis in deserto.*

86. In Greek, *phōnē boōntos en tē erēmō.*

87. Similarly to the "angel of Yahweh," who designates both Yahweh and a distinct character pointing to the future Messiah (Exod 3:4).

88. In Hebrew, *derek.*

89. Regarding Malachi 3:1, the reader is directed to the detailed discussion of this text above, in "Part B. The Rising Messiah. II. The Birth of Messiah. 3. Time of Birth."

90. For our previous comments regarding this text, see "I. The Preexistence of Messiah. 1. Within the Godhead. (6) 'Son of Man' or 'Son of Weakness.'"

91. In Genesis 9:27 Japheth is living in Shem's "tents."

92. Walter Brueggemann, *Genesis,* Interpretation (Louisville: John Knox Press, 1982), 91.

93. The word *škynh* means literally "dwelling," from the root *š-k-n,* "to dwell."

94. The word "tents" was replaced with the word "schools."

95. In Hebrew, *ʾabrām* means "the father is exalted."

96. In Hebrew, *ʾabrāhām.*

97. From the root *y-ṣ-ʾ,* "to go forth."

98. From the root *h-l-k,* "to go, walk."

99. From the same root, *h-l-k,* "to go, walk," as was used in Yahweh's imperative to Abram (Gen 12:1).

100. That is, *ʾēšet zĕnûnîm,* "woman of fornications" (cf. the common term *zônâ,* "prostitute"), and note the silence surrounding the identity of the prophet's future wife.

101. The MT uses the Niphal (reflexive) conjugation of the root *b-r-k,* "to bless."

102. The meaning is therefore "to wish on oneself a blessing like that of Abram."

103. The Septuagint reads, *eneulogēthēsontai,* which means, "[tribes] will be blessed through you."

104. The Sirach text is rendered, "The Lord therefore promised him [Abram] on oath so that the nations may be blessed [*eneulogēthēnai*] through his seed [*spermati*]."

105. Specifically, this is the Pual conjugation.

106. Except for the Priestly material in vv. 34–35.

107. The Hithpael of the root *b-r-k* used in Genesis 26:4b (the Masoretic Text) has the same meaning as the Niphal attested in Genesis 12:3b, i.e., "to wish on oneself a blessing like that of…"; but note the Septuagint, which, again, has a passive, *eneulogēthēsontai,* and hence the reading, "(tribes) will be blessed (through your seed)."

108. For further details concerning this text, see above, "Part B. The Rising Messiah. II. The Birth of Messiah. 3. Time of Birth."

109. The genealogy in Matthew mentions Jesse as one of the forefathers of Christ (Matt 1:5–6).

110. For our previous discussion of this text, see above, "Part B. The Rising Messiah. II. The Birth of Messiah. 4. Place of Birth and Other Places in Christ's Itinerary."

III

The Suffering, Death, and Resurrection of Messiah

IT IS MORE THAN SIMPLY AXIOMATIC that the totality of Scripture is inspired by God and therefore must be accurate in the prophetic instance. We hold it to be true also that the singular unity of Scripture is reflexive; that is, it witnesses to its own ultimate fulfillment in the person and activities of Jesus Christ. We maintain that Christ himself acknowledged the prophetic value of the Old Testament on the road to Emmaus (Luke 24:25–27), that the evangelist John (13:18–19) interpreted Psalm 41:9 as a reference to Judas's act of deception, which we will explore below, and that the psalm therefore has messianic implication. In this light, the veracity of the existence of scriptural precursors intended to indicate Christ, his birth, life, death, and resurrection seems obvious.

Above all, the prophetic message, the human significance, and the divine conveyance of Scripture all point to the Messiah and the sum of his incarnate being. The prophetic Messiah is, of course, the historical Christ. In addition to the interpretive corroboration found within the writings of the New Testament authors, John confirms for us that the revelator on the throne, the Lord, is "the alpha and the omega, the beginning and the end" (Rev 1:8; 21:6; 22:13). The essence of this nomenclature suggests completeness, the power of God. It seems apparent in the Christian tradition that this power and status were bestowed by the Almighty upon his Son, the Christ (Matt 28:18). The linguistic essence of these phrases also carries the implication of unity: between the persons of the Godhead; between the events of salvation history; and in the scriptural corroboration of the reality of Christ as both Son of God and Son of Man, and as our Savior.

Christ's suffering and resurrection are indicators for us that pain and betrayal can bring us the opportunity for growth and deification. His ministry leads us to an understanding of greater depth and clarity of the role of suffering in our lives. Not by single moments of his life alone is faith in Christ realized. By the totality of his birth, suffering, death, and resurrection are we brought to a thorough and inclusive faith in him as the Son of God. In this way, the singular unity of the life of Christ mirrors the singular unity of Scripture. The fulfillment of his mission echoes the realizations found in the law and the prophets.

There are several elements of Christ's passion as it is portrayed in the gospel accounts. These elements include betrayal, forsakenness (both by his disciples and by God), accusation by false witnesses, ridicule and humiliation, physical abuse, agony and crucifixion, and death. All of these elements, as well as Christ's responses—his sacrifice and his unfailing commitment to his purpose and his Father's will—are all alluded to in Old Testament prophetic writings and recorded in New Testament parallels. In this chapter, we will address the major points of reference that foreshadow the passion of Christ.

Betrayal evokes myriad affective sentiments and carries with it a sense of such depth and breadth of pain as is experienced only in the destruction of an intimate friendship for unimaginable reasons. It conjures up loneliness, isolation, and humility on behalf of the betrayed; it conjures up depravity, immorality, and corruption on behalf of the betrayer. These are the mystifying elements that accost us in the narratives of the end of Christ's journey to the cross. The visceral sorrow we experience from the story is at once heightened and mitigated by the knowledge that such was the fate of the Son of God, and that he chose to suffer this fate for our sake, in spite of the knowledge that humanity is a peculiar, vengeful, compassionate, and puzzling lot. Christ's suffering was intended for all, even for the betrayer.

How then are we to prepare for and understand the betrayal of Christ by Judas Iscariot? Was it necessary? Was it foreseen? What clues are we offered in order to make sense of the passion of the incarnate Son of God? How can something so inconceivable happen? There is substantial evidence in the Old Testament that the passion was necessary and foreseen. As such, humanity needed (and needs still) the vital information that serves to open our hearts and minds to the reality of the passion, crucifixion, and resurrection of Christ. Christ's intent in acceding to his mission of suffering, death, and resurrection was to redeem fallen humanity. One of the outgrowths of this is the restoration of our complete faith. In order to rise from the dead, Christ had to die; in order for humanity to believe in him as a person of the triune Godhead, Christ had to rise. Faith is, therefore, our wisdom born of Christ's pain. God deemed it essential to prepare us for the inconceivable. In the Old Testament we find pointers that lead to the apprehension of Christ, and his passion and death. These pointers also illuminate personalities and situations involved in the course of his life and death. We include two caveats, however: (1) messianic prophecies should be read as parallels to the gospels, since Christ's saving work supersedes both the Old Testament's foreshadowings and the New Testament's accounts; and (2) the prophecies of the Old Testament must necessarily be understood in qualitative terms. That is, they are indicators of events of fulfillment, but they ought not to be viewed as rigid categories of prediction. One should strike a balance between the historical and typological meanings of these texts.

1. The Betrayal

The most evocative component of the episodes of Christ's suffering is perhaps the ambivalence of the incident of betrayal. At once we witness the valleys and the peaks of the human condition and we are drawn into a polemic that challenges us to glimpse the light amidst a deep darkness. Within the ambivalence, then, there exists this antagonism, which only exacerbates the humanness of the story, and ought to give us greater pause. There is breadth of emotional dimension present in the various gospel accounts of the betrayal: friendship and trust, juxtaposed with greed, deceit, and fear. Not only does Christ have the onus of Judas's perfidy to bear, but he is also beset by abandonment by others of his chosen twelve. Perhaps the most poignant of the recallings is the fleeing by the others in Mark's narrative (Mark 14:50–52). Not only did they forsake their master, but they left everything behind in doing so; this is in stark contrast to the original call of Christ to leave everything and join him (Matt 8:22; Mark 10:29). For the disciples, the fear of condemnation and death was greater even than the impact of the discarding of the one in whom they sought their salvation. Against this backdrop of disturbance and melee, we see the tremendous potential for humanity as Christ is led to and endures his sacrifice. These various dimensions should beget in us a keen perception of the vagaries of our humanness; that our individual, small efforts are insufficient to the task of our own improvement; and that our hope lies in turning over our lives to the one who took on our flesh and redeemed us from the darkness. By referring to the events and person of the Messiah, the Old Testament made available for the faithful of the early common era the apparatus of belief and understanding by which the perception of Christ as the Messiah could be conceived. It continues to make this apparatus available for contemporary readers of faith.

(1) Betrayer's Profile (Ps 41:10 [Eng. 41:9]; 55:13–15 [Eng. 55:12–14])

***Ps 41:10:** Even my colleague, in whom I trusted, who ate of my bread, lifted up [his] heel against me.*

***Ps 55:13–15:** For it is not an enemy who taunts me, that I could bear; he who hates me did not lift his heel against me, then I could hide from* *him. But it is you, a person of my own rank, my compatriot, my confidant. For we used to sweeten our secret together in the house of God.*

Christ's suffering begins with Judas Iscariot's treachery; Jesus is sold by his trusted disciple. In looking at the prophetic hints of the betrayal, two questions arise: (1) Who was the one who *delivered*? And (2) How does the Old Testament portray the betrayer and the events leading up to Christ's death on the cross?

John tells us of Christ's words to Pilate, the man who would ultimately sentence Christ and order his death, "[He] who delivered me to you has the greater sin" (John 19:11). For the sake of a presentation that parallels the elements of the gospel narratives, we will begin with a profile of the betrayer himself. What are the passages of the Old Testament that give us an indication that the Messiah would be betrayed? That he would be turned over to the authorities? That, as a result of the betrayer's actions, he would be killed? We can specify the attributes of "the one who delivered" Jesus to the Jewish authorities and eventually to Pilate, the Roman governor. We will turn first to an examination of the Old Testament portrayals of the most famous betrayer.

The texts that refer specifically to the betrayer are Psalm 41:10 and Psalm 55:13–15. In the following pages, we shall explain these texts in their prophetic light and establish a profile of the betrayer in order to demonstrate the veracity of the prophetic message vis-à-vis the events of the gospel narratives. The substance of both Old Testament passages is King David's great disappointment, not only by the actions of his enemies but by the actions of his intimate friend and counselor, who sided with his enemies. The imbricated identity of the betrayer in these psalms is unfolded gradually, as it is in the gospel fulfillment account.

In its typological interpretation, Psalm 41 is messianic in both wide and narrow senses. In the wide sense, it conveys general statements of betrayal and humiliation to be suffered by the Messiah in the carrying out of his royal, prophetic, and priestly tasks. Narrowly construed, it also conveys, as seen in verse 10, the specific image of David, the royal persona, betrayed by a close and trusted friend. The imagery and sentiment are repeated in the gospel narratives, and the duplicity of Psalm 41:10 is fulfilled by the chronicling of Christ and Judas and the scene of betrayal in Gethsemane. To view the prophetic message of our passage in its fullness, we must evaluate the signal components of the text.

a. Colleague

King David refers to the betrayer as "my colleague" (*ʾîš šālôm*), a phrase that, in Hebrew, is attended by undertones of significant relationship. In the Septuagint, the Hebrew idiom is rendered literally as "the man of my peace" (*ho anthrōpos tēs eirēnēs mou*). Similarly, the Vulgate version delivers to us *homo pacis meae,* a virtually identical image. That *ʾîš šālôm* is a difficult idiom can be seen from the fact that the Targum on Psalm 41 inserts the word *dtbʿ,* "who seeks," the whole phrase meaning, "the man who seeks my welfare (peace)," which actually fits quite well with Ahithophel's profile. The original Hebrew idiom, however, means "colleague, comrade, companion"; in short, it connotes a specific and deep bond of shared intimacy. Neither the Greek nor the Latin translation adequately brings forward the original metaphorical value of the Hebrew idiom; both render unsatisfactorily the idea of the close relationship between betrayed and betrayer.

In the garden of Gethsemane, at the time of his arrest, Christ called Judas "comrade, companion" (*hetairos*), which clarifies Judas's status as one of the apostles and sums up his position as a co-worker of Christ. Matthew (26:47–50) relates the scene in the garden with a particular clarity and juxtaposes the act of betrayal by Judas with Christ's commendation of him as "comrade." The crowd, the kiss, and the arrest of Christ as he poses his poignant question to Judas, "Comrade, why are you here?" give a particularly weighty flavor to Judas's deception and intensify the agonizing aspect of the incident.

b. Trusted One

The trusted one (*bāṭaḥtî,* "[the one on whom] I trusted") of Psalm 41:10 has been identified with Ahithophel the Gilonite, David's counselor, who sided with Absalom in his rebellion against his father the king (2 Sam 15:12). David wrote Psalm 41 after he learned that his friend had joined Absalom in his conspiracy (2 Sam 15:31; 16:23). The full psalm situates David in the context of bodily illness and calumny brought upon him by surrounding enemies and, most bitterly, by his colleague. In spite of his lament, David successfully crushed Absalom's rebellion, and his colleague, Ahithophel, hanged himself in remorse and abnegation (2 Sam 17:23).

In its realization in the New Testament equivalent, Judas was entrusted with the finances of the group (John 13:29), which gives us insight into the trust placed in him by Christ. As the fulfillment of the antitype Ahithophel, Judas joined in the conspiracy of the priests and scribes who sought Jesus' life. It is significant that Judas paid the same price as Ahithophel for his mistake: he hanged himself (Matt 27:5). We should also note that none can avoid judgment when standing before Jesus: not Judas, not Pilate, and not the gospel reader of today. We must be careful not to exempt ourselves from the implications of faith and of being part of the Christian community. The gospel accounts are not historic exhortations to extinct communities; rather, they are intended for every generation of faith, to be understood and incorporated into the daily living of one's personal and communal faith.

c. Meal Sharer

The relationship lamented in Psalm 41 has been posited to be that between David and Ahithophel. This was a cherished relationship of trust and mutual confidence, as indicated by the referent "colleague," and further indicated by the act of eating together. The act of sitting at table with one's closest companions is a nearly universal theme of hospitality, trust, and deep emotional connection between the sharers of the meal.

In the Hebrew text ("the one who was eating my bread"), the form of the verb used for "eating" (*ʾōkēl*) is a participle, which expresses continuous or habitual activity, and some scholars suggest that it was a covenantal meal, shared in order to consecrate the friendship of David and Ahithophel. The use of the term "bread" (*leḥem*) supports this hypothesis.

These themes of repetitive, continuous activity and communion take on greater significance in the New Testament context of the relations between Christ and his disciples and their shared life. For example, the habitual activity of the meal of Psalm 41 can be understood as an indicator of the several occasions when Jesus and his disciples used to eat together. The suggestion of a relationship based on a covenantal meal in Psalm 41 may also hint at the revelation Jesus made at the Last Supper regarding the identity of the betrayer and the institution of the Eucharist (see, e.g., Matt 26:20–29; John 13:21–30). Typologically, "my bread" (Ps 41:10) may be a reference to "my body" (Matt 26:26–29); that is, it may refer to Jesus' body, the Eucharist.

d. Despiser

The Hebrew reading *higdîl ʿal ʿāqēb,* "to lift the heel against somebody," is a *hapax legomenon,* an idiom found only in Psalm 41:10. It suggests, perhaps, a stamping with the heel of a boot, or giving a great kick spitefully. The main idea is that David and the royal family are rejected and humiliated by both a rebellious son and an intimate friend turned overnight into an enemy.

Christ himself witnesses to the scriptural reference to him in the Gospel of John, "I am not speaking of all of you; I know whom I have chosen. But it is to fulfill the scripture, 'The one who ate my bread (*ho trōgōn*) has lifted his heel against me.' I tell you this now, before it occurs, so that when it does occur, you may believe that I am he (i.e., Yahweh, the Lord)" (John 13:18–19 NRSV). John continues, "After saying this Jesus was troubled in spirit, and declared, 'Very truly, I tell you, one of you will betray (*paradōsei*) me"' (13:21 NRSV).

It takes little imaginative process to conjure the sentiment of betrayal. The poignancy of Judas's act against Christ is augmented by the metaphorical reference to the kingdom of God as found in helplessness, rather than through the wielding of power over others. Jesus demonstrated the greatest vulnerability in his endurance of the trial, the humiliation, physical torture, and death. Crucifixion was deliberately designed to display the victim's lowliness and the disdain in which he was held by the authorities. It was the most ignoble method of putting criminals to death.

e. Co-equal

Psalm 55:14 adds an additional layer of detail to the profile of the betrayer. Interestingly, the Targum on Psalm 55 inserts the name of Ahithophel in order to clarify the identity of David's "equal." The Septuagint renders the Hebrew phrase *ʾĕnôš kĕʿerkî*, "a person according to my valuation, my equal," or "a person such as I," as *isopsychou*, "of equal spirit," underscoring the point of shared intent of purpose, although not necessarily of the same rank. It is an ideological equivalence, distinct from the Hebrew idiom, which implies political and social equality. No longer is he simply a comrade of the Messiah; he is also, according to this psalm, an equal of the Messiah, his close friend and confidant. Coupled with the hues of meaning implicit in the sharing of bread between intimate friends (see above), this additional layer of significance further belies the great accord of the friendship to which the psalmist refers.

As with Psalm 41:10, the idea remains that it is tolerable to be jostled and oppressed by one's enemies, for it is expected from those who hate. The bitter gall of betrayal by one as intimate as the psalmist indicates, however, is all but unbearable. The lament of loss is the psalmist's appeal to God, his effort to lay bare the extent of his soul and plead for compassion. This petition made to God by the injured man as a result of the betrayal stands in stark relief to the betrayal itself. The brokenness of heart is the point of convergence for God and the brokenhearted, the point at which the psalmist finds solace. Destroyed by one so intimate as his "equal," the psalmist lifts up his eyes to God. He turns to his faith in the eternal Judge when his belief in his friends has been shattered.

The New Testament alludes to the intent of the psalmist in defining this broken relationship. In John 15:15, Jesus names his disciples "friends," and treats them as equals and co-workers, rather than as ignorant servants, "I have called you friends, because I have made known to you everything that I have heard from my Father" (NRSV). A "friend" (*philos*) is more than a "comrade" (*hetairos*). The former designates a close relationship based on equality between two persons; the latter refers to a professional cooperation.

f. Compatriot

The Hebrew term *ʾallûp* I means "close (family) friend," and is related to the term *ʾelep,* which means "clan, tribe, settlement, region," and hence confers the sense of "compatriot." However, in the Septuagint we find *ho hēgemōn mou,* meaning "my leader, commander." This presupposes the Hebrew homonym *ʾallûp* II, "tribal chief, leader," which does not fit well into the context of Psalm 55, because the betrayer is described as equal to David.[1]

This raises the question of whether Judas Iscariot, the New Testament betrayer, could be called a compatriot of Christ; that is, can we find evidence that Judas came from the same region as Christ?

The first element of the betrayer's name, Judas (*Ioudas*), is the Hellenized form of the Hebrew name Judah (*yĕhûdâ*). As for Iscariot, this appears to be a nickname used to distinguish this apostle from others also bearing the name Judah (Luke 6:16; Acts 1:13; John 14:22). There are several interpretations surrounding this nomenclature. The following two of these interpretations are the most discussed.

(a) The first assumes that Iscariot is a compound word, which derives from the Hebrew term *ʾîš* for "man" or "the one of," and *Qĕriyyôt,* a town, probably the hometown of Judas. If this interpretation is correct, then Judas, probably alone among the twelve, was a Judean (from the village of Kerioth; cf. Josh 15:25), as Jesus was.

(b) Other scholars believe that the Aramaic name Iscariot means "man from the City" (*qiryĕtāʾ*), namely, from Jerusalem. According to either of these interpretations, Judas Iscariot seems to be the only apostle originally from Judea, and a good candidate for the title of "compatriot" of our Lord. These two readings support the sites in the psalms where the betrayer is called "close friend, colleague, compatriot" of the Messiah, who shall be from the tribe of Judah (Gen 49:10).

g. Confidant

As with the analysis of "a person of my rank," examination of the term *mĕyuddāʿ,* "confidant" (from the Hebrew verb *yādaʿ,* "to know"), reveals that the psalmist is referring to a person entrusted with the knowledge of one's private affairs. This title is very close in meaning to *rēaʿ,* "friend," and points to the new appellation given by Christ to his disciples at the Last Supper, "I have called you friends because I have made known to you everything I have heard from my Father" (John 15:15 NRSV). The implication is that the Father has revealed pertinent and specific information to Jesus, and that Jesus has, in turn, shared this information with his disciples:

"Then the disciples came and asked him, 'Why do you speak to them in parables?' He answered, 'To you it has been given to know the secrets of the kingdom of heaven, but to them it has not been given'" (Matt 13:10–11 NRSV). The mysteries are not for general consumption, but are given to the closest of the collaborators of Christ. We might guess at the content of this revelation, but it is not vital for our task. It was, of course, privileged information and required enormous trust for disclosure. Despite his impending duplicity, Judas was graced with this trust; because of this, he fits the description as confidant.

h. Participant in a Secret Gathering

This clause serves as a conclusion and a rationale for all the titles and attributes of the betrayer vis-à-vis his master. The Hebrew phrase *namtiq sôd* means literally "we used to sweeten together [our] secret," which conveys the sense of "we held close company together." The rendering of the clause in the LXX reads, "who in companionship with me sweetened [our] food."

The Hebrew word *sôd* in this phrase means "secret council" and designates either the gathering of individuals joined to conduct secret business or the secret content of their discussions. Here again we find themes of community and trust. This "secret" or "mystery" may hint at the Eucharist instituted by Jesus at the Last Supper prior to Judas's leaving the upper room (Luke 22:19–23; but note Mark 14:18b–21, which places the betrayal before the institution account). A compelling facet of this possibility is the intent of the term for "sweetening," which means to make the mystery (e.g., the sacrificed body and blood of Christ) accessible to a community of believers.

The betrayer is emerging very clearly as the trusted, intimate friend. He is relied upon by his victim. He is a sharer of fellowship and the confidential details of his victim's life. He is the one who originates from the same tribe. In essence, the betrayer and his victim were accustomed, during their relationship, to coming together to share a meal, perhaps a covenantal meal; to sharing converse of secret content, including the revelation of God the Father to his Son, and the institution of the most sacred of worshiping mysteries; to sharing in the redemptive work of God. These are immense dual interests, and the familiarity necessary to the successful disposition of such a reciprocal association is plain. We are challenged, then, to delve into the depth of the sedition perpetrated in prophetic allusion in the Old Testament by Ahithophel against King David and consummated in the New Testament by the abhorrent activities of Judas against Jesus Christ.

(2) Sold for Thirty Pieces of Silver (Zech 11:12–13//Matt 26:15–16; 27:3–10)

> *Zech 11:12–13: I then said to them, "If you see fit, give me my wages; if not, never mind." So they weighed out my wages: thirty shekels of silver. Yahweh said to me, "Throw it to the potter, this princely sum at which I was valued by them!" Taking the thirty shekels of silver, I threw them into the Temple of Yahweh, for the potter.*

The duality of the relationship shared by Jesus and Judas Iscariot, as shown in the previous section, is accentuated by the valuation and sale of Jesus. His life is bargained away for a pittance paid to one who esteems his value as virtually nothing, even though he knows the most intimate details of Christ's life and his true nature as the Son of God. Even in light of such immeasurable knowledge, Judas prefers to violate the sacred bonds of intimacy and deep knowledge for the value of insignificant wages, as the ruling class sees fit to pay. Indeed, the price is not even paid to Jesus, the prophet of God, but to Judas. This inverts the relationship of remittance as found in Zechariah and further illustrates the mistreatment of God's servant at the hands of those who trade in the work of their human subjects.

The historical significance of the passage from Zechariah is to remind us that the ruler always has the right to calculate and levy appropriate remuneration (cf. Neh 5:15). The price placed on Christ was assessed by the ruling class on the prophet/shepherd and represents a slave's value (cf. Exod 21:32). It is an insulting amount. In the connection made to this passage by Matthew, the evangelist clearly intends to demonstrate that Christ is esteemed substantially below his true value. His true value, of course, is beyond any price, and we are given the scene in order to illustrate the great evidence of human arrogance and ungratefulness, and the willingness to barter God's redemptive work for merely a slave's stipend.

This passage has been interpreted as a messianic prophecy by one of the Midrashim, which saw in the thirty pieces of silver a reference to thirty precepts of the law, "For what purpose will the royal Messiah come, and what will he do? He will come to assemble the exiles of Israel and to give them [the Gentiles] thirty precepts, as it (i.e., Zech 11:12) says" (*Genesis Rabbah* 98:9). Matthew (27:3–10; cf. 26:15–16) applies Zechariah 11:12–13 to Jesus, whom the prophet (playing the part of Yahweh) seems to prefigure; the rejection of the shepherd in Zechariah corresponds to the suffering of the "Servant of Yahweh" (*ʿebed Yahweh*) in Isaiah 53.

Matthew (27:9) attributes the quotation from Zechariah 11:12–13 to Jeremiah 32:6–15 ("The word spoken through the prophet Jeremiah was then fulfilled"). We should note that the passage in Jeremiah is similar, but not identical, to that of Zechariah. In any case, Matthew applies the text to

Jesus, whom the prophet seems to prefigure. In addition, the rejection of the shepherd in Zechariah corresponds to other cases in the Old Testament of prophets rejected as servants of Yahweh (cf. Isa 53).

There is no betrayal explicit in Zechariah, but there is the idea of undervaluing the worth of a person and the mistreatment this precipitates. This is odious in the case of the slave or the prophet, and it is exceptionally heinous in the case of Christ. This idea of the mistreatment of others is, in fact, foundational in Zechariah's texts. This idea was coopted by the evangelist and molded to fit the specifics of Jesus' situation. The prophet Zechariah himself is mistreated, and his worth is undervalued by the people and the ruling class. Yahweh, in response, advises Zechariah to throw out the sum they have pledged to him. The "price," since it has been assessed against the prophet and his work, has in fact been levied against Yahweh himself. The prophet, by virtue of his rapport with Yahweh is, of course, in a filial relationship with him, which heightens the inappropriateness of his mistreatment and low payment. This couples with the notion of Christ as the prophet and the Son of God, and therefore equal with God. Christ foretells his followers that such ingratitude and abuse are endemic among the people of this world and that they should expect the same treatment he himself has received at their hands, "If they persecuted me, they will persecute you; if they kept my word, they will keep yours also" (John 15:20 NRSV). This demonstrates Christ's connection with Yahweh, with the prophet, and with his followers, and links all of them in an organic unity of intimate and personal fellowship. The correlation between this notion and the passage from Zechariah is to show that the prophet, who ought to be valued for his work at God's behest, is not. In the assessment of value, this should apply even more strongly in the consideration of Christ, the actual Son of God, but it is instead even more underrated. An inverse relationship is thus presented: The closer one is to God, the less will one's worth be esteemed by the people of the world. The prophet Zechariah at least was paid, even though Yahweh told him to toss away the price. In the case of Jesus, the price was given to the one who betrayed him, and Christ was not a participant in the negotiations or the receipt of the price. There is an increasing intensity in the abuse of God's worker and therefore of God himself. His redemptive work in this world is forsaken in favor of human concerns.

Zechariah (11:12) said, "If you see fit, give me my wages; if not, never mind." In other words, if the people saw him as the prophet of God, they were to pay him as such. The people, however, took the middle way. They paid him, but it was significantly less than the customary prophet's wages; they did not reject him outright, but they accepted him only to a lesser degree than as a prophet. This applies also to Christ: the thirty shekels of the evangelist's phrase was an effort to elide the experience of Zechariah with the experience of Jesus. He was not totally rejected, but was received by some, and even his enemies put some value on his life, tiny though it was. Both Zechariah and Jesus were shepherds dispatched by God to protect and to lead his flock, but they were both accepted only in part, and only in part were they understood as God's agents. It was also only in part that they were paid for their work on God's behalf, but they were thoroughly mistreated in light of their commission and their work.

Yahweh exhorts Zechariah to receive the price and to give it over to him, in recognition that the people can see and understand at least some of God's activity on their behalf. Given this, however, Yahweh's reference is to the "price" (Hebrew *yĕqār*) offered to Zechariah by the people. God has perceived the intent of the people to treat Zechariah and therefore God himself, as an object, a commodity to be trafficked in. The price offered is for the object; the people do not offer a payment commensurate with the extraordinary work of God's prophet. The price received for Judas's treachery is a glaring affront to Yahweh's work in the world.

This is one underlying message of Zechariah and its connection in Matthew. The servant of God is made to suffer because he is not recognized as such by the people of the world. They underestimate his true meaning, his intentions, and his purpose in their midst. His value is calculated by the human community based on their own incomplete understanding. At issue is the arrogance and presumptiveness of emphasizing human rationality over that of the message of Yahweh. We are willing to pay much less for the Word of God than his true worth.

In the end, the ruling class of Matthew's account actually pays the betrayer, not Jesus the prophet and Son of God. The value of the prophet's work is held in low esteem, and payment for it is, finally, given to Judas, who betrays his Master. It is not a total rejection of the prophet; rather it highlights the exploitation and abuse of the prophet. Just as in Zechariah, as the ruling class recognizes Zechariah's prophetic nature, but not his intimate, filial relationship with God. He is just like any other worker, and valued as such.

In Zechariah there is a sort of irony in Yahweh's reference to the "princely (magnificent) sum" (*ʾeder hayqār*), which is actually the price of a slave, and in his reference to the potter. There is a double entendre in Yahweh's use of the term "potter" (*yôṣēr*): on the one hand, it can be understood as the mundane worker; on the other hand, the deeper meaning of the term is as one of the appellations of Yahweh, as found in several Old Testament texts (Isa 45:18; 49:5; Jer 18:2–4, 6; Amos 4:13; Zech 12:1; Ps 2:9; Lam 4:2). Yahweh doubtlessly intends himself in his use of the term "potter," which is to say the Creator.[2] In his ironic discourse, Yahweh finally emphasizes that the value of the prophet's work is to be attributed to Yahweh himself, to his work through the prophet. In the case of Zechariah, this ultimate value end is recognized, at least in part, and compensated to a small extent; in the case of Christ, the ultimate value is noticed and disregarded. For the people who surround Jesus in the passion narratives, his work on behalf of Yahweh is worthless, but the work Judas performs in betraying him is worth something. In the final analysis, however, this indicates that the people have placed a "price" on God's work in the world, even if it is primarily seen through the lens of hatred for Christ.

The evangelist uses the same term for the amount of the "price" that is found in Zechariah (thirty pieces). The substance of this is that Yahweh himself exercises his prerogative and makes the judgment regarding the amount and the intent behind its payment. The prophet does not assess the valuation made against his work, but Yahweh does, and he sees that it is an insult to him.

2. The Passion

The second stage in the suffering and death of Christ is the passion itself. By *passion*, I mean the trial of Christ, the crucifixion, and the entombment. The betrayal is the abandonment of Christ, as we have seen, but the theme of the passion is the enmity toward Christ, and the enemies of Christ are brought to the forefront in the narratives of the passion. Those who demand his trial and execution are highlighted in their character and their behavior. There is a secondary theme that is revealed in the providing of the tomb by Joseph of Arimathea, one of Jesus' secretive disciples. This theme demonstrates the respect his followers had for Christ, their acknowledgment of his humanity and his divinity, and the singular hope that will be revealed in the cross.

There is a crescendo in the passages that moves from the betrayal and abandonment of Christ to the antagonism and the passion. The evil is finally overcome by the power of the cross, of course, and even in the midst of the darkness, there is a light that shines in Joseph and his willingness to come forward under conditions of great hostility and offer his own new tomb for the burial of Christ.

(1) Forsaken by His Disciples (Zech 13:7//Mark 14:27)

> *Zech 13:7: Sword, awake against my shepherd, against my fellow man—declares Yahweh Sabaoth! Strike the shepherd and the sheep will be scattered! Then I shall turn my hand against the young.*

The phrase *geber ʿămîtî*, "the man of my community,"[3] illustrates the dual nature of the messianic agent. On the one hand, his humanity is emphasized (*geber* refers to both "human" and "male"), and, on the other hand, the divine aspect is also underscored, because this agent is part of God's community—he is God's "fellow man." This is reinforced in alternative and complementary texts. Note the *Targum Jonathan*'s reading of Zechariah 13:7, "against the ruler, his companion who is like him." As one can see, the Targum replaces *geber*, "man," with *šlṭwnʾ*, "ruler, rule," and the anthropomorphic *ʿămîtî*, "my community," with a more abstract term *ḥbrʾ*, "companion, friend."

Strike the shepherd and the sheep will be scattered.

The general opinion is that the shepherd of Zechariah 13:7 is neither the good shepherd of Zechariah 11:4–14 nor the bad one of Zechariah 11:15–16, but he is the "leader" of the people and the representative of Yahweh on earth.[4] What is interesting in the passage is that Yahweh himself orders the annihilation of this leader. It is Yahweh himself who is speaking in Zechariah 13:7, and he is the one who decides to destroy his representative and the leader of the people. The same idea is found in Isaiah 53:10, "Yahweh has been pleased to crush him [the Servant] with suffering."

This leader of the people is evidently very close to Yahweh on earth (as is every king in Israel, an adopted son of God [cf. Ps 2:7]), but is still far away from him. This binary and complementary relationship, near to God and yet far from him, is expressed by the phrase "my fellow man." That is, the subject is simultaneously "man" and "my community" (i.e., God's). Even so, however, in his efforts in the world, God must take what seems to us to be harsh action: the leader of the people (Yahweh's agent) is destroyed, and the entire nation is punished by God in retaliation for disobedience, vanity, and iniquity. The punishment of the nation is illustrated by the phrase "Then I shall turn my hand even against the young ones," which I will treat in more detail below.

This text in Zechariah 13:7 was considered from a very early age in both the Christian and the Judaic traditions to be a messianic text. The premessianic age is seen as a national ordeal in which God plays an important role. For Christians this is an important text because it presents the Messiah as a man, but at the same time as very close to God. It is in the same vein of thought as Psalm 110:1, in which there is a mysterious, enigmatic person playing the role of counselor or confidant positioned between the king of Israel (David) and God. In Psalm 110 the intermediary is not portrayed as a man (that is, as a human), but certainly as close to God, and it is significant that this person is introduced as operative between God and his representative on earth, namely, David in Psalm 110.

Another text to be brought into discussion is Daniel 7:13ff., in which we learn that the messianic agent is named the "Son of Man." In this context, the "Son of Man" is seen not in his male form but rather in the general sense of humanity, weakness. He is an agent who receives all power from Almighty God, the one who lasts until the end of days.

Then I shall turn my hand against the young.

The "young ones, the small ones (of the flock)" (*ṣōʿărîm*) represent the entire community that is affected by God's intervention against his own Messiah. One may add that the Septuagint (*mikrous poimenas*) interprets the Hebrew word as referring to "shepherd lads." In this case, God's wrath aims at Messiah's disciples. There are few places where God is said to work against his Messiah, so this is a crucial element of the text. As Paul puts it (Gal 3:13; cf. Deut 21:23), Jesus, in fact, became a "curse" through his taking on of humanity and human sinfulness, and God must take action against the defilement. Christ asks God to take away the cup (Matt 26:36–39), but the Father instead abandons Christ on the cross (Matt 27:45–46).

There is here a gradation of intent that begins with the command, "Sword, awake," and culminates with God's exact command to strike against his own Messiah (the "shepherd"). In one New Testament application of this, in Mark 14:27, we read the following, "And Jesus said to them, 'You will all become deserters; for it is written, "*I will strike* the shepherd, and the sheep will be scattered"'" (NRSV). This reading is based on some Greek manuscripts that depart from the Hebrew text and from the main channels of transmission of the Septuagint. The main texts have "Strike!" (imperative), and the alternate reading is "I shall strike," as we find in the New Testament application. This is an important interpretive deviation, because it is one thing to say "Strike!" and something else entirely to say "I shall strike," which is an emphatic declaration of God's intervention in Messiah's dramatic end.

(2) Accused by Fanatic Witnesses (Ps 35:11–12; 109:2; 38:13–15 [Eng. 38:12–14]; 39:2; Isa 53:7//Matt 26:59–60; 27:12, 14; 1 Pet 2:23)

Ps 35:11–12: *Fanatic witnesses* (ʿēdê ḥāmās) *appear who question me about things I do not know. They repay me evil for good, [seeking] my bereavement.*

> *Matt 26:59–60: Now the chief priests and the whole council were looking for false testimony* (pseudomartyrian) *against Jesus so that they might put him to death, but they found none, though many false witnesses* (pseudomartyrōn) *came forward. (NRSV)*

The Hebrew phrase *ʿēdê ḥāmās* should be rendered "fanatic (malicious) witnesses," not "false witnesses," as many modern translations do probably under the influence of the New Testament (e.g., Matt 26:59–60) application of Psalm 35:11–12. The rendition "fanatic witnesses" is required by the term *ḥāmās,* "violence" or "wrong," which should be related to Arabic *ḥamisa,* meaning "to be persistent in battle and in religion" or "to be a religious fanatic." These witnesses to which Matthew refers, in connection with Psalm 35:11–12, are motivated by fanatical ideology and not by the bringing of false witness for material gains.

The Septuagint text of Psalm 35:11 uses *adikoi,* which means "unjust," and is close, in a way, to the Hebrew text. The evilness is rooted in the nature and character of the witnesses, and they come forth on account of their own evilness and unjust demands. There is no contradiction between the Old Testament prophecy and the New Testament application; on the contrary, we have here two slightly different views of the witnesses who testified against the Messiah. The Old Testament text points to their character or nature and their violent, fanatical, and unjust dispositions, whereas the New Testament application insists on their behavior as liars.

The Old Testament precedes the New Testament, of course, and often casts new and illuminating light on the reporting of the New Testament. This is a case in point: the understanding of the character of the witnesses against Christ is significantly broadened when we consider that not only are they liars, but they are also, by nature, malicious and fanatical.

> *Ps 109:2–3: For they opened (their) wicked and deceitful mouth against me; they spoke to me with lying tongue. They surrounded me with words of hate; they fought against me without a cause.*

In other passages in the Old Testament, these witnesses are understood to be wicked and deceitful. So, as can be seen above in Psalm 109:2–3, the author emphasizes both the character and the behavior of the witnesses, that is, their wickedness and their lying.

> *Ps 38:13–15: Those who seek my life lay snares; those who seek my misery speak of destruction; they plan deceit all day long. But I, like a deaf man, do not hear, like a dumb man who does not open his mouth; I am like one who does not hear, and in whose mouth there are not arguments.*

***Ps 39:2:** I was dumb, quiet, speechless even from good. My pain was stirred up.*

***Isa 53:7:** He was oppressed, yet he was submissive, and he did not open his mouth; like a sheep was led to the slaughter, like a dumb ewe before its shearers, he did not open his mouth.*

What is the reaction of Messiah[5] to the deposition of these witnesses? The answer may be found in Psalms 38 and 39 and Isaiah 53. Messiah is dumb, does not open his mouth in protest, shows no reaction to the acts perpetrated against him. In the New Testament we also see the silent response of the Messiah. Thus, 1 Peter 2:23 reads, "When he was abused, he did not return abuse; when he suffered, he did not threaten; but he entrusted himself to the one who judges justly" (NRSV).

The Old Testament texts emphasize the nature and character of the witnesses testifying against Messiah, thus shedding some light on the New Testament accounts of Jesus' trial. These accounts present the witnesses as being convinced against Jesus' claim to be the Messiah, and being motivated by this conviction to bring false testimony against him in order to see through his execution. That is, the witnesses disbelieved him, and they desired a certain outcome, and were willing to lie to achieve their end.

(3) Smitten with a Rod upon His Cheek (Mic 4:14 [Eng. 5:1]; Isa 50:6a//Matt 26:67–68; 27:30)

***Mic 4:14:** Now you gash yourself daughter of the troop. They have laid siege to us. They strike the ruler of Israel on the cheek with a staff.*

This text was probably written in connection with the invasion of Judah by the Assyrian king Sennacherib in 701 BC, when he camped at Lachish (2 Kgs 18:13–16) and from this encampment sought to besiege and conquer Jerusalem. Here also Micah contrasts the pride of the fortified (old) capital (Jerusalem) with the humble state of Ephrathah from which salvation is to come. Immediately after this prophecy, Micah (5:1) continues, "And you, O Bethlehem of Ephrathah, least among the clans of Judah, from you shall come forth to me the one to be ruler in Israel, one whose goings forth are from primeval times, from everlasting…." This verse prophesies the birth of the Messiah in Bethlehem, which I have detailed previously in this work.[6] The humility and inauspiciousness of Bethlehem and Ephrathah illustrate the contrast with haughty and pompous Jerusalem.

Now you gash yourself.

The practice of gashing the body was a custom of the Phoenicians (see 1 Kgs 18:20–40), that is, it is a non-Israelite practice. The intent of the passage is probably to indicate that Lachish at the time was full of different religious worshipers, especially the followers of Baal, and the exhortation to gash was to dare the Lachish inhabitants to invoke their own god against the God of Israel. The point is that the Assyrians and the inhabitants of Lachish can make as many gashes as they desire on their bodies, but their fate is already sealed and Yahweh will be finally triumphant. This passage contrasts the present king of Jerusalem (Hezekiah) with the ideal king of Israel, who will come from Bethlehem.

The phrase *bat gĕdûd,* "daughter of the troop," could refer to a garrison, but the Septuagint adopts for *gĕdûd* the alternate meaning ("wall, fence") of a smaller fortified city in contrast with Jerusalem, the larger, well-fortified capital.

They have laid siege to us. They strike the ruler of Israel on the cheek with a staff.

Yahweh is seen to have been humiliated by the success of the nonsraelite invaders in Lachish, and their accomplishment was analogous to a strike on the king's cheek with his own scepter. In effect, Yahweh's power was diminished, and the hit on his face is a symbolic reference to victory. It also presages the smiting of Christ mentioned in Matthew 26:67–68; 27:30.

Matt 26:67–68: *Then they spat in his face and struck him; and some slapped him, saying, "Prophesy to us, you Messiah! Who is it that struck you?" (NRSV)*

Matt 27:30: *They took the reed and struck him on the head. (NRSV)*

These New Testament applications do not specifically mention the staff or scepter, as Micah does, but Matthew 26:67–68 uses the verb *kolaphizō,* meaning "to beat, strike"; and Matthew 27:30 uses the term *kalamon,* "reed," as the weapon with which Jesus was struck. The implication is clear: just as God's representative on earth, the king, was struck on the cheek by his enemies camped in Lachish, so was the incarnate Son of God by his enemies in Jerusalem, and he suffered the same humiliation.

Isa 50:6a: *I offered my back to the floggers, and my cheeks to those who injure.*

Many modern translations render the end of Isaiah 50:6a, "those who pull out the hair." This reading relies on the Masoretic Text, which has *mōrĕṭîm,* active participle of the verb *māraṭ,* "to pull out hair." Yet the Isaiah Scroll found at Qumran (1QIs[a]) reads *mṭlym* [vocalized *maṭlîm*], "those who injure," the Hiphil participle of the verb *ṭālal,* "to injure" (cf. Arabic *ṭalla*). The Qumran reading is supported by the Septuagint, *rapismata,* "slaps (blows) in one's face," and by the first member of the parallelism in Isaiah 50:6a, where we have *makkîm,* "floggers." Moreover, the New Testament accounts speak of "slapping" (*rapisma*) (John 18:22; cf. John 19:3) or "striking" (*ekolaphisan*) (Matt 26:67) rather than "pulling out hair" with respect to the Lord's passion.

(4) Spat upon (Isa 50:6b//Matt 26:67a; 27:30a)

Isa 50:6b: *I did not hide my face from insults and spittle.*

The passage Isaiah 50:4–11 is part of the third song of the "Servant of the Lord" (*ᶜebed Yahweh*). Israel is reluctant to listen to God, to trust him, based on the acts of the past, that God is able to redeem his people (vv. 1–3). The Servant of the Lord is depicted in verses 4–11 as a substitute for a stubborn people. The Servant receives a skilled tongue and a listening ear ready to heed the Creator. Moreover, the Servant is willing to endure suffering in the place of his people and to act as God's representative vis-à-vis a stubborn Israel. Since he endured persecution (vv. 5–6), God will grant him final triumph (vv. 9–11).

The Servant of the Lord is willing to accept not only the slaps and blows but also the most obvious sign of humility and condescension, the spittle of his enemies, both Jews and Romans, who were competing in spitting upon his precious face.

Matt 26:67: *Then they spat in his face....*

Matt 27:30: *And they spat upon him....*

The New Testament application of Isaiah 50:6b is that Matthew refers back to Isaiah and reduplicates the scene of the passive Messiah who endures the brutality of the crowd and his enemies as he awaits his trial and execution. The links between Isaiah and Matthew are evident: being spat upon, offering his cheeks and his back to those who slap and flog him, and the reed that is used to beat him on the head. In addition, the enemies add insults to these injuries by mocking his position as prophet. (Note, however, that the Septuagint takes the Hebrew words *kĕlimmôt wā-rōq,* "insults and spitting," in Isaiah 50:6b as a construct state, *aischynēs emptysmatōn,* "shame of spitting.")

(5) Pierced in Hands and Feet (Ps 22:17 [Eng. 22:16]//John 20:25)

Ps 22:17: For dogs surrounded me; a pack of evildoers encircled me; they pierced my hands and feet.

Psalm 22 is the messianic Psalm par excellence, considered by both Jews and Christians to refer to Messiah. It is also appropriated by Jesus to himself, and because of this we can be sure that the text actually alludes to our Lord. The Psalm is like a dream or a film and contains all the details of the Messiah's last moments on earth. Especially significant is the prophesying of the crucifixion.

This particular verse refers to two categories of people surrounding the Messiah: the dogs and the pack of evildoers. Everywhere in the Bible, the word *kĕlābîm,* "dogs," designates the Gentiles, or non-Hebrews; here it is probably an indication of the Roman soldiers present at the crucifixion (cf. John 19:23).

The "pack of evildoers" (*ʿădat mĕrēʿîm*) could be an allusion to the assembly of priests and scribes gathered together on Friday morning and fomenting the trial against Jesus (John 11:47: "The chief priests and Pharisees gathered the council"). But this phrase may also hint at the council of the evil spirits deliberating over Jesus' death during his last moments on the cross.

It is interesting that both the dogs and the evildoers "encircle" (root *s-b-b*) the suffering one. This is probably an allusion to the crucifixion; that is, the sufferer's body is elevated on a pole and surrounded by his opponents. We must note, however, that this could only be an allusion by inspiration, because this type of punishment, crucifixion, was introduced to the region by the Persians around the sixth century BC, and the text is attributed to the Davidic era (tenth century BC).

The second part of the verse differs in the Masoretic Text and the Septuagint. In the Masoretic Text we have "like a lion, my hands and my feet," in which the verb "encircle" is understood, and the indication is that "they" are powerful and the Messiah is at their mercy in this position. The alternate interpretation is rendered in the New Jewish Publication Society translation "like lions (they maul) my hands and my feet": the depiction here is of the mauling of the hands and feet of the Messiah, which offers a hunting image.

The Septuagint has "they dug (pierced) my hands and feet," and the

Septuagint reading is supported by the (Syriac) Peshitta (*bzʿw*) and Vulgate (*foderunt*). It is generally accepted as the correct rendition. What we have in the Masoretic Text is an error due to the masoretic vocalization. The Septuagint presents us with the verb *oryssō,* which means "to dig" (understood as different from "to pierce"). If we accept the Septuagint reading, we should revocalize the Masoretic Text as *kāʾrê(y)*, instead of current *kāʾărî,* "like a lion."[7] The emended form *kāʾrê(y)* is an infinitive absolute from *kārâ* < **k-r y,* "to dig," with the archaic ending *y* (*yod*), as obtains with another verb in Genesis 30:8 (*naptûlê[y],* "to get entangled with one another") and an inserted *ʾ* (*aleph*) as a *mater lectionis* for the vowel [a].

The author chose[8] the verb "to dig" instead of, for instance, "to pierce" in order to emphasize the graphic and brutal nature of the method of crucifixion: driving wedges through the hands and feet to attach the punished to the wood of the cross. It is emphasized in the text because it was a new punishment; it was unknown prior to the sixth century BC, and the author made a special effort to describe it.

The Septuagint reading was not used in the gospels' passion narratives, which may indicate that the reading was unknown. This is a powerful testimony to the reality of Christ's crucifixion and to the authenticity of the prophecy, and it presents a powerful paradox. On the evening of the Sunday of the resurrection, Jesus entered the upper room where his disciples were gathered and said to them, "'Peace be with you!' And after saying this," continues John, "he showed them his hands and his side" (John 20:19–20). The theological significance of the juxtaposition of Jesus' words and showing of the marks of crucifixion is that "peace" (the word *šālôm* connotes the idea of "completeness"), repeated twice and pointing to John 14:27, understood as reconciliation with God cannot be attained but by Christ's salutary passion. The gospels do not use this Septuagint text in the passion narratives, but it is later referred to in John 20:20, which is the first reference to the nails (only assumed because Christ displays his hands and his side to his disciples to assure them that he is who he claims to be). The reference to piercing or nailing is explicit in John 20:25, "So the other disciples told him, 'We have seen the Lord.' But he [Thomas] said to them, 'Unless I see the mark of the nails in his hands, and put my finger in the mark of the nails and my hand in his side, I will not believe'" (NRSV).

(6) Crucified with Thieves (Isa 53:9, 12//Mark 15:27, 28; Luke 22:37; 23:39–43)

Isa 53:9, 12: And he set his grave with the wicked, and with the rich, his death, though he had done no violence and treachery was not in his mouth....Assuredly, I will give him a portion with the many. He will share the spoil with the mighty. For he poured out his soul unto death and was numbered with the rebellious....

The fourth song of the "Servant of the Lord" (*ʿebed Yahweh*) (Isa 52:13–53:12) takes up the theme of suffering (cf. Ps 22). In life as in death, Messiah remains the same rejected prophet.[9] Isaiah prophesies that Messiah's "grave" (*qibrô*) will be among the guilty. This saying alludes to Christ's death, rather than his entombment; use of the word "death" would have been more appropriate. Specifically, it refers to his death among robbers, and more precisely, the two rebels or thieves crucified alongside of him on Golgotha, "And with him [Jesus] they crucified two bandits (*lēstas*), one on his right and one on his left" (Mark 15:27 NRSV). Luke labels the bandits (thieves) in Mark *kakourgōn*, "criminals," a term closer to Isaiah's "rebellious outlaws," "One of the criminals who were hanged there kept deriding him and saying, 'Are you not the Messiah? Save yourself and us!'" (Luke 23:39 NRSV).

The significance lies not only in the death of the rejected prophet along with the "guilty" but also in that he was considered by his contemporaries as "rebellious" and was therefore subject to the rebel's punishment, namely, crucifixion. The significance deepens when we consider that Jesus went to this punishment and was willing to die for many and to make intercession for the rebellious.

The Hebrew term *pōšĕʿîm*, "rebellious," found in Isaiah 53:12 was rendered by the Septuagint as *anomois*, "transgressors," and in this we find the New Testament application of the Isaianic text, "For I tell you that this scripture must be fulfilled in me, 'And he was considered with transgressors'; for what is written about me has its fulfillment" (Luke 22:37). Yet Jesus was considered a transgressor even before his trial and execution; even on the day of his baptism he was perceived as such. Accepting baptism by John (Matt 3:13–17), Jesus willingly identified himself with our sinful nature and assumed the task of humbly bearing our iniquities (Isa 53:6–7, 12).

(7) He Prayed for His Persecutors (Ps 109:4–5; Isa 53:12//Luke 23:34; cf. Acts 7:59)

Ps 109:4–5: They are my adversaries because of my love; yet, I am all prayer. They repaid me with evil for good, with hatred for my love.

The precise meaning of the Hebrew term *tĕpillâ* is "intercessory prayer."[10] The Septuagint interprets this line by reading "but I continued to pray (*proseuchomen*)."[11] The Hebrew short nominal clause *ʾănî tĕpillâ* may be translated "All I can do is pray!" or "I, myself, am a prayer." When we talk of the power of prayer, the image of the praying psalmist identifying himself with the very notion of prayer is one of the most beautiful metaphors in the entire Old Testament. Intercessory prayer is the anointed psalmist's breath of life, his reason to be, his supreme ideal. In the context of Psalm 109:4–5, prayer also acts as a protective fence against all adversaries.

The Masoretic Text reading *yiśṭĕnûnî,* "they are my adversaries" (similarly LXX: *endieballon*), goes back to *śāṭan,* "to be at enmity with, be hostile toward, become an adversary," probably a denominative verb from *śāṭān,* "adversary, opponent, Satan."

> ***Isa 53:12:*** *But he, himself, bore the guilt for sin of many and he made intercession for the rebellious.*

The Septuagint's rendition is much different from the Masoretic Text, "And he was delivered because of their iniquities"; yet the Masoretic Text fits better in the context of Isaiah 53:12, where the Servant of Yahweh is depicted as bearing the guilt of many and interceding for the rebellious.

The intercessory function of Messiah is underscored by Isaiah with the use of verb *yapgîaᶜ,* "he made intercession." This text may allude to Jesus' prayer on the cross. While bearing the guilt for sin, the incarnate Son of God prays for those who crucified him ("rebellious, criminals" in Isa 53:12), "Father, forgive them; for they know not what they do" (Luke 23:34). Later, Stephen, the first martyr of the church, will utter almost the same intercessory prayer, "While they were stoning Stephen, he prayed, 'Lord Jesus, receive my spirit.' Then he knelt down and cried out in a loud voice, 'Lord, do not hold this sin against them'" (Acts 7:59–60).

(8) He Became the Object of Ridicule (Ps 109:25; 22:7, 8, 13 [Eng. 22:6, 7, 12]; Isa 52:14; 53:2–3//Matt 27:39; Luke 23:35)

> ***Ps 109:25:*** *I am the object of their scorn; when they see me, they shake their head.*

> ***Ps 22:7, 8, 13:*** *But I am a worm, and not man; scorned by men, despised by people. All who see me mock me; they open wide (their) mouths, they shake their heads.…Many bulls surround me, mighty ones of Bashan encircle me.*

> ***Isa 52:14:*** *His appearance was inhumanly deformed, his form beyond human semblance.*

> ***Isa 53:2–3:** Without beauty, without majesty (we saw him), no looks to attract our eyes; despised and abandoned by men.*

The texts underscore three ideas. (1) The deformation of Messiah's appearance during his suffering. There is a certain gradation in Messiah's deformation: from lack of beauty, majesty, and attractiveness to a physical "ugliness." The term *mišḥat,* "deformed" (Isa 52:14), with *mēʾîš,* "from/ more than a man," may be rendered "inhumanly deformed." Messiah is the disfigured Servant.

(2) Messiah's willingly accepted humility. Messiah describes himself as a "worm" (*tôlaʿat*). The metaphorical use of animal names is attested as early as in Ugaritic epics, where, for instance, *zby,* "gazelle," designates a dignitary (cf. Isa 23:9: *ṣĕbî*). In Psalm 22:7, "worm" stands in contrast with the term *ʾîš,* "man, male, husband." And, as *ʾîš* derives from a verbal root *ʾ-w-š,* meaning "to be strong, powerful," the contrast produced by "worm" is meant to suggest the humbleness, the humility of Messiah (cf. Job 25:6; Isa 41:14).[12] Commenting on Psalm 22:7, the Talmud praises David's genuine humbleness (*Ḥullin* 89a). The suffering Messiah became willingly an object of scorn and despise for his contemporaries. But scorn is only a step toward the bitter abandonment experienced by Messiah in the last moments of his earthly existence.

(3) Commoners and elite are both involved in ridiculing the suffering Messiah. The terms "bulls" and "mighty ones of Bashan" allude to the Jews, commoners and ruling class, witnessing Christ's agonizing death and ridiculing him. "Lion" and "ox" are conventional pairs to connote the epitome of power ("dogs" refers to Roman [soldiers], while "bulls" designates the Jewish mob). The bulls surround Messiah. The "nearness" of the enemies contrasts with the "farness" of God (Ps 22:1). These enemies ridicule the suffering Messiah by imitating the last agonizing moments of his precious life (Ps 22:8). The idiomatic expression *yapṭîrû bĕśāpâ* (the Septuagint interprets as "they spoke with [their] lips")[13] should be rendered "they open wide (their) mouths" in a derisory gesture. The Targum on Psalm 22 reads, "they were attacking (*mtgryn*) me restlessly (*mtnddyn*) with their lips." Perhaps those present at Christ's crucifixion tried to imitate the Lord who was, as any crucified person, opening his mouth wide and raising his chest in short, sudden movements, as he struggled to breathe in his last moments.

The New Testament application may be found in Matthew 27:39, "Those who passed by derided him, shaking their heads" (NRSV). In addition, Luke 23:35 refers, similarly to Psalm 22, to the two groups, commoners and ruling class, ridiculing Messiah's final moments, "And the people stood by, watching; but the leaders scoffed at him, saying, 'He saved others; let him save himself if he is the Messiah of God, his chosen one'" (NRSV).

(9) His Garments Were Gambled for (Ps 22:19 [Eng. 22:18]//John 19:23–24)

Ps 22:19: They divide my garments among themselves, casting lots for my tunic.

The use of the imperfective aspect of the verb (*yĕḥallĕqû,* "they divide") suggests that the partition of garments occurred as the suffering psalmist watched, and was unable to stop the absurd, millennial *rehearsal* of Christ's crucifixion. Even so, the psalmist was eager to herald this antecedent detail.

The plural *bĕgādāy,* "(outer) garments" (*beged* designates all kinds of communal garb, i.e., cultic, social, cultural), alludes to the fact that there were several pieces of outer clothing grasped by the psalmist's enemies on the day they harassed him. This explains also the New Testament account about the four soldiers who divided Jesus' vestments among themselves, "When the soldiers had crucified Jesus, they took his clothes and divided them into four parts, one for each soldier" (John 19:23a NRSV).

The additional term in Psalm 22:19, *lĕbûšî,* designates the "undergarment, tunic," which in Jesus' case was seamless, "Now the tunic (*chitōna*) was seamless, woven in one piece from the top. So they said to one another, 'Let us not tear it, but cast lots for it to see who will get it.' This was to fulfill what the scripture says, 'They divided my clothes (*himatia*) among themselves, and for my clothing (*himatismon*) they cast lots'" (John 19:23b, 24 NRSV).

(10) Abandoned by God (Ps 22:2 [Eng. 22:1]; Isa 49:14; 54:7–8//Matt 27:46; Mark 15:34–35)

Ps 22:2: My God, my God why have you forsaken me? How far from my salvation, the words of my roaring!

In Psalm 22, "a pack of evildoers" symbolizes either humans or demons who "were encircling him," pushing in on him, eager to see the outcome of the awesome, unpredictable confrontation between light and darkness, between the serpent's seed and the woman's seed (Gen 3:15); eager to see if the sufferer would be able to overcome the last temptation.

The psalmist's suffering in Psalm 22:2 is amplified by his perception of having been abandoned by God. The psalmist has been accused by violent, fanatic witnesses; condemned by enemies; forsaken by friends; and ridiculed by bystanders, both commoners and ruling class. Even in the face of such malevolence, the psalmist trusts in the God of the fathers, and in the final analysis this trust does not waver. At his moment of suffering, however, the questions occur: Has he the strength to resist the last and the greatest test of all? Is he truly abandoned by the very same God whom he has served passionately, even reluctantly? Will he be another Job evading the act of cursing God and thus depriving himself of that last exploit of freedom and human pleasure, the *art of cursing* another, of blaming one's ill fortune on anyone other than oneself?

Anyone who reads Psalm 22:2 and its New Testament parallels is puzzled by the despairing tone of Messiah's question, "My God, my God, why have you forsaken me?" It is often likened to a child's repeated yet hopeless plea; entreaties whimpered just prior to his bursting into tears and hiding in his room. A careful examination of the context, however, recalls that the question in Psalm 22:2 is a cry of genuine distress rather than of hopelessness or despair.

Psalm 22 may be divided into two clear sections: the first twenty-two verses (Eng. twenty-one verses) express desertion, humiliation, threats of death, and the despairing reactions to these; verses 23–32 (Eng. 22–31) contain praise and commitment to Yahweh, as well as a universal view of Yahweh's victory and dominion on earth and in heaven. There is also an old tradition that says that Jesus, hanging on the cross, began his recitation of prayer with Psalm 22:2 and continued through the following psalms, giving up his Spirit when he came to Psalm 31:6, "Into your hand I commit my Spirit, you have redeemed me, Yahweh, faithful God." It is critical to realize in the messianic reading of the psalms that Jesus experienced the full array of human emotions; he was not merely stoic in the face of his own death; he lived and died as a member of humanity, but expressed his true divinity and relationship to the eternal Father at the end of his humble life. While agonizing in his last moments on cross, he experienced just what any one of us might experience, from a moment of despair and seeming solitude, to trust and joy that led to praise of Yahweh and a missionary enthusiasm. The fullness and depth of his humanity, as revealed in his experience of the cross, ought to bring us all to his humility and perseverance. Like the psalmist, Jesus, the Messiah, did not die in solitude, abandoned by God, but rather he went to his death awash in a jumble of feelings, which were ultimately overshadowed by his trust that the God of the fathers has already redeemed him, "From between the horns of the rams you answered me!" (Ps 22:22; cf. Ps 31:6).

The repetition *ʾēlî ʾēlî*, "My God, my God," indicates the depth of King David's spiritual suffering and agony, but it also suggests that on the cross

Jesus addressed the other two persons of the Holy Trinity, the Father and the Holy Spirit. A similar case is found in Exodus 34:6, where Yahweh, in a concrete manifestation of the preexistent Logos, appears to Moses and invokes twice the name Yahweh, "Yahweh passed before him [i.e., Moses], and proclaimed, '*Yahweh, Yahweh*, a God merciful and gracious, slow to anger, and abounding in steadfast love and faithfulness....'" On the cross, Messiah invites the other two persons of the Holy Trinity to share in the work of salvation that belongs primarily to the Son. Similarly, "in the beginning," the Father's creative work was shared by the Son (Word) and the Holy Spirit (Gen 1).

In this passage, the use of the personal pronoun "my" in the sufferer's invocation of "My God" shows the close relationship between the psalmist and Yahweh and, simultaneously, in the messianic reading, between Messiah and God. The phrase "you have forsaken me" refers historically to David fleeing away from King Saul of Judah (1 Sam 19:8–31:13). Stalked by death, the lonely David foreshadows Jesus' taste of God's abandonment on the cross.

If the first half of Psalm 22:2 reveals an almost despairing Messiah, the second half underscores his strength. One may note that the term *mîšûʿātî*, "from saving me/my salvation" (from the root *y-š-ʿ*, "to help, assist, save"), points to the name *Jesus*, spelled the same in Hebrew (*yĕšûʿâ*, "help, salvation"). Surprisingly, the suffering Messiah finds enough energy to roar his question. The term *šaʾăgātî* means "my roaring" (from the root *š-ʾ-g*, "to roar")[14] and designates a loud, strong sound, not a faint one, as many modern translations suggest through the rendering of "groaning." Messiah's question on the cross resembles the sound of a lion, a common biblical metaphor for Yahweh (cf. Judg 14:5; Isa 15:29; Jer 2;15; Amos 3:4, 8). In Hosea 11:10, as in other parts of the Old Testament, God is likened to a lion "roaring," that is, summoning the scattered Israelites through the strength of his voice. In this light, Psalm 22:2 describes Messiah as a suffering human, yet strong, divine, and able to overcome that critical moment both bodily and spiritually.

Accordingly, when they record Jesus' last hours, the Synoptic evangelists underscore the fact that "he cried with a loud voice" (Matt 27:46; Mark 15:34; Luke 23:46). Christ, though suffering, is still the Son of the eternal God, and as God, he "roars" in his effort to summon his children to salvation. The different reading offered by the Septuagint (*paraptōmatōn mou*, "my transgressions"), due perhaps to a scribal error[15] would suggest that the psalmist (and by extension, Messiah) was abandoned by God as punishment for his own transgressions. In order to support the sinless nature of Christ, Theodoret of Cyrus, who used the Septuagint as a study text, came forward with his own interpretation of the implications of the Greek text. In Theodoret's view, Psalm 22:2b alludes to the fact that Christ took on his shoulders the sins of humanity, so the use of "my transgressions" points to fallen humanity rather than to Messiah himself. Psalm 22:2 should be read along with the following two Isaianic texts, which show that the desertion was exceedingly brief, as the twinkling of an eye.

> ***Isa 49:14:*** *Zion said, "Yahweh has forsaken me, my Lord has forgotten me. Can a woman forget her suckling, or have no compassion of her womb? Yet even if these can forget, I myself will never forget you."*

> ***Isa 54:7–8:*** *For a brief moment, have I forsaken you, but with great mercies will I gather you. In a flood of wrath, for a moment, I hid my face from you. But with love everlasting will I have compassion on you, says Yahweh, your redeemer.*

The text of Psalm 22:2 poses one of the most difficult questions of theology: How and in what sense was our Lord forsaken by his Father? In what sense was his human nature forsaken by, or separated from, the Logos? Overall, the ancient Christian interpreters saw in Jesus' words a sign of divine condescension. Christ, the incarnate Son of God, suffered, while the Word, the second person of the Trinity, became *quiescent,* "dormant" (Jerome), in order to represent humanity, which was in reality abandoned by God (Gregory of Nazianzus).

(11) He Agonized with Thirst (Ps 22:16 [Eng. 22:15]; 69:3, 21//John 19:28; Matt 27:34, 48)

> ***Ps 22:16:*** *My palate is drier than a potsherd and my tongue is stuck to my jaws.*

> ***Ps 69:3, 21:*** *I am worn out with calling, my throat is scorched, my eyes are strained, waiting for my God.... They gave me poison for food, and for thirst they gave me vinegar to drink.*

> ***John 19:28:*** *After this, Jesus knew that everything had now been completed, and to fulfill the scripture perfectly he said, "I am thirsty."*

> ***Matt 27:34, 48:*** *They gave him wine to drink mixed with gall, which he tasted but refused to drink...and immediately one of them ran to get a sponge which he dipped in vinegar and putting it on a reed, gave it him to drink.*

There are three elements to be considered in order to uncover the messianic nuance of these passages: (1) the thirst of Messiah; (2) the cause of this thirst, namely, Messiah's persistent appeals to God; and (3) Messiah given vinegar to drink by his enemies.

The Masoretes vocalized the third word in the Hebrew text of Psalm 22:16 as *kōḥî,* "my strength," which is consistent with the Septuagint reading (*ischys*). The editors of the *Biblia Hebraica Stuttgartensia* suggest the reading *ḥikkî,* "my palate," instead of "my strength," which virtually all modern translations have taken into consideration. Mouth, or palate, is the preferred reading in the context and lends greater meaning to the messianic content of the passage.

Psalm 69:3 probably refers to Psalm 22:16, and most likely alludes to the general indication of Christ's suffering and his plea to God: Why have you forsaken me? His calling, the very act of summoning the energy and physically producing the noise, causes the hoarseness of his throat, which greatly exacerbates his thirst. His palate, already dry, is aggravated by his calling to God for so long a time, yet receiving no answer.

In Psalm 69:21 the enemies of Messiah surround him and offer him vinegar to drink instead of water. This is fulfilled in the New Testament (John 19:28; Matt 27:34, 48). The text of John 19:28 reveals that the Messiah is thirsty, and Jesus' statement "I am thirsty" fulfills the prophecy given in Psalm 22:16, and echoed in Psalm 69:3. The style in which John writes this passage is indicative of his intent to demonstrate the fulfillment of Scripture. There is a doublet of fulfillment in Matthew 27:34, 48, where we are first told that in spite of his thirst, Messiah refuses to taste the gall and wine. Then Matthew elucidates the prophetic content of Psalm 69:21 with the offer of vinegar to Messiah by his enemies. In both of these New Testament texts the fulfillment of the christological indicators of Psalm 22:16 and Psalm 69:3 are brought to completion.

(12) He Entrusted His Spirit to God (Ps 22:21 [Eng. 22:20]; 31:6//Matt 27:43; Luke 23:46; Acts 7:59)

> ***Ps 22:21:*** *Deliver my life* (napšî) *from the sword; my only one* (yěḥîdātî) *from the paw of the dog.*

> ***Ps 31:6:*** *Into your hands I entrust my spirit* (rûḥî); *you have redeemed me, Yahweh God of truth* (ʾěmet).

In this section, Messiah speaks of his life as a whole. After he cries out that God forsook him, he realizes that he has no way of preserving his earthly life and body, and he resorts to praising God, focusing on the only remaining element of value, his eternal soul. In the hope of saving this last remaining and most important essence of life, he beseeches God to snatch it out of the enemies' paws.

In the second part of Psalm 22:21, there is a parallel term for soul, *yĕḥîdātî,* which is best rendered as "my only unique one."[16] This is a poetic term for soul, the one unique and priceless reality that can never be replaced. Another rendition of the term is "I am," which might indicate the combination of the human soul and the divine Logos. If we accept this latter meaning, then Messiah asks God that the hypostatic union between the human soul and the divine Logos, the second person of the Holy Trinity, be not destroyed by death but preserved for eternity. That is, Messiah is the hypostatic union, he is the unique "I am" of the passage, the one to be saved and preserved.

In Psalm 22:21, the enemy is represented as "dog" and the weapon as "sword." Dogs, according to Old Testament convention, symbolize the Gentiles; in the New Testament vernacular they typically refer to Roman soldiers, which is especially evident in the case of Jesus' trial and execution.

In terms of the weapon, the Hebrew word for "sword," *ḥereb,* could also be translated as "lance" or "spear," according to Semitic philology.[17] In messianic terms, this provides us with a nice antecedent reference to the piercing of Jesus' side by the Roman solider with his lance in John 19:34.

In Psalm 31:6, in the phrase "Into your hands I entrust my spirit," Messiah refers to his spirit using the term *rûaḥ,* not *nepeš.* The term *rûaḥ* in the Old Testament is applied mostly in reference to God, to divinity, and not merely to the human soul or earthly being. We see from the context of Psalm 31:6 that this is the meaning intended by the psalmist. The New Testament application shows Christ's co-opting of the term in reference to his own spirit.

The Hiphil (causative conjugation) of the root *p-q-d,* "to commit, hand over, entrust," expresses an important theological idea: Though in suffering Jesus Christ remains the Son of God, he has power over his life; so he causes his spirit to return to God the Father. John 10:17–18 explains, "For this reason the Father loves me, because I lay down my life in order to take it up again. No one takes it from me, but I lay it down of my own accord. I have power to lay it down, and I have power to take it up again. I have received this command from my Father" (NRSV).

> ***Acts 7:59:*** *As they were stoning Stephen, he said, invoking, "Lord Jesus, receive my spirit."*

One may note that Stephen does not entrust his spirit, as Jesus did, but rather he is "invoking" (*epikaloumenon*) God to "receive" (*dexai*) his spirit.

As we see from John 10:17–18, Jesus, unlike mortal humans, is in control of the disposition of his spirit. In Psalm 31:6, Messiah entrusts his spirit to God. The depth of meaning here must be understood in contrast to other humans, who can only ask God to receive their souls. The implication highlights Jesus' power over, or his ability to control, his own spirit; it is in fact an indication of his divine nature. There is a crescendo of meaning building in this passage, which denotes an increasing emphasis on the divinity of Messiah. This is somewhat paradoxical, in that the emphasis comes at the last moment of his life, rather than in the beginning during his conversation with God. The ultimate expression of his divinity shows as he entrusts his spirit to God in the final moments of his earthly existence.

The attribute of God that we know as *ʾĕmet*, "truth," has a much greater breadth of meaning and includes firmness, faithfulness, and reliability. The God of the suffering servant in the Psalms is, above all, reliable. He covenants with his people, and he maintains his promises. God is the God of consistency and steadfastness, on whom we can always depend, and this is demonstrated in the final moments of Messiah's life. In the Old Testament prophecy (Ps 31:6), Messiah entrusts his soul to God because he is absolutely certain that God can be depended on; in the New Testament application (Luke 23:46), Christ takes the risk of entrusting his soul into the hands of the Father, because he knows that God will keep his word and that he will be redeemed.

***Matt 27:43:** He put his trust in God; let God rescue him if he wants him.*

Christ recited several psalms on the cross. He began with Psalm 22 and continued to Psalm 31:6 before he expired. It is significant that Psalm 31:6 is his final quotation from the Psalms as he died. The text points to the God of truth and reliability, as well as to Christ's own divinity. We see here, in sum: Messiah's divinity, as he is in control of committing his spirit to God; Messiah's willingness to entrust his spirit to the God in whom he believes and who, he knows, will care for him; and most importantly, God's providence and dependability. This dependability is stated as such by Christ, as his own affirmation, in response to the taunting of his enemies as they remind him that he has put his trust in God. The enemies of Christ invoke his actions; Christ then entrusts the spirit; and God upholds his responsibility to his Son.

There is a parallel between Psalm 22:21 and Psalm 31:6. The intent of this parallel is to demonstrate that God has already completed the salvific event: He has saved Jesus and redeemed him. But this raises the question: In what sense has Jesus been redeemed? It seems to mean that God had already made his decision, and in the midst of his suffering, Jesus took note of this fact. It is a moment of confidence for the Messiah in the reality of his own salvation.

Luke 23:46: And Jesus, crying with a loud voice, said, "Father, into your hands I entrust my spirit." Having said this, he breathed his last.

The passage from Luke 23:46 is the New Testament application of Psalm 31:6. It records that Jesus completed his recitation of the Psalms through (and including) Psalm 31:6, and it couples with a concomitant fulfillment of Old Testament prophecy in its connection with Matthew 27:34, 48.

(13) His Friends Stood Afar Off (Ps 38:12; 88:8; Isa 63:3//Luke 23:49)

Ps 38:12: My admirers and my neighbors stood at a distance from my stroke, even my relatives stood afar off.

"Admirers" (*ʾōhăbay*), "compatriots" (*rēʿay*), and "relatives" (*qĕrôbay*), all stand far away from the distressed Messiah. Those who accompanied the Lord in his trips throughout the country are in a state of confusion, mingled with fear, at the sight of their teacher's anguish. The word *nigʿî*, "stroke, plague, mark," alludes probably to a disease viewed by Messiah's contemporaries as divine chastisement. A similar opinion is reflected in Isaiah's "Servant of Yahweh" (*ʿebed Yahweh*) song, "As for us, we thought of him as struck (*nāgûaʿ*), smitten, and afflicted by God. Yet, he was pierced for our transgressions, crushed for our iniquities" (Isa 53:4, 5). The term *qĕrôbay*, "kinsmen, relatives," as it appears in our passage, might designate the human race, to which Christ, the Son of Man, belongs.

Ps 88:9: You have removed my friends from me and made me an abomination to them.

There are two ideas in this text, if we read it carefully, as the ancient interpreters did. The first idea is the removal of the sufferer's friends; the second is to make him repulsive to them. God, seemingly in contradiction to himself, is working in both actions. As in Zechariah 11:17, in which the prophet relates the shepherd with God's sword, in Psalm 88:9, God takes an active role in the suffering of his servant. At the same time, he caused Messiah to look like an abomination (repulsive) to all, even to those who knew him and cared for him. "Abomination" (*tôʿēbôt*) in this passage seems to be in parallel to Job 22:13, in which Job became repulsive to his wife; that is, Job suffers as the Messiah suffers. There is a fugue here, in which Job foreshadows Messiah: removed from friends and repulsive to wife and friends.

The word *mĕyuddāʿay*, "my friends, confidants," is attested in the singular in Psalm 55:14 as a prophetic hint to the Messiah's betrayer (Judas).

> ***Isa 63:3:*** *I have trodden the winepress alone. Of the peoples no man was with me.*

The term *ʿammîm* means "peoples," but also refers to one's "kinsmen." Although Messiah belongs to the human race, no one, not even his own family, came to his aid as he suffered for their redemption; he was left alone to accomplish the saving work. The poem in Isaiah 63:1–6 is applied to the suffering of Messiah (crimson and winepress allude to blood and suffering); but he suffers alone, and no human is willing or able to share his suffering. The New Testament application of this passage is Luke 23:49, "All his friends (*gnōstoi*), including the women who had accompanied him from Galilee, stood at a distance, seeing these." Deserted and isolated on a wooden cross, Jesus the Messiah sees his friends distance themselves from him and his passion, as foretold.

(14) They Did Not Break His Bones (Ps 22:18 [Eng. 22:17]; 34:20–21 [Eng. 34:19–20]; Exod 12:46; Num 9:12//John 19:36)

> *Ps 22:18: I can count all my bones while they look and stare at me.*

Messiah could count his bones, which indicates either his thinness or the lack of any broken bones in his tortured body. One may also assume that he was naked if he could examine himself. While the sufferer was counting his bones, his enemies were looking and staring at him, perhaps, to make sure that their victim was dead. This insistent looking (MT: *yabbîṭû*; cf. LXX: *katenoēsan*, "they observed") at the sufferer may be a hint of the Roman soldiers' puzzlement occasioned by Jesus' quick death. The Roman soldiers were commissioned to accelerate the death of the crucified in the eve of the Sabbath; "But when they came to Jesus and saw that he was already dead, they did not break his legs. Instead, one of the soldiers pierced his side with a spear, and at once blood and water came out" (John 19:33–34 NRSV).

> *Ps 34:20–21: Many are the hardships of the righteous, but Yahweh snatches him out of them all; he guards all his bones; not one of them will be broken.*

Psalm 34:20–21 should be read in conjunction with Psalm 22:18; the common theological idea is that God will not abandon his servant; the latter's body will be preserved in its entirety; the unbroken bones are a sign of God's intervention on the side of his servant.

From Ezekiel 37 we learn that bones are essential for life; not only are they the support and framework of the living, earthly body, but their wholeness is also divinely insisted upon for bodily resurrection in the afterlife. The Hebrew word *ʿeṣem,* "bone," derives from a root *ʿ-ṣ-m,* which means "to be powerful" and may designate the entire being. Thus, bones must be unbroken for vivification. Life is in the bones. Everything is possible, if you have bones! Building the body on the bones, and having the breath of life are foundational ideas for the bodily resurrection of Christ, and of all humanity.

> ***John 19:36:*** *For these happened to fulfill the scripture, "None of his bones will be broken."*

The "scripture" (*graphē*), mentioned here, may designate in addition to the texts quoted above, the following biblical witnesses that talk about the unbroken bones of the paschal lamb.

> ***Exod 12:46:*** *It [the paschal lamb] shall be eaten in one house; you shall not take any of the meat outside the house; nor shall you break any bone of it.*

> ***Num 9:12:*** *They shall leave none of it until morning; nor shall they break any bone of it; they shall keep it according to all the regulations of the Passover.*

All four gospels agree that Jesus' sacrificial death occurred during the Passover festivities. If the Synoptics depict Jesus as eating the Passover meal at the Last Supper, John insists on the theological equation Christ—the paschal Lamb. Other New Testament texts that make use of the same equation are the following:

> ***1 Cor 5:7:*** *Clean out the old yeast so that you may be a new batch of dough, since you are unleavened. For Christ, our Passover has been sacrificed.*

Here Jesus is considered "our Passover." This text brings to mind the sacrifice, the lamb, the wholeness of his body, the redemption of God's children, and the imminent resurrection of Messiah.

1 Pet 1:19: *...but with the precious blood of Christ, as of a lamb without blemish and without spot.*

Jesus is here compared with the paschal lamb of Easter, evoking again the sacrifice, the lamb, the salvation of the Israelites, and the event of the exodus.

The restriction against the breaking of bones is in anticipation, as it were, of the resurrection of Christ: it alludes to the possibility of resurrection, the promise of resurrection, and it makes deeper the connection between the lamb and Messiah, as evidenced in the directions for the slaughter and consumption of the paschal lamb in the Book of Exodus. The bones of the sacrificial lamb must not be broken; neither are the bones of Christ to be broken at his sacrificial crucifixion.

(15) He Was Pierced between His Hands (Zech 12:10; 13:1, 6//John 20:25–27; cf. 19:34; Rev 1:7)

Zech 12:10: *But over the House of David and the citizens of Jerusalem I will pour out a spirit of grace and supplication. Then they will look* (hibbîṭû) *on me, the one whom they have pierced* (dāqārû); *they will mourn for him as for an only son, and weep for him bitterly as people weep bitterly for a first-born.*

First, we learn that those responsible for this "piercing" of the suffering Messiah are the "house of David" and the "inhabitants of Jerusalem." Eventually, God, out of mercy, will fill the culprits with a spirit of grace and supplication so that, at the realization that the one whom they pierced is Messiah, they will mourn as does a parent after an only child. And this because they failed the only chance for salvation offered by God to a lost humanity. Interestingly, the Talmud applies Zechariah 12:10 to Messiah. However, the rabbis are divided with respect to the question: What is the cause of such a mourning? The answer is either the slaying of Messiah or the slaying of the "evil inclination" (cf. *Sukkah* 52a).

Zech 13:1: *On that day, a well* (māqôr) *will be opened for the house of David and for the citizens of Jerusalem, for sin and impurity.*

The Septuagint has *pas topos,* "every place," where the Masoretic Text reads *māqôr,* "well." The word *well* refers to the pierced (opened) side of Messiah, whence blood and water poured out. The side of Messiah becomes a well or a spring of living water for those who believe in him. The term *māqôr*, "well, spring," denotes the source of water found by digging up the ground. The "well of water" offered by Jesus (John 4:14) becomes a reality only after being "pierced" by the Roman soldier's lance (John 19:33–34).[18]

> ***Zech 13:6:*** *And if anyone asks him, "Then, what are these wounds* (hammākkôt) *between your hands* (bên yāde[y]kā)*?" He will reply, "These with which I was wounded in the house of my friends* (mĕʾahăbāy)*."*

> ***John 19:33–34:*** *But coming to Jesus and noticing that he was already dead, they did not break his legs, but one of the soldiers pierced his side with a lance, and at once blood and water came out.*

> ***Rev 1:7:*** *Look, he is coming on the clouds and every eye will see him, even those who pierced him, and all the tribes of the earth will mourn over him. This is the truth. Amen.*

According to Zechariah 13:1, it is Yahweh whom the Davidites have pierced and for whom, when looking on him, they mourn; in the view of Isaiah 53, it is the descendant of David who is afflicted and put to death. Christ, the Word incarnate, is, of course, the one whom both passages refer to: he is God, and he is the descendant of David. It is now Yahweh himself who suffers. What may at first glance appear to be a contradiction between Zechariah and Isaiah is resolved by accepting the fact that, as Isaiah said, the descendant of David, Messiah, is to be God almighty (Isa 9:5–6 [Eng. 9:6–7]).

In Zechariah 13:6, the prophet states "between your hands," which means "on your body" (i.e., back or chest). In antiquity, the prophets used to gash their bodies (see 1 Kgs 18:28) to demonstrate their position. The man who bears such scars is accused of being a prophet; "between your hands" in this passage is possibly a hint at the wound Jesus received in his side (cf. John 19:33–34). The piercing indicates two things: (1) Christ's prophetic nature; and (2) the idea that the piercing of the Messiah will be in his body, not merely in his hands and feet, for which a different verb is used.[19] The piercing in his side, done by his contemporaries, indicates that he is the Messiah.

(16) Darkness over the Whole Earth (Amos 8:9; Ps 22:3 [Eng. 22:1]//Matt 27:45)

> ***Amos 8:9:*** *That day—the saying of my Lord Yahweh—I will make the sun go down at noon, and darken the earth in broad daylight.*

***Ps 22:3:** O my God, I cry in the daytime, but you do not answer me: and by night-season also I have no rest.*

***Matt 27:45:** From the sixth hour there was darkness over all the land until the ninth hour.*

Amos (8:9) departs from the Israelite tradition in which the "day of Yahweh" (*yôm Yahweh*) is seen as the day of glory for Israel. Amos presents this day as one of gloom and punishment, a day of judgment in which the sun will go down, and the earth will be darkened.

The text of Psam 22:3 refers to the daytime period. In this messianic text par excellence, the one recited by Christ on the cross, we pay special attention to the content and related texts. In the second part of verse 3, Messiah refers to the "night season...with no rest"; what this actually refers to is the darkness that fell during the day, at noon, as we see in the New Testament application. Darkness occurs at an unexpected and confusing time of the day, and therefore Christ is not prepared for or in need of rest; in fact, it is daytime, a day during which the sun has become darkened.

The text in Amos 8:9 alludes to a total eclipse visible at Jerusalem shortly after noon, on February 9, 784 BC. Although Amos indicates the starting point of such a sudden darkening, he does not say anything about its duration. Since a solar eclipse cannot last longer than a few minutes, the darkness over all the land (Judea) from the sixth to the ninth hour (from noon until three in the afternoon) during Christ's crucifixion (Matt 27:45), cannot be an eclipse as prophesied by Amos, for it lasted three hours. This darkness at Christ's crucifixion was rather nature's reaction to human injustice committed against the Creator's Son.

3. The Death

(1) He Died a Voluntary, Substitutionary Death (Isa 53:5, 6, 11, 12; 50:6; Dan 9:26//John 10:11, 18; Matt 20:28; 1 Cor 15:3; Gal 2:20; Heb 1:3; 1 Pet 2:24; Rev 1:5)

Since the very early Christian era, the substitutionary death of Christ became part of the apostolic *kerygma*, "For I handed on to you as of first importance what I in turn had received: that Christ died for our sins in accordance with the scriptures" (1 Cor 15:3; cf. John 10:11, 18; Matt 20:28; Gal 2:20; Heb 1:3; Rev 1:5). The "scriptures" mentioned here may be the following Old Testament texts.

Isa 53:5: *But he was pierced for our transgressions, he was crushed for our iniquities; the chastisement for our peace was upon him, and by his stripes we were healed.*

The concrete meaning of the verb *ḥālal*, "to wound," according to other biblical occurrences and the cognate root *ḫalla* in Arabic, is "to pierce." Hence the allusion to Christ being pierced because of "our transgressions." He was also "crushed," namely, "murdered" (cf. Akkadian *dâku*, "to kill"). There is a certain gradation in the Isaianic text with respect to the last moments of Messiah, beginning with the piercing or wounding of the messianic agent and culminating with the killing or exterminating of him. We may mention at this juncture that when it speaks of the suffering of Messiah, the Talmud calls him the "leper scholar" (*Sanhedrin* 98b).

We are told that discipline, as chastisement, fell upon the shoulders of Messiah, who through his perfect obedience repaired Adam's fault of disobedience (cf. Gen 3), thus procuring for Adam and his race the primordial completeness, that is, the lost relationship between humanity and its Creator.

Messiah's stripes (*ḥăburātô*, "his slashes, wounds," a hint at slashes on Jesus' body caused by the whip's blows [John 19:1]) would heal us or, more precisely, restore us to the first state of grace. This is the very meaning of the verb *rāpāʾ*, "to heal," namely, "to restore, to make whole."

Isa 53:11: *He shall see some of the labor of his soul; he shall be satisfied. Through his knowledge, my righteous one, my Servant, will make the many righteous. For he himself will carry their iniquities.*

As a slave carries heavy burdens, so will Messiah bear his people's iniquities,[20] but heavy burden, or travail, will not stop Messiah from foreseeing the glorious future, the fruit of his labor, and this alone could make the cross bearable.

"Knowledge" (Hebrew *daʿat*) is a relational concept in the old Testament referring to a personal communion between God and men, which is made possible again through Messiah's righteousness (obedience toward God's plan). Peter declares, "He himself bore our sins in his body on the cross, so that, free from sins, we might live for righteousness; by his wounds you have been healed" (1 Pet 2:24 NRSV).

As to the value of his sacrificial death, Christ remarks, "Very truly, I tell you, unless a grain of wheat falls into the earth and dies, it remains just a single grain; but if it dies, it bears much fruit" (John 12:24 NRSV). Christ's prescience helped him endure the cross, "Looking to Jesus the pioneer and perfecter of our faith, who for the sake of the joy that was set before him endured the cross, disregarding its shame, and has taken his seat at the right hand of the throne of God" (Heb 12:2 NRSV).

> ***Isa 53:12:*** *Assuredly, I will give him a portion with the many. He will share the spoil with the mighty. For he poured out his soul unto death and was numbered with the rebellious. But he, himself, bore the guilt for sin of many and he made intercession for the rebellious.*

Isaiah uses here a courageous image: Messiah pours out his soul unto death.[21] In other words, Messiah empties himself in front of death, to signify his extreme condescension or, as Paul puts it in Phil 2:7–8, "But he emptied himself (*ekenōsen*), taking the form of a slave, being born in human likeness. And being found in human form, he humbled himself and became obedient to the point of death—even death on a cross" (NRSV).[22]

The text says then that Messiah "bore the guilt for sin of many." Note that the verb translated here "to bear" is not *sābal* (as might be expected, and as is found in Isaiah 53:11), but rather *nāśāʾ*, which means "to lift, raise." We have here a possible hint at crucifixion. This could be true if one takes into account Paul's words in Colossians 2:14, "He [Christ] has erased the record of our debt to the Law, which stood against us; he has destroyed it by nailing it to the cross."

> ***Dan 9:26:*** *And after those sixty-two weeks, Messiah shall be cut off, but he has no....The people of a leader that shall come shall destroy the city and the sanctuary, and its end* shall be *through a flood. Desolation is decreed until the end of war.*

In this passage, Daniel adds two new details to the description of Messiah's substitutionary death. The verb *kārat* ("to cut off") hints at a violent death, a murder. Messiah will be murdered *wĕ-ʾên lô*, "but he has no...," namely, "with no cause." A similar idea may be found in Jesus' observation, "They [people's leaders] hated me without reason" (John 15:25).

These Old Testament passages, pointing toward the substitutionary death of Messiah, find their New Testament application especially in John 10:11, 18 and Matthew 20:28. John reminds us of Jesus' own words, "I am the good shepherd. The good shepherd lays down his life for the sheep....No one takes it from me, but I lay it down of my own accord. I have power to lay it down, and I have power to take it up again. I have received this command from my Father" (NRSV). The death Jesus awaited was intended to be a substitution to remedy the illness that afflicts humanity. Jesus knew this and acceded to his fate. Not just acceded, but willingly, even blissfully went forward to his death. He directed his efforts on earth and among his disciples to the end of healing and repairing the breach with God the Father; the final rapprochement was, of course, his own death, and he unreservedly went to it for our sake.

Matthew (20:28) also hands down to us Jesus' speech, in which he states, "Just as the Son of Man came not to be served but to serve, and to give his life a ransom for many" (NRSV). The substitution of one life for the sake of many is explicit here in the notion of ransom. Humanity is held hostage, captive to the machinations of Satan. Christ condescended to incarnate as one of us and, as Messiah, to volunteer his human life for the cause of liberating his mortal brethren from the shackles of devilry and death. His service was his ransom, which restored the communion of God with his children.

Paul assures us of the extraordinary value of Christ's substitutionary death in 1 Corinthians 15:3 and Hebrews 1:3. He also makes it clear that this was the intended aim of Christ's healing work on earth. Similarly, 1 Peter 2:24 recalls to our minds the essence of the Old Testament prophecies of Messiah and the necessity of his death as the sole substitution for mending the rift between the Creator and his creatures, so that "through his wounds you have been healed." The culmination of New Testament references to the substitution of Christ on the cross for our iniquity is found in Revelation 1:5, where John asserts the healing nature of Messiah's blood and its power to wash away our sins.

(2) He Was Buried with the Rich (Isa 53:9//Matt 27:57–61)

> *Isa 53:9: And he set his grave* (qibrô) *with the wicked* (rĕšāᶜîm), *and with the rich* (ᶜāšîr), *his death* (mōtāyw), *though he had done no violence and treachery was not in his mouth.*

The term *ᶜāšîr*, "rich," alludes to Joseph of Arimathea's kind offering. Joseph, a clandestine disciple of Jesus, was a member of the religious council in Jerusalem. He courageously went to Pilate and asked for Jesus' body, in order to put it in his own new tomb (Matt 27:57–61). Perhaps we should replace *bĕ-mōtāyw,* "in his death," as was vocalized by the Masoretes, with the reading *bomŏtô,* "his tomb," based on the Isaiah Scroll of Qumran (1QIs[a]), *bwmwtw*. Thus emended, the text would read "he set his tomb with the rich," which would enhance the meaning in view of Joseph's offering. The essential messianic point is that Christ, the Messiah, was interred in a place reserved for the wealthy of the community. His ignominious death was brought to its prophetic fullness by the faithfulness of his disciple, and the vision of Messiah's resting place was fulfilled.

4. Resurrection

The Third-Day Resurrection and the "Sign of Jonah" (Hos 6:1–3; Jonah 1:17//Matt 12:39–40; 1 Pet 3:18–20)

The teaching of the bodily resurrection in the Old Testament is embedded in the anthropological view of the content and is reflected so well by the Yahwist narrative of Genesis 2:7. Having been fashioned as the "living breath" (*nepeš ḥayyâ*) of God, humanity was called from its very beginning toward life. Yet, out of fear of insecurity, Adam and Eve chose not the "tree of life" but the "tree of knowledge of good and evil," the metaphorical equivalent of power; hence death entered the world. Taking into account the peculiarity of this anthropological view, for an ancient Israelite the life of the soul beyond the tomb could be nothing other than miserable survival in a place of gloom and cold, far from God. That is why there was no perceived need of the demarcation between *bliss* and *punishment* in the realm of the afterlife, as obtains, for example, in Christian teaching dealing with this topic. Sheol (the abode of the dead)[23] was for everyone, wicked and righteous alike. According to the earliest traditions of the Hebrew Bible, no one can have a genuine life out of his or her body. As a matter of fact, from the very first moment of creation, body and soul, understood as "living breath" of God, have been so tightly intertwined that nothing could destroy their unity. Thus, when Scripture speaks of the inhabitants of Sheol, it uses the term "shadows" (*rĕpāʾîm*).[24] The souls in Sheol are "shadows" (Isa 14:9; Ps 88:10; Job 26:5) because they are only mirrored reflections of those who once lived or who were, to use the Yahwist's beautiful metaphor, the "living breaths" of God (Gen 2:7). We may assume that there was a continuous, though silent and not clearly articulated, belief and longing after a time when God would make this happen, namely, when he will bring together his breathing of life with those in Sheol. The conviction that human bodies could be brought back to life after a period of time is evidenced in ancient Israel as early as eighth century BC, if we take into account the prophet Hosea's liturgical song (Hos 6:1–3). Into the same interpretive framework we may add the classic text of Ezekiel about the "dry bones," which are to be infused with the Spirit of Yahweh in order to move around (Ezek 37). Yet the most articulate testimonia with respect to the physical resurrection are to be found in two distinctive texts coming to us from different periods of Israel's history. These texts are Daniel 12:1–3, from the Hellenistic period (323–63 BC), and Isaiah 26:19, part of the Great Apocalypse (Isa 24–27), from the end of the Persian period (538–323 BC).

The general opinion is that the articulation of this tenet of faith as the bodily resurrection was triggered by the persecution initiated and led by

Antiochus IV Epiphanes (167–164 BC) in Palestine, as well as by the idea of martyrdom born on that occasion and, more precisely, with the sacrificial death of the seven brothers Maccabees (2 Macc 7). Between the two sets of texts, Hosea 6 and Daniel 12, there are other Old Testament passages that allude to resurrection in general terms, though not necessarily to a return of God's breathing to the bodies that have already entered the state of decomposition.

Here are some of the pertinent texts.

(a) The Hebrew Bible speaks of two exceptions from physical death, Enoch (Gen 5:24) and Elijah (2 Kgs 2:1–15). As a reward for their pious lives, Enoch and Elijah were "translated" with their bodies to heaven; hence they avoided death as separation of breath from the body. The technical term used for these "translations" is the root *l-q-ḥ,* "to take." Some of the psalms allude to a similar phenomenon when they praise God's ability to "snatch out" (*n-ṣ-l*) or "take" (*l-q-ḥ*) the souls out of Sheol (Ps 49:16; 73:24). The theme of "translations" is well attested in Hellenistic Judaism (Wis 2:22–24; 3:1–9).

(b) Resurrections as healing sessions. There are three Old Testament texts (1 Kgs 17:17–24; 2 Kgs 4:31–37; 13:20–21) that mention the resurrections performed by two prophets from the northern kingdom, namely, Elijah and Elisha. In fact, in these cases, Elijah and Elisha are involved in bodily resurrection that could also be seen as healing sessions. For instance, Elisha mounted the bed where the lifeless child was lying and made his mouth, eyes, and hands match those of the child (2 Kgs 4:34). This episode reminds one of mouth-to-mouth resuscitation. In any event, these cases of resurrection may be treated within the larger context of healings from bodily ailments. Likewise, in the New Testament, examples of resurrection on the same day of death could well have been regarded by Jesus' contemporaries with suspicion as merely healing sessions (e.g., Jairus's daughter, Mark 5:21–24, 35–43). Lazarus's resurrection (John 11) is the only example that can have no explanation other than resurrection, because it concerns a corpse that had already entered the state of decomposition. Jesus' own resurrection is to be placed in the same category as that of Lazarus.

(c) Job's *credo* (Job 19:25–27). This testimony articulates the Old Testament faith in bodily resurrection. Here bodily resurrection is contingent on God's power. The speaker testifies that God, his redeemer, is alive. Thus, bodily resurrection is not only possible but, more than that, we may add, inescapable. Even in the case of natural decomposition, so graphically depicted by Job with reference to his physically deteriorating ailment (v. 26: "after my skin will have been peeled off"), the Redeemer will find a way to restore his dialogical creatures so that they may behold him in their same flesh, with their own eyes. So strong was Job's feeling that, he adds, "My kidneys are consumed within me" (v. 27).

Hos 6:1–3: *Come, let us return to Yahweh, for he has torn and he will heal us; he has struck us and he will bind us up. He will revive us after two days; on the third day he will raise us up that we may live in his presence. Let us know, let us strive to know Yahweh; as sure as the dawn is his going forth. He will come to us like rain, like spring showers that water the land.*

This passage comes from Hosea son of Beeri, the only prophet of northern Israel who lived in the second part of the eighth century BC. Hosea describes here one of the several attempts by Israel to abandon the multitude of idols and syncretistic practices used in worship, and to return sincerely to Yahweh.

Verse 1 represents the first of two exhortations by which an afflicted Israel recognizes that only Yahweh, the one who chastises (Hos 5:12ff.), is able to heal its wounds (cf. Deut 32:39; Job 5:18). Thus, punishment is not a goal in itself but a way chosen by Yahweh to instruct the people, to bring them back to him.

"He will revive us" (Hos 6:2a). Is this line referring to people's revival (resurrection) as in Ezekiel 37? The answer depends on how one deals with another question: Is the nation in Hos 5:14–6:1 ill or dead? Both verbs in verse 1, *ṭ-r-p,* "to tear," and *n-k-h,* "to strike," point to the second situation. "To tear to pieces" means that the victim is lifeless, while "to strike, to give a fatal blow" suggests killing, not maiming. In this case, "he will raise us up" (v. 2b) presupposes the prior cessation of life. Moreover, "that we may live in his presence" (v. 2b) can barely parallel "to preserve alive" (v. 2a). The image, depicted by the latter clause, of a debilitated nation preserved in life, would considerably diminish the vigor of the phrase "living in the presence of Yahweh," which points to a full, personal relationship with God. Conversely, the imagery of the people's revival (resurrection) would correspond well to such a vigorous relationship. Thus, the nuance of the Piel conjugation of the root *ḥ-y-h,* "to live," is better rendered "to make alive, to revive," than "to preserve alive."

"After two days...on the third day." Alone, "the third day" indicates a short period of time (Gen 22:4; 40:20; Exod 19:11). Here, connected with "two days," it looks oddly like a repetition, since the use of "after" (Judg 11:4) points to the day following the initial two days. This period probably refers to the time when a revival was still possible, before the body begins to decompose (John 11:39; cf. Jonah 2:1). What could signify the recovery or even the revival of a nation after such a short interval? This sequence of numerals remains meaningless unless the text is read as a messianic prophecy regarding Christ's third-day resurrection: the "two days" refer to the time the body of Jesus lay in the tomb, and "the third day" points to the moment of his glorious resurrection. Writing to the Corinthians, Paul mentions that Jesus "was raised on the third day in accordance with the scriptures" (1 Cor 15:4), which doubtless alluded to Hosea 6:2.

The Targum interprets the Hosean text in connection with the final resurrection, "He will give us life in the days of consolations that will come; on the day of the resurrection of the dead he will raise us up and we shall live before him." Yet, owing to the polemic with Christian circles, the author of the Aramaic translation replaced the references to the number of days with his own interpretation, namely, an eschatological view of the resurrection of the dead at the end of time, rather than an allusion to Jesus' resurrection on the third day. We may mention that the topic of resurrection is often debated in the Talmud.[25] Yet, according to the Talmud, the coming of Messiah, or more precisely the "pangs of Messiah," that troublesome period that will announce the coming of Messiah, will anticipate the universal resurrection (*Pesaḥim* 118a).

As for the ancient Christian interpreters, they are in line with Paul's conviction that Jesus' third-day resurrection was foretold in the Scriptures. Theophylact of Bulgaria explains Hosea 6:1–3 thus:

> Certainly, it alludes to the mystery according to nature. For he [i.e., God] has stricken nature by death and gave those who sin to death. But he inserted his Son in the stricken nature like some precious thing, who, since he was in the wound of death, he healed us and rose on the third day. For by raising the acquisition he assumed from us, he bestowed upon us all the resurrection, which each one of us will have in his own time, and we will live. For if one died for all, the same one also rose for all, and, since we are not far off from him since we are seen in his face, we will have a more perfect knowledge.[26]

Historically, Hosea 6:2 may be read as a reference to Israel's future restoration following a short ("after two days") captivity (cf. Ezek 37:1–14). But typologically this text foreshadows Christ's third-day resurrection. The transition from historical to typological is possible since Christ in his life and activity embodied Israel. For instance, the forty days that Jesus fasted in the wilderness parallel Israel's forty-year journey. Thus, the Lord's resurrection is a *typological embodiment* of Israel's revival, which will be literally fulfilled at the end of time when the New Israel, that is, all who believe in Christ, will be raised up (1 Thess 4:13–17).

Verse 3 introduces the second exhortation centered on the theme of *daʿat,* "knowledge" (Hos 4:1; 6:6). "Let us know," in this context and according to Hosea's theology, means "acknowledging" Yahweh as the Lord of life and death. This "acknowledgment" is based on concrete experiences, such as the national calamities occasioned by the Syro-Ephraimite War (733–732 BC), and recorded in Hosea 5:14–6:1.

The second part of verse 3 spells out the people's trust in Yahweh's bounty. His intervention[27] is as sure as the breaking of the "dawn," and Israel's visitation by Yahweh is likened to the beneficial rains of winter (December–February) and spring (March–April) that water the land. The same Theophylact of Bulgaria offers at this juncture a typological interpretation:

> Therefore, God will come to us as an early rain, when he will begin to liberate us from captivity. And like the late [rain], when reestablishing us in our homeland, he treats us with great care, and he is anxious for us. After his resurrection, Christ revealed himself early in the morning to the women, and in the evening, although the doors were shut, to the disciples (John 20:26).[28]

But this prophetic saying on Messiah's third-day resurrection has to be separated from another archaic tradition, namely, that which refers to Jesus' stay in Sheol for three days and three nights. This tradition draws on a text from Matthew, "But he answered them, 'An evil and adulterous generation asks for a sign, but no sign will be given to it except the sign of the prophet Jonah. For just as Jonah was three days and three nights in the belly of the sea monster, so for three days and three nights the Son of Man will be in the heart of the earth'" (Matt 12:39–40 NRSV). The "sign of Jonah" refers to Jesus' sojourn for three days and three nights not in the tomb, followed by resurrection, but rather "in the heart of the earth," where, according to the ancient Israelites, the netherworld, Sheol, was located. This was a dark, cold place, far away from the life-giving presence of the Almighty. The time spent by Jonah in the belly of the fish foreshadowed the time spent by Jesus in Sheol. As odd as this might seem, the "sign of Jonah" refers not to the resurrection alone but rather to the stay of Christ in Sheol and his subsequent victorious emergence, which is the most important sign performed by our Lord. His victory over death and the powers of death lurking in Sheol makes him Lord over death and life.

Jonah 1:17: *Yahweh appointed a huge fish to swallow Jonah; and Jonah was in the fish's belly three days and three nights.*

Jonah's experience can be offered as an example of bodily resurrection only by extension. The prophet did not die, but rather he survived and came out of the fish's belly unhurt and as a victor. This text speaks of Jonah's three days and three nights spent in this dark place, and hence it can be considered a foreshadowing of Christ's sojourn in the netherworld, from where he returned victorious, taking with him to heaven Adam and Eve and the righteous people of the Old Testament times.

The Christian *kerygma* about Jesus' descent to the netherworld can be found in 1 Peter 3:18–20:

> For Christ also suffered for sins once for all, the righteous for the unrighteous, in order to bring you to God. He was put to death in the flesh, but made alive in the spirit, in which also he went and made a proclamation to the spirits in prison, who in former times did not obey, when God waited patiently in the days of Noah, during the building of the ark, in which a few, that is, eight persons, were saved through water. (NRSV)

NOTES

1. One of the Midrashim connects the word *ʾallûp* to the root *ʾ-l-p* I, "to learn," by explaining that Ahitophel was an educated man, someone familiar with Torah (*Numbers Rabbah* 18:17).

2. Genesis 2:7 uses the root *y-ṣ-r,* "to fashion," from which the word *yôṣēr,* "potter," derives, to describe God's "fashioning" humanity out of the "dust."

3. The word *ʿāmît* means "community, association of people" (cf. Arabic *ʿāmmat,* "people," and perhaps Akkadian *emūtu,* "family" < *emu,* "father-in-law"); hence the whole phrase *geber ʿămîtî* may be rendered "my partner" or "my fellow man." We might mention that the word *ʿāmît,* "community," without *geber,* "man," appears only in Leviticus (5:21; 6:2; etc.) and conveys the idea of a "near neighbor, fellow."

4. The *Targum Jonathan*'s reading is a good illustration of this point; the MT's reading *rōʿî,* "my shepherd," corresponds to the Targum's choice, *mlkʾ,* "king."

5. That the immediate literary context of Isaiah 53:7 refers to Messiah's sufferings can be deduced from one of the Midrashim (*Ruth Rabbah* 5:6).

6. See "Part B. The Rising Messiah. II. The Birth of Messiah. 4. Place of Birth and Other Places in Christ's Itinerary."

7. Earlier than the MT's vocalization, there is the Targum's consonantal reading of Psalm 22:17, *kʾryʾ,* "like a lion," with an emphatic *ʾ* (*aleph*) at the end of the noun.

8. We may assume the author's choice based on the LXX's and pre-Masoretic readings.

9. The Midrashim read Isaiah 53:12 as a messianic text referring to a new world at the end of time when those who have "busied themselves with Torah" will be rewarded (cf. *Numbers Rabbah* 13:2).

10. The noun *tĕpillâ* derives from a root *p-l-l,* meaning "to speak up for someone, to intercede."

11. Similarly, the *Targum Jonathan* reads *wʾnʾ ʾṣly,* "As for me, I pray."

12. This is the understanding of the Targum on Psalm 22, which offers an interpretive reading of what we have in the MT, *wʾnʾ zḥyl ḥlš,* "a weak creeping thing."

13. In Greek: *elalēsan en cheilesin.*

14. The MT's reading ("roaring") is supported by the Targum's lexical choice, *ʾklywty,* "my cry."

15. That is, metathesis: *šāʾag* (root *š-ʾ-g*), "to roar," was replaced with *šāgāʾ* (root *š-g-ʾ*), "to err," by a mere change in the *aleph*'s position (from medial to final).

16. Note the Targum's reading, *rwḥʾ dgwšmy,* "the spirit of my body."

17. Note the Arabic *ḥarbat,* "lance"; see Friedrich W. Schwarzlose, *Die Waffen der alten Araber aus ihren Dichtern dargestellt* (1886; Hildesheim/New York: Georg Olms Verlag, 1982), 213.

18. On the imagery of the "well," see under "Part B. The Rising Messiah. I. The Preexistence of Messiah. 1. Within Godhead (1). Poured Out as a Libation."

19. See above under "2. The Passion. (5) Pierced in Hands and Feet."

20. The basic meaning of Hebrew *ʿăwōnôt* is "distorted ways."

21. The Hiphil of verb *ʿārâ,* "to pour out, empty," means "to uncover, tip out, throw."

22. On the similar image of divine Wisdom being "poured out [as a libation]," see "Part B. The Rising Messiah. I. The Preexistence of Messiah 1. Within Godhead (1). Poured Out as a Libation."

23. Even though the etymology of *Sheol* (*šĕʾôl*) is still debated, the best option remains to relate this Hebrew word to the root *š-ʾ-l,* "to ask, inquire"; if this etymology holds true, then the semantic development will be: inquire > call to account > punish (see the detailed study of R. Rosenberg, "The Concept of Biblical Sheol Within the Context of ANE Beliefs" (Ph.D. dissertation; Harvard University, 1980).

24. The term *rĕpāʾîm* derives most likely from a root *r-p-ʾ* (*r-p-h*), "to be weak, to grow slack"—hence the idea of "dead spirits" or "shadows," in any event, something without substance or consistency.

25. The expression *tḥyt hmtym,* "resurrection of the dead," appears forty-one times in the Talmud.

26. PG 126:673C-D.

27. That is, "his going forth," probably from his "place"; cf. Hos 5:15.

28. PG 126:676B-C.

Bibliography

For further study and literature cited

Anderson, Gary A. *The Genesis of Perfection: Adam and Eve in Jewish and Christian Imagination*. Louisville: Westminster John Knox Press, 2001.

Botterweck, G. Johannes, Helmer Ringgren, and Heinz-Josef Fabry, eds. *Theological Dictionary of the Old Testament*. Translated by John T. Willis. 14 vols. Grand Rapids: Eerdmans, 1974–.

Brueggemann, Walter. *Genesis*. Interpretation. Louisville: John Knox, 1982.

———. "That the World May Be Redescribed." *Interpretation* 56, no. 4 (2002): 359–67.

———. *Theology of the Old Testament: Testimony, Dispute, Advocacy*. Minneapolis: Fortress Press, 1997.

Cathcart, Kevin, Michael Maher, and Martin McNamara, eds. *The Aramaic Bible: The Targums*. 22 vols. Collegeville, MN: Liturgical Press, 1987–.

Charlesworth, James H. "From Jewish Messianology to Christian Christology: Some Caveats and Perspective." In *Judaism and Their Messiahs at the Turn of the Christian Era,* edited by Jacob Neusner, William S. Green, Ernest Frerichs. Cambridge: Cambridge University Press, 1996.

Charlesworth, James H., ed. *The Old Testament Pseudepigrapha*. 2 vols. New York: Doubleday, 1983–85.

Childs, Brevard S. *Introduction to the Old Testament as Scripture*. Philadelphia: Fortress Press, 1979.

Clements, Ronald E. "Messianic Prophecy or Messianic History?" *Horizons in Biblical Theology* 1 (1979): 87–104.

Collins, John J. *The Scepter and the Star: The Messiahs of the Dead Sea Scrolls and Other Ancient Literature*. Anchor Bible Reference Library. New York: Doubleday, 1995.

Congar, Yves. *Jesus Christ*. Translated by Luke O'Neill. New York: Herder & Herder, 1966.

Danby, Herbert. *The Mishnah: Translated from the Hebrew with Introduction and Brief Explanatory Notes*. London: Oxford University Press, 1933.

Edersheim, Alfred. *The Life and Times of Jesus the Messiah*. 2 vols. Grand Rapids: Eerdmans, 1953.

Epstein, Isidore, ed. *The Hebrew/English Babylonian Talmud*. 30 vols. New York: Soncino, 1990.

Fitzmyer, Joseph A. *Essays on the Semitic Background of the New Testament.* Missoula, MT: Scholars Press, 1974.

Friedman, H., and Maurice Simon, eds. *The Midrash Rabbah.* 10 vols. New York: Soncino, 1992.

García Martínez, Florentino, and Eibert J. C. Tigchelaar, eds. *The Dead Sea Scrolls: Study Edition.* 2 vols. Leiden: Brill, 2000.

Gelb, I. J., et al., eds. *The Assyrian Dictionary of the Oriental Institute of the University of Chicago.* Chicago, IL: University of Chicago Press, 1956–.

Goppelt, Leonhard. *Typos: The Typological Interpretation of the Old Testament in the New.* Grand Rapids: Eerdmans, 1982.

Hanson, Paul D. *Isaiah 40–66.* Interpretation. Louisville: Westminster John Knox Press, 1995.

Hengstenberg, E. W. *Christology of the Old Testament.* Grand Rapids: Kregel, 1970.

Hurtado, Larry W. *Lord Jesus Christ: Devotion to Jesus in Early Christianity.* Grand Rapids: Eerdmans, 2003.

Jastrow, Marcus. *A Dictionary of the Targumim, the Talmud Babli and Yerushalmi, and the Midrashic Literature.* 2 vols. New York: Judaica Press, 1992.

Juel, Donald. *Messianic Exegesis: Christological Interpretation of the Old Testament in Early Christianity.* Philadelphia: Fortress Press, 1988.

Kaiser, Walter C., Jr. *The Messiah in the Old Testament.* Studies in Old Testament Biblical Theology. Grand Rapids: Zondervan, 1995.

Koehler, Ludwig, and Walter Baumgartner. *The Hebrew and Aramaic Lexicon of the Old Testament.* 5 vols. 3rd edition. Revised by Walter Baumgartner and Johann Jakob Stamm. Translated and edited under the supervision of M. E. J. Richardson. Leiden: Brill, 1994–2000.

Kugel, James L. *The Bible as It Was.* Cambridge, MA: Belknap Press of Harvard University Press, 1997.

Levenson, Jon D. *The Hebrew Bible, the Old Testament, and Historical Criticism.* Jews and Christians in Biblical Studies. Louisville: Westminster John Knox Press, 1993.

Lockyer, Herbert. *All the Messianic Prophecies of the Bible.* Grand Rapids: Zondervan, 1973.

Louth, Andrew, ed. *Genesis 1–11.* Ancient Christian Commentary on Scripture, Old Testament 1. Downers Grove, IL: InterVarsity, 2001.

Mays, James L. *Psalms.* Interpretation. Louisville: John Knox Press, 1994.

Moltmann, Jürgen. *The Way of Jesus Christ: Christology in Messianic Dimensions.* Minneapolis: Fortress Press, 1993.

Moore, G. F. *Judaism in the First Centuries of the Christian Era.* 2 vols. New York: Schocken, 1971.

Moran, William L., ed. *The Amarna Letters.* Baltimore/London: Johns Hopkins University Press, 1992.

Murphy-O'Connor, Jerome. *The Holy Land: An Archaeological Guide from Earliest Times to 1700.* New York: Oxford University Press, 1987.

Payne, J. Barton. *Encyclopedia of Biblical Prophecy.* New York: Harper & Row, 1973.

Pentiuc, Eugen J. "Messianism in the Book of Hosea in the Light of Patristic Interpretations." *Greek Orthodox Theological Review* 46 (2001): 35–56.

Rendtorf, Rolf. *Canon and Theology*. Overtures to Biblical Theology. Minneapolis: Fortress Press, 1993.

Schimanowski, Gottfried. *Weisheit und Messias: Die jüdischen Voraussetzungen der urchristlichen Präexistenzchristologie*. Wissenschaftliche Untersuchungen zum Neuen Testament 2/17. Tübingen: Mohr Siebeck, 1985.

Schürer, Emil. *The History of the Jewish People in the Age of Jesus Christ*. Revised and edited by G. Vermes, F. Millar, and M. Black. 3 vols. Edinburgh: Clark, 1973–87.

Segal, Alan F. *Two Powers in Heaven: Early Rabbinic Reports about Christianity and Gnosticism*. Studies in Judaism in Late Antiquity 25. Leiden: Brill, 1977.

Simon, Maurice, ed. *The Zohar*. 5 vols. New York: Soncino Press, 1984.

Skarsaune, Oskar. "The Development of Scriptural Interpretation in the Second and Third Centuries—Except Clement and Origen." In *Hebrew Bible/Old Testament: The History of Its Interpretation:* vol. 1, *From the Beginnings to the Middle Ages,* edited by Magne Saebo. Göttingen: Vandenhoeck & Ruprecht, 1996.

———. *The Proof from Prophecy: A Study in Justin Martyr's Proof-Text Tradition: Text Type, Provenance, Theological Profile*. Supplements to Novum Testamentum 66. Leiden: Brill, 1987.

Stylianopoulos, Theodore G. *Justin Martyr and the Mosaic Law*. Society of Biblical Literature Dissertation Series 20. Missoula, MT: Scholars Press, 1975.

Trakatelis, Demetrius C. *The Pre-Existence of Christ in Justin Martyr: An Exegetical Study with Reference to the Humiliation and Exaltation Christology*. Harvard Dissertations in Religion 6. Missoula, MT: Scholars Press, 1976.

Whiston, William, ed. *The Works of Josephus: Complete and Unabridged*. New updated edition. Peabody, MA: Hendrickson, 1985.

Woollcombe, K. J. "The Biblical Origins and Patristic Development of Typology." In *Essays on Typology,* edited by G. W. H. Lampe, and K. J. Woollcombe. Studies in Biblical Theology 22. London: SCM Press, 1957.